Citizenship Now

Other readers featured in the "Longman Topics" series include:

Issues of Gender
Ellen Friedman and Jennifer Marshall

Language and Prejudice
Tamara Valentine

Translating Tradition
Karen E. Beardslee

The Counterculture Reader
E. A. Swingrover

Considering Cultural Difference
Pauline Uchmanowicz

Citizenship Now

JON FORD
College of Alameda

MARJORIE FORD
Stanford University

PEARSON
Longman

New York   San Francisco   Boston
London   Toronto   Sydney   Tokyo   Singapore   Madrid
Mexico City   Munich   Paris   Cape Town   Hong Kong   Montreal

Senior Vice President and Publisher: Joseph Opiela
Senior Acquisitions Editor: Lynn M. Huddon
Marketing Manager: Deborah Murphy
Managing Editor: Bob Ginsberg
Project Coordination, Text Design, and Electronic Page Makeup:
    Sunflower Publishing Services
Senior Cover Design Manager: Nancy Danahy
Cover Image: Houses and American flag, Tangier Island, Virginia,
    USA, © Stone/Getty Images, Inc.
Manufacturing Buyer: Roy L. Pickering, Jr.
Printer and Binder: RR Donnelly & Sons Company
Cover Printer: Lehigh Press, Inc.

For permission to use copyrighted material, grateful acknowledgment is made to the copyright holders on pp. 257–258, which are
hereby made part of this copyright page.

Library of Congress Cataloging-in-Publication Data
    Ford, Jon.
        Citizenship now: rethinking our roles in 21st century America /
    Jon Ford and Majorie Ford.
            p. cm.
        ISBN 0-321-11767-0
            1. Readers—United States. 2. English language—Rhetoric—
    Problems, exercises, etc. 3. Citizenship—United States—
    Problems, exercises, etc. 4. Report writing—Problems,
    exercises, etc. 5. Readers—Citizenship. 6. College readers.
    I. Ford, Marjorie (Marjorie A.) II. Title.

PE1127.H5F47 2003
808'.0427—dc21   2003050652

Please visit our website at http://www.ablongman.com

ISBN 0-321-11767-0

678910—DOH—1009080706

CHAPTER 4
The Media and the Citizen 155

CHAPTER 5
The Public Citizen 207

PREFACE

Citizenship Now is a short anthology of readings for college writing students that focuses on an extraordinarily relevant topic as our country moves into the New Millennium: the changing and increasingly more crucial role of the citizen in the democratic process and in the crucial task of revitalizing our communities. How many Americans today think seriously and consciously about their role as citizens? How many of us understand the extent of our civil liberties and the way they are being curtailed in the name of national security? Do we, as citizens, have a positive responsibility to act to effect social change? Many people are beginning to ask such questions today; and it is important that students, the citizens of tomorrow, begin to consider these issues as well.

Citizenship Now makes the assumption that we, as citizens, need to examine the changing meaning of citizenship. The selections that we have chosen for this anthology will help students think carefully about historical and timely issues that require careful consideration. The essays open a dialogue about how citizens can take an active part in our changing society. While some of the readings discuss the need for a compromise in our quest for personal freedom with the necessity of better security in many aspects of our communities and our lives, other writers argue for an increased vigilance about our civil liberties and freedom at a time when security concerns have already led to an increase in domestic spying. The selections also ask student readers to think about how consumerist values often privilege individual needs for self-fulfillment over allegiance to a larger sense of community or national responsibility. At the same time, we need to find ways to cope with the new influx of immigrants into our country through social services and educational reform. How do we provide access to quality schools for all of our citizens while considering the ways that the mass media are increasingly influencing the way Americans are educated about social and political realities?

Citizenship Now is divided into five chapters, each examining a distinct aspect of modern citizenship and democracy. The chapters and topics include "Citizenship and Diversity" (Chapter One),

"Education and Citizenship" (Chapter Two), "Citizenship and Civil Liberties" (Chapter Three), "The Media and the Citizen" (Chapter Four), and "The Public Citizen" (Chapter Five). Each chapter features five or six essays of varying lengths and reading levels and a brief but useful apparatus. This apparatus is designed to help students read and write more perceptively in response to the selections and to think more critically about their roles as citizens.

Special features of our book include the following:

- Twenty-nine essays, many of them written within the past two to three years, each of which emphasizes a different aspect of the chapter theme and reflects on the larger questions about the meaning of citizenship in America today.
- Essays chosen to reflect a balance of political, gender, and cultural perspectives, as well as literary styles and reading level.
- Five chapters, each of which explores a different question or issue related to modern citizenship.
- Classic historical quotations about the themes in each chapter, followed by chapter introductions which examine the historical issue of citizenship in the chapter, explaining how such issues are being redefined in recent times in the essays included.
- Author biographies for each selection and suggestions for further readings by the author.
- Four "Questions for Discussion" for each essay in the book, designed to facilitate close reading and to encourage students to take critical positions on the essay and its issues.
- Two "Ideas for Writing" questions for each essay that encourage argument and analysis, as well as asking students to apply the concerns of the professional writers to their own lives and communities.
- Four or five "Extending the Theme" end-of-chapter questions for each chapter. These questions call either for a synthesis of several different concerns or for further research involving Internet/library-oriented or field research or participation in organizations of citizens devoted to community revitalization, education, and social/political change.

ACKNOWLEDGMENTS

First we would like to thank our editor Lynn Huddon, who was instrumental in helping us define the theme of this text, for working with us to keep the project in focus and on schedule in the midst of our very busy lives. We would like to thank our reviewers for their insightful questions and their various perspectives: Alan Ainsworth, Houston Community College; Greg Beatty, University of Phoenix online; Jan Strever, Spokane Community College; and Bianca Tredennick, University of Oregon.

JON FORD
MARJORIE FORD

CHAPTER 1

Citizenship and Diversity

"The United States should be an asylum for the persecuted lovers of civil and religious liberty."   THOMAS PAINE

"Everywhere immigrants have enriched and strengthened the fabric of American life."   JOHN F. KENNEDY

Immigration . . . has required a process of racialization so that the prevailing national identity could be maintained. . . . Immigrants of color . . . largely remained outside Americanism."   LINDA MARTINEZ

The American dream for immigrants involves a search for liberty, equality, and opportunity by acquiring the full benefits of American citizenship. As Thomas Paine states, many immigrants come here for asylum: They have been denied basic rights in their native culture or previous country of residence, and they wish to make a contribution to American life with their skills and determination to succeed. Traditionally, according to the assimilationist view, that opportunity was acquired by getting a job, often within an immigrant community, then gradually acquiring English language skills, training, and contacts with American natives, who would open the doors to better jobs as the immigrants the cultural traits and values of mainstream America.

Increasingly, newer immigrants and native citizens of color are questioning this approach, in part because of the pride they take in maintaining their own culture and religious beliefs; in part because, as Linda Martinez points out in her quotation above, they have felt rebuffed by mainstream society in their efforts to become fully accepted as Americans. In addition, rapid transportation and international electronic communications make it easy for immigrants to remain connected to their original cultures, even to the extent that some see themselves as "hyphenated Americans" or members of the global community rather than simply as American citizens.

The readings in this chapter probe for a definition of what an American is in a changing society, and how we "belong" as Americans if we are below the poverty line, recent immigrants, or bicultural/bilingual. Also revealed in this chapter's essays are the ideological struggles over the role immigrants and new citizens should play in this society. Some writers, such as Lewis Lapham, in "Who and What Is American?", present an image of Americans based neither on loyalty to a particular cultural/ethnic group nor on the melting-pot theory of passive assimilation into a conformist culture; instead, these authors emphasize the need for individualism and the creative metamorphosis of identity and culture.

However, as Anna Quindlen points out in her essay, "A Quilt of a Country: Out of Many, One?" our nation has always experienced a conflict between the needs of the individual and the needs of the community, as in the case of those immigrants and people of color who struggle to achieve American-style individuality yet come up against the resistance of their neighbors. For example, Andrew Pham, in his essay "Viet-Kieu," reflects on his physical abuse and humiliation while growing up Vietnamese-American in San Jose, California, one of our country's most multicultural communities.

If immigrants are fully accepted by the larger community, we will move closer to John F. Kennedy's view of immigrants enriching and strengthening "the fabric of American life." The ultimate dream of Kennedy's contemporary, Martin Luther King, Jr., is an America free from racism where black and white youth can join hands as equals. This dream, presented in King's famous speech, "I Have a Dream," delivered in 1963 at a civil rights rally in Washington, D.C., still shines as a hopeful vision that has not been fully realized for many minorities (including African Americans) or by recent immigrants.

In a more recent essay, "Hispanics and the American Dream," conservative activist Linda Chavez presents a positive picture of the advances made by certain members of the Hispanic community. However, she admits that recent Mexican-American immigrants who come to the United States without English skills do not fare so well, although they have certain strong cultural values such as a stable, child-centered family structures that help them to attain stability and make progress toward obtaining some portion of the American dream.

Unlike Chavez, who does not accept bilingual education and believes that Hispanics need to master English as quickly as possible in order to enter the workforce, Professor Robert D. King, in his essay "Should English Be the Law?", is concerned about how the resistance to immigrants who persist in maintaining their own languages has led to the rise of the "English Only" movement to make English the official American language. King argues that America has so many unique national qualities and cultural beliefs that the use of languages other than English by some groups will in no way diminish our strength and unity as a nation.

The struggles that immigrants must overcome to feel accepted and comfortable in their lives as American citizens are an inextricable part of the American way of life for all citizens. We have much to gain from the integration of immigrants into American life, for diversity has always been at the foundation of the American dream and the success that we, as Americans, have achieved.

Who and What Is American?

Lewis Lapham

Lewis Lapham (b. 1935) received a B.A. from Yale University in 1956 and has had a long career as a news reporter, essayist, television personality, and social critic. Since 1971 he has been editor of *Harper's Magazine*. His essays have been collected in several volumes, including *Money and Class in America* (1988), *Hotel America: Scenes in the Lobby of the* Fin-de-Siecle (1995), and *Theater of War* (2002). Lapham is one of the best-known essayists in America. With his sharp wit and satirical view of American society, he has been compared to Mark Twain and Tom Wolfe. In the essay that follows, Lapham defines the American character in a way that rejects the modern tendency to identify oneself primarily with a particular group, race, or social class.

———————— ✦ ————————

Were I to believe what I read in the papers, I would find it easy to think that I no longer can identify myself simply as an

American. The noun apparently means nothing unless it is dressed up with at least one modifying adjective. As a plain American I have neither voice nor authentic proofs of existence. I acquire a presence only as an old American, a female American, a white American, a rich American, a black American, a gay American, a poor American, a native American, a dead American. The subordination of the noun to the adjectives makes a mockery of both the American premise and the democratic spirit, but it serves the purposes of the politicians as well as the news media, and throughout the rest of this election year I expect the political campaigns to pitch their tents and slogans on the frontiers of race and class. For every benign us, the candidates will find a malignant them; for every neighboring we (no matter how eccentric or small in number), a distant and devouring they. The strategies of division sell newspapers and summon votes, and to the man who would be king (or president or governor) the popular hatred of government matters less than the atmosphere of resentment in which the people fear and distrust one another.

Democratic politics trades in only two markets—the market in expectation and the market in blame. A collapse in the former engenders a boom in the latter. Something goes wrong in the news—a bank swindle of genuinely spectacular size, a series of killings in Milwaukee, another disastrous assessment of the nation's schools—and suddenly the air is loud with questions about the paradox of the American character or the Puritan subtexts of the American soul. The questions arise from every quarter of the political compass—from English professors and political consultants as well as from actors, corporate vice presidents, and advertising salesmen—and the conversation is seldom polite. Too many of the people present no longer can pay the bills, and a stray remark about acid rain or a third-grade textbook can escalate within a matter of minutes into an exchange of insults. Somebody calls Jesse Helms a fascist, and somebody else says that he is sick and tired of paying ransom money to a lot of welfare criminals. People drink too much and stay too late, their voices choked with anecdote and rage, their lexicons of historical reference so passionately confused that both Jefferson and Lincoln find themselves doing thirty-second commercials for racial quotas, a capital gains tax, and the Persian Gulf War.

The failures in the nation's economy have marked up the prices for obvious villains, and if I had a talent for merchandising I would go into the business of making dolls (black dolls, white dolls, red-necked dolls, feminist dolls, congressional dolls) that each of the candidates could distribute at fund-raising events with a supply of color-coordinated pins. Trying out their invective in the pre-season campaigns, the politicians as early as last October were attributing the cause of all our sorrows to any faction, interest, or minority that could excite in their audiences the passions of a beloved prejudice. David Duke in Louisiana denounced the subsidized beggars (i.e., black people) who had robbed the state of its birthright. At a partisan theatrical staged by the Democratic Party in New Hampshire, Senator Tom Harkin reviled the conspiracy of Republican money. President Bush went to Houston, Texas, to point a trembling and petulant finger at the United States Congress. If the country's domestic affairs had been left to him, the President said, everybody would be as prosperous and smug as Senator Phil Gramm, but the liberals in Congress (blind as mollusks and selfish as eels) had wrecked the voyage of boundless opportunity.

The politicians follow the trends, and apparently they have been told by their handlers to practice the arts of the demagogue. Certainly I cannot remember an election year in which the political discourse—among newspaper editorialists and the single-issue lobbies as well as the candidates—relied so unashamedly on pitting rich against poor, black against white, male against female, city against suburb, young against old. Every public event in New York City—whether academic appointment, traffic delay, or homicide—lends itself to both a black and a white interpretation of the news. The arguments in the arenas of cultural opinion echo the same bitter refrain. The ceaseless quarrels about the canon of preferred texts (about Columbus the Bad and Columbus the Good, about the chosen company of the politically correct, about the ice people and the sun people) pick at the scab of the same questions. Who and what is an American? How and where do we find an identity that is something other than a fright mask? When using the collective national pronoun ("we the people," "we happy few," etc.) whom do we invite into the club of the we?

Maybe the confusion is a corollary to the end of the Cold War. 5 The image of the Soviet Union as monolithic evil held in place the image of the United States as monolithic virtue. Break the circuit of energy transferred between negative and positive poles, and the two empires dissolve into the waving of sectional or nationalist flags. Lacking the reassurance of a foreign demon, we search our own neighborhoods for fiends of convincing malevolence and size.

The search is a boon for the bearers of false witness and the builders of prisons. Because it's so easy to dwell on our differences, even a child of nine can write a Sunday newspaper sermon about the centrifugal forces that drive the society apart. The more difficult and urgent questions have to do with the centripetal forces that bind us together. What traits of character or temperament do we hold in common? Why is it that I can meet a black man in a street or a Hispanic woman on a train and imagine that he and I, or she and I, share an allied hope and a joint purpose? That last question is as American as it is rhetorical, and a Belgian would think it the work of a dreaming imbecile.

What we share is a unified field of emotion, but if we mistake the sources of our energy and courage (i.e., if we think that our uniqueness as Americans rests with the adjectives instead of the noun) then we can be rounded up in categories and sold the slogan of the week for the fear of the month. Political campaigns deal in the commodity of votes, and from now until November I expect that all of them will divide the American promise into its lesser but more marketable properties. For reasons of their own convenience, the sponsors of political campaigns (Democratic, environmental, racial, Republican, sexual, or military-industrial) promote more or less the same false constructions of the American purpose and identity. As follows:

> That the American achieves visible and specific meaning only by reason of his or her association with the political guilds of race, gender, age, ancestry, or social class.

The assumption is as elitist as the view that only a woman endowed with an income of $1 million a year can truly appreciate the beauty of money and the music of Cole Porter. Comparable theories of grace encourage the belief that only black people can know or teach black history, that no white man can play jazz piano, that blonds have a better time, and that Jews can't play basketball.

America was founded on precisely the opposite premise. We were always about becoming, not being; about the prospects for the future, not about the inheritance of the past. The man who rests his case on his color, like the woman who defines herself as a bright cloud of sensibility beyond the understanding of merely mortal men, makes a claim to special privilege not unlike the divine right of kings. The pretensions might buttress the cathedrals of our self-esteem, but they run counter to the lessons of our history.

We are a nation of parvenus, all bound to the hopes of tomor-   10
row, or next week, or next year. John Quincy Adams put it plainly
in a letter to a German correspondent in the 1820s who had written on behalf of several prospective émigrés to ask about the requirements for their success in the New World. "They must cast
off the European skin, never to resume it," Adams said. "They
must look forward to their posterity rather than backward to
their ancestors."

We were always a mixed and piebald company, even on the
seventeenth-century colonial seaboard, and we accepted our
racial or cultural differences as the odds that we were obliged to
overcome or correct. When John Charles Frémont (a.k.a. The
Pathfinder) first descended into California from the East in 1843,
he remarked on the polyglot character of the expedition accom-
panying him south into the San Joaquin Valley:

"Our cavalcade made a strange and grotesque appearance, and
it was impossible to avoid reflecting upon our position and composition in this remote solitude. . .still forced on south by a desert on
one hand and a mountain range on the other; guided by a civilized
Indian, attended by two wild ones from the Sierra; a Chinook from
the Columbia; and our own mixture of American, French, German—all armed; four or five languages heard at once; about a hundred horses and mules, half-wild; American, Spanish and Indian
dresses and equipments intermingled—such was our composition."

The theme of metamorphosis recurs throughout the whole
chronicle of American biography. Men and women start out in one
place and end up in another, never quite knowing how they got
there, perpetually expecting the unexpected, drifting across the
ocean or the plains until they lodge against a marriage, a land deal,
a public office, or a jail. Speaking to the improvised character of
the American experience, Daniel Boorstin, the historian and former Librarian of Congress, also summed up the case against the
arithmetic of the political pollster's zip codes: "No prudent man
dared to be too certain of exactly who he was or what he was about;
everyone had to be prepared to become someone else. To be ready
for such perilous transmigrations was to become an American."

That the American people aspire to become more nearly alike.

The hope is that of the ad salesman and the prison warden, but
it has become depressingly familiar among the managers of political campaigns. Apparently they think that no matter how different

the native songs and dances in different parts of the country, all the tribes and factions want the same beads, the same trinkets, the same prizes. As I listen to operatives from Washington talk about their prospects in the Iowa or New Hampshire primary, I understand that they have in mind the figure of a perfect or ideal American whom everybody in the country would wish to resemble if only everybody could afford to dress like the dummies in the windows of Bloomingdale's or Saks Fifth Avenue. The public opinion polls frame questions in the alphabet of name recognitions and standard brands. The simplicity of the results supports the belief that the American citizen or the American family can be construed as a product, and that with only a little more time and a little more money for research and development all of us will conform to the preferred images seen in a commercial for Miller beer.

15   The apologists for the theory of the uniform American success sometimes present the example of Abraham Lincoln, and as I listen to their sentimental after-dinner speeches about the poor country grown to greatness, I often wonder what they would say if they had met the man instead of the statue. Throughout most of his life Lincoln displayed the character of a man destined for failure—a man who drank too much and told too many jokes (most of them in bad taste), who was habitually late for meetings and always borrowing money, who never seized a business opportunity and missed his own wedding.

The spirit of liberty is never far from anarchy, and the ur-American is apt to look a good deal more like one of the contestants on *Let's Make a Deal* (i.e., somebody dressed like Madonna, or Wyatt Earp, or a giant iguana) than any of the yachtsmen standing around on the dock of Kennebunkport. If America is about nothing else, it is about the invention of the self. Because we have little use for history, and because we refuse the comforts of a society established on the blueprint of class privilege, we find ourselves set adrift at birth in an existential void, inheriting nothing except the obligation to construct a plausible self, to build a raft of identity on which (with a few grains of luck and a cheap bank loan) maybe we can float south to Memphis or the imaginary islands of the blessed. We set ourselves the tasks of making and remaking our destinies with whatever lumber we happen to find lying around on the banks of the Snake or Pecos River.

Who else is the American hero if not a wandering pilgrim who goes forth on a perpetual quest? Melville sent Ahab across the world's oceans in search of a fabulous beast, and Thoreau followed the unicorn of his conscience into the silence of the Maine woods. Between them they marked out the trail of American literature as well as the lines of speculation in American real estate. To a greater or a lesser extent, we are all confidence men, actors playing the characters of our own invention and hoping that the audience—fortunately consisting of impostors as fanciful or synthetic as ourselves—will accept the performance at par value and suspend the judgments of ridicule.

The settled peoples of the earth seldom recognize the American as both a chronic revolutionary and a born pilgrim. The American is always on the way to someplace else (i.e., toward some undetermined future in which all will be well), and when he meets a stranger on the road he begins at once to recite the summary of the story so far—his youth and early sorrows, the sequence of his exits and entrances, his last divorce and his next marriage, the point of his financial departure and the estimated time of his spiritual arrival, the bad news noted and accounted for, the good news still to come. Invariably it is a pilgrim's tale, and the narrator, being American, assumes that he is addressing a fellow pilgrim. He means to exchange notes and compare maps. His newfound companion might be bound toward a completely different dream of Eden (a boat marina in Naples, Florida, instead of a garden in Vermont; a career as a Broadway dancer as opposed to the vice presidency of the Wells Fargo bank), but the destination doesn't matter as much as the common hope of coming safely home to the land of the heart's desire. For the time being, and until something better turns up, we find ourselves embarked on the same voyage, gazing west into the same blue distance.

> That the American people share a common code of moral behavior and subscribe to identical theories of the true, the good, and the beautiful.

Senator Jesse Helms would like to think so, and so would the enforcers of ideological discipline on the vocabulary of the doctrinaire left. The country swarms with people making rules about what we can say or read or study or smoke, and they imagine that we should be grateful for the moral guidelines (market-tested and government-inspected) imposed (for our own good) by a centralized bureau of temporal health and spiritual safety. The would-be reformers of the national character confuse the American sense of equality with the rule of conformity that governs a police state.

It isn't that we believe that every American is as perceptive or as accomplished as any other, but we insist on the preservation of a decent and mutual respect across the lines of age, race, gender, and social class. No citizen is allowed to use another citizen as if he or she were a means to an end; no master can treat his servant as if he or she were only a servant; no government can deal with the governed as if they were nothing more than a mob of votes. The American loathing for the arrogant or self-important man follows from the belief that all present have bet their fortunes (some of them bigger than others, and some of them counterfeit or stolen) on the same hypothesis.

20   The American premise is an existential one, and our moral code is political, its object being to allow for the widest horizons of sight and the broadest range of expression. We protect the other person's liberty in the interest of protecting our own and our virtues conform to the terms and conditions of an arduous and speculative journey. If we look into even so coarse a mirror as the one held up to us by the situation comedies on prime-time television, we see that we value the companionable virtues—helpfulness, forgiveness, kindliness, and, above all, tolerance.

The passenger standing next to me at the rail might be balancing a parrot on his head, but that doesn't mean that he has invented a theory of the self any less implausible than the one I ordered from a department-store catalogue or assembled with the tag lines of a two-year college course on the great books of Western civilization. If the traveler at the port rail can balance a parrot on his head, then I can continue my discussion with Madame Bovary and Mr. Pickwick, and the two gentlemen standing aft of the rum barrels can get on with the business of rigging the price of rifles or barbed wire. The American equation rests on the habit of holding our fellow citizens in thoughtful regard not because they are exceptional (or famous, or beautiful, or rich) but simply because they are our fellow citizens. If we abandon the sense of mutual respect, we abandon the premise as well as the machinery of the American enterprise.

That the triumph of America corresponds to its prowess as a nation-state.

The pretension serves the purposes of the people who talk about "the national security" and "the vital interest of the American people" when what they mean is the power and privilege of government. The oligarchy resident in Washington assumes that all Americans own the same property instead of taking part in the same idea, that we share a joint geopolitical program instead of a common temperament and habit of mind. Even so faithful a servant of the monied interests as Daniel Webster understood the distinction: "The public happiness is to be the aggregate of individuals. Our system begins with the individual man."

The Constitution was made for the uses of the individual (an implement on the order of a plow, an ax, or a surveyor's plumb line), and the institutions of American government were meant to support the liberties of the people, not the ambitions of the state. Given any ambiguity about the order of priority or precedence, it was the law that had to give way to the citizen's freedom of thought and action, not the citizen's freedom of thought and action that had to give way to the law. The Bill of Rights stresses the distinction in the two final amendments, the ninth ("The enumeration in the Constitution, of certain rights, shall not be construed to deny or disparage others retained by the people") and the tenth ("The powers not delegated to the United States by the Constitution, nor prohibited by it to the States, are reserved to the States, respectively, or to the people").

What joins the Americans one to another is not a common nationality, language, race, or ancestry (all of which testify to the burdens of the past) but rather their complicity in a shared work of the imagination. My love of country follows from my love of its freedoms, not from my pride in its fleets or its armies or its gross national product. Construed as a means and not an end, the Constitution stands as the premise for a narrative rather than a plan for an invasion or a monument. The narrative was always plural. Not one story but many stories.

That it is easy to be an American.

I can understand why the politicians like to pretend that   25
America is mostly about going shopping, but I never know why anybody believes the ad copy. Grant the existential terms and conditions of the American enterprise (i.e., that we are all bound to invent ourselves), and the position is both solitary and probably lost. I know a good many people who would rather be British or Nigerian or Swiss.

Lately I've been reading the accounts of the nineteenth-century adventures and pioneers who traveled west from

Missouri under circumstances almost always adverse. Most of them didn't find whatever it was they expected to find behind the next range of mountains or around the next bend in the river. They were looking for a garden in a country that was mostly desert, and the record of their passage is largely one of sorrow and failure. Travelers making their way across the Great Plains in the 1850s reported great numbers of dead horses and abandoned wagons on the trail, the echo of the hopes that so recently preceded them lingering in an empty chair or in the scent of flowers on a new grave.

Reading the diaries and letters, especially those of the women in the caravans, I think of the would-be settlers lost in an immense wilderness, looking into the mirrors of their loneliness and measuring their capacity for self-knowledge against the vastness of the wide and indifferent sky.

Too often we forget the proofs of our courage. If we wish to live in the state of freedom that allows us to make and think and build, then we must accustom ourselves to the shadows on the walls and the wind in trees. The climate of anxiety is the cost of doing business. Just as a monarchy places far fewer burdens on its subjects than a democracy places on its citizens, so also bigotry is easier than tolerance. When something goes wrong with the currency or the schools, it's always comforting to know that the faults can be easily found in something as obvious as a color, or a number, or the sound of a strange language. The multiple adjectives qualifying the American noun enrich the vocabulary of blame, and if the election year continues as it has begun I expect that by next summer we will discover that it is not only middle-aged Protestant males who have been making a wreck of the culture but also (operating secretly and sometimes in disguise) adolescent, sallow, Buddhist females.

Among all the American political virtues, candor is probably the one most necessary to the success of our mutual enterprise. Unless we try to tell each other the truth about what we know and think and see (i.e., the story so far as it appears to the travelers on the voyage out) we might as well amuse ourselves (for as long as somebody else allows us to do so) with fairy tales. The vitality of the American democracy always has rested on the capacity of its citizens to speak and think without cant. As long ago as 1838, addressing the topic of *The American Democrat*, James Fenimore Cooper argued that the word "American" was synonymous with the habit of telling the truth: "By candor we are not to understand trifling and uncalled for expositions of truth; but a sentiment that proves a conviction of the necessity of speaking truth, when speaking at all; a contempt for all designing evasions of our real opinions.

"In all the general concerns, the public has a right to be   30 treated with candor. Without this manly and truly republican quality . . . the institutions are converted into a stupendous fraud."

If we indulge ourselves with evasions and the pleasure of telling lies, we speak to our fears and our weaknesses instead of to our courage and our strength. We can speak plainly about our differences only if we know and value what we hold in common. Like the weather and third-rate journalism, bigotry in all its declensions is likely to be with us for a long time (certainly as long as the next hundred years), but unless we can draw distinctions and make jokes about our racial or cultural baggage, the work of our shared imagination must vanish in the mist of lies. The lies might win elections (or sell newspapers and economic theories) but they bind us to the theaters of wish and dream. If I must like or admire a fellow citizen for his or her costume of modifying adjectives (because he or she is black or gay or rich), then I might as well believe that the lost continent of Atlantis will rise next summer from the sea and that the Japanese will continue to make the payments—now and forever, world without end—on all our mortgages and battleships.

Among all the nations of the earth, America is the one that has come most triumphantly to terms with the mixtures of blood and caste, and maybe it is another of history's ironic jokes that we should wish to repudiate our talent for assimilation at precisely the moment in time when so many other nations in the world (in Africa and Western Europe as well as the Soviet Union) look to the promise of the American example. The jumble of confused or mistaken identities that was the story of nineteenth-century America has become the story of a late-twentieth-century world defined by a vast migration of peoples across seven continents and as many oceans. Why, then, do we lose confidence in ourselves and grow fearful of our mongrel freedoms?

The politician who would lift us to a more courageous understanding of ourselves might begin by saying that we are all, each and every one of us, as much at fault as anybody else, that no matter whom we blame for our troubles (whether George Bush, or Al Sharpton, or David Duke) or how pleasant the invective (racist, sexist, imperialist pig), we still have to rebuild our cities and revise our laws. We can do the work together, or we can stand around making strong statements about each other's clothes.

Questions for Discussion

1. Why does Lapham believe that expressions containing the word "American" in which there is "subordination of the noun to the adjectives" (as in expressions like "Asian-American") both mock the idea of America and advance the agenda of politicians? Do you agree with his thesis?

2. Beginning in paragraph 8, Lapham takes up four "false constructions" of the American purpose and identity. What are these false constructions, and how does Lapham attempt to refute them? Do you agree that all of these constructions or statements are as unfounded as Lapham believes? Explain your point of view.

3. In paragraph 11, Lapham makes references to historical examples and quotations from history to support his claim that America's main cultural premise is one of metamorphosis or change, a looking to a new identity in the future. Does the evidence he presents for this concept of American identity seem convincing? Explain your response.

4. Lapham states in paragraph 22 that Americans tend to hold our "fellow citizens in thoughtful regard . . . simply because they are our fellow citizens." Do you agree that the essence of American citizenship involves such blanket acceptance of one's fellow Americans, regardless of their values or ethnicity?

5. In his closing paragraphs, Lapham emphasizes the importance of honesty and candor as we try to unify our country as citizens working together for the common good. Is it clear what he means by candor, as opposed to "the mist of lies"? Does he seem to mean the same thing by truth and lying as James Fenimore Cooper does in the quotation in paragraph 29? Is it always possible to be truthful in a civil society?

Ideas for Writing

1. Write an essay in which you develop the idea of "shared work" that Lapham believes will bring us together. What types of shared work would you use as examples or participate in? What sort of shared work has been proposed in the wake of 9/11? Do you think that shared work has helped our country recover from the tragedy of 9/11?

2. One of Lapham's major points concerns the destructiveness to our country and its shared values of change and transfor-

mation that come about when there is an overemphasis on taking one's identity from race, origins, or class. Write an argument essay in which you give your own views on this issue.

A Quilt of a Country: Out of Many, One?

ANNA QUINDLEN

Anna Quindlen (b.1953) graduated from Barnard College in 1974 and worked at the *New York Times* as a reporter and editor from 1977 to 1985. She then began writing her own column for the *New York Times*. Quindlen has been awarded many prizes for journalism and in 1992 received the Pulitzer Prize for commentary. She has published many books including several collections of her columns such as *Living Out Loud* (1988) and *Thinking Out Loud* (1993). Her most recent novels include *Black and Blue* (1998) and *Blessings* (2002). The following selection was first published in *Newsweek* on September 27, 2001, as a response to the tragedy of 9/11 and as a look at the diverse American society that she believes is our strength.

---- ✦ ----

America is an improbable idea. A mongrel nation built of ever-changing disparate parts, it is held together by a notion, the notion that all men are created equal, though everyone knows that most men consider themselves better than someone. "Of all the nations in the world, the United States was built in nobody's image," the historian Daniel Boorstin wrote. That's because it was built of bits and pieces that seem discordant, like the crazy quilts that have been one of its great folk-art forms, velvet and calico and checks and brocades. Out of many, one. That is the ideal.

The reality is often quite different, a great national striving consisting frequently of failure. Many of the oft-told stories of the most pluralistic nation on earth are stories not of tolerance, but of bigotry. Slavery and sweatshops, the burning of crosses and the ostracism of the other. Children learn in social-studies class and in the news of the lynching of blacks, the denial of rights to women, the murders of gay men. It is difficult to know how to convince them that this amounts to "crown thy good with brotherhood," that amid all the failures is something spectacularly successful. Perhaps they understand it at this moment, when enormous tragedy, as it so often does, demands a time of reflection on enormous blessings.

This is a nation founded on a conundrum, what Mario Cuomo has characterized as "community added to individualism." These two are our defining ideals; they are also in constant conflict. Historians today bemoan the ascendancy of a kind of prideful apartheid in America, saying that the clinging to ethnicity, in background and custom, has undermined the concept of unity. These historians must have forgotten the past, or have gilded it. The New York of my children is no more Balkanized, probably less so, than the Philadelphia of my father, in which Jewish boys would walk several blocks out of their way to avoid the Irish divide of Chester Avenue. (I was the product of a mixed marriage, across barely bridgeable lines: an Italian girl, an Irish boy. How quaint it seems now, how incendiary then.) The Brooklyn of Francie Nolan's famous tree, the Newark of which Portnoy complained, even the uninflected WASP suburbs of Cheever's characters: they are ghettos, pure and simple. Do the Cambodians and the Mexicans in California coexist less easily today than did the Irish and Italians of Massachusetts a century ago? You know the answer.

What is the point of this splintered whole? What is the point of a nation in which Arab cabbies chauffeur Jewish passengers through the streets of New York—and in which Jewish cabbies chauffeur Arab passengers, too, and yet speak in theory of hatred, one for the other? What is the point of a nation in which one part seems to be always on the verge of fisticuffs with another, blacks and whites, gays and straights, left and right, Pole and Chinese and Puerto Rican and Slovenian? Other countries with such divisions have in fact divided into new nations with new names, but not this one, impossibly interwoven even in its hostilities.

5   Once these disparate parts were held together by a common enemy, by the fault lines of world wars and the electrified fence of communism. With the end of the cold war there was the creeping concern that without a focus for hatred and distrust, a sense of national identity would evaporate, that the left side of the hyphen—African-American, Mexican-American, Irish-American—would overwhelm the right. And slow-growing domestic traumas like

economic unrest and increasing crime seemed more likely to emphasize division than community. Today the citizens of the United States have come together once more because of armed conflict and enemy attack. Terrorism has led to devastation—and unity.

Yet even in 1994, the overwhelming majority of those surveyed by the National Opinion Research Center agreed with this statement: "The U.S. is a unique country that stands for something special in the world." One of the things that it stands for is this vexing notion that a great nation can consist entirely of refugees from other nations, that people of different, even warring religions and cultures can live, if not side by side, than on either side of the country's Chester Avenues. Faced with this diversity there is little point in trying to isolate anything remotely resembling a national character, but there are two strains of behavior that, however tenuously, abet the concept of unity.

There is that Calvinist undercurrent in the American psyche that loves the difficult, the demanding, that sees mastering the impossible, whether it be prairie or subway, as a test of character, and so glories in the struggle of this fractured coalescing. And there is a grudging fairness among the citizens of the United States that eventually leads most to admit that, no matter what the English-only advocates try to suggest, the new immigrants are not so different from our own parents or grandparents. Leonel Castillo, former director of the Immigration and Naturalization Service and himself the grandson of Mexican immigrants, once told the writer Studs Terkel proudly, "The old neighborhood Ma-Pa stores are still around. They are not Italian or Jewish or Eastern European any more. Ma and Pa are now Korean, Vietnamese, Iraqi, Jordanian, Latin American. They live in the store. They work seven days a week. Their kids are doing well in school. They're making it. Sound familiar?"

Tolerance is the word used most often when this kind of coexistence succeeds, but tolerance is a vanilla-pudding word, standing for little more than the allowance of letting others live unremarked and unmolested. Pride seems excessive, given the American willingness to endlessly complain about them, them being whoever is new, different, unknown or currently under suspicion. But patriotism is partly taking pride in this unlikely ability to throw all of us together in a country that across its length and breadth is as different as a dozen countries, and still be able to call it by one name. When photographs of the faces of all those who died in the World Trade Center destruction are assembled in one place, it will be possible to trace in the skin color, the shape of the eyes and the noses, the texture of the hair, a map of the world. These are the representatives of a mongrel nation that somehow, at times like this, has one spirit. Like many improbable ideas, when it actually works, it's a wonder.

Questions for Discussion

1. According to Quindlen, what are the two conflicting ideals that form the foundation of our country? What evidence does she present to show that the American character is changing and yet also staying the same?
2. Why does Quindlen believe that bigotry is a defining fact of life in the United States? Do you agree with her when she says that we are unwilling to admit "that most men consider themselves better than someone"? Explain why you agree or disagree with her.
3. Why does Quindlen claim that terrorism has led us back to unity? Do you agree or disagree with her? Explain your point of view.
4. How does Quindlen define the American character and psyche in this article? How does the metaphor of the quilt help to clarify her definition? Does her definition seem accurate or stereotypical?

Ideas for Writing

1. Write an essay in which you express your point of view on how the concept of citizenship has been altered as a consequence of 9/11. Do you believe that the United States is becoming more or less tolerant of differences, in race, religion, gender, and country of origin?
2. Write an essay about the metaphors that have been used to describe our society. Examine Quindlen's metaphor of the quilt and compare it to some of the dominant metaphors that have been used to describe American society and the roles immigrants play in it: the assimilationist metaphors of the melting-pot or stew, the salad-bowl metaphor (related to cultural pluralism), the mosaic metaphor, etc. What is different about Quindlen's metaphor?

I Have a Dream

MARTIN LUTHER KING, JR.

Martin Luther King, Jr. (1928–1968) received a Ph.D. in theology from Boston University. After graduation, King became a pastor and founded the Southern Christian Leadership Conference, developing the concept, derived from the teachings of Thoreau and Gandhi, of nonviolent civil disobedience or planned resistance to obtain civil rights and put an end to segregation. King won the Nobel Peace Prize in 1964. Although his life ended in a tragic assassination, King wrote many speeches and essays on race and civil rights that are collected in books such as *I Have A Dream: Writings and Speeches That Changed the World* (1992) and *The Papers of Martin Luther King, Jr.* (1992). "I Have a Dream," King's most famous speech, was originally delivered in 1963 in front of the Lincoln Memorial in Washington, D.C., before a crowd estimated at 300,000. Notice how King uses powerful language, images, and comparisons to move his massive, diverse audience and to express his idealistic dream for America's future citizens.

———————— ✦ ————————

I am happy to join with you today in what will go down in history as the greatest demonstration for freedom in the history of our nation.

Five score years ago, a great American, in whose symbolic shadow we stand today, signed the Emancipation Proclamation. This momentous decree came as a great beacon light of hope to millions of Negro slaves who had been seared in the flames of withering injustice. It came as a joyous daybreak to end the long night of their captivity.

But one hundred years later, the Negro still is not free; one hundred years later, the life of the Negro is still sadly crippled by the manacles of segregation and the chains of discrimination; one hundred years later, the Negro lives on a lonely island of poverty in the midst of a vast ocean of material prosperity; one hundred years later, the Negro is still languished in the corners of American society and finds himself in exile in his own land.

So we've come here today to dramatize a shameful condition. In a sense we've come to our nation's capital to cash a check. When the architects of our republic wrote the magnificent words of the Constitution and the Declaration of Independence, they were signing a promissory note to which every American was to fall heir. This note was the promise that all men, yes, black men as well as white men, would be guaranteed the unalienable rights of life, liberty, and the pursuit of happiness.

5   It is obvious today that America has defaulted on this promissory note in so far as her citizens of color are concerned. Instead of honoring this sacred obligation, America has given the Negro people a bad check, a check which has come back marked "insufficient funds." But we refuse to believe that the bank of justice is bankrupt. We refuse to believe that there are insufficient funds in the great vaults of opportunity of this nation. And so we've come to cash this check, a check that will give us upon demand the riches of freedom and the security of justice.

We have also come to this hallowed spot to remind America of the fierce urgency of now. This is no time to engage in the luxury of cooling off or to take the tranquilizing drug of gradualism. Now is the time to make real the promises of democracy; now is the time to rise from the dark and desolate valley of segregation to the sunlit path of racial justice; now is the time to lift our nation from the quicksands of racial injustice to the solid rock of brotherhood; now is the time to make justice a reality for all of God's children. It would be fatal for the nation to overlook the urgency of the moment. This sweltering summer of the Negro's legitimate discontent will not pass until there is an invigorating autumn of freedom and equality.

Nineteen sixty-three is not an end, but a beginning. And those who hope that the Negro needed to blow off steam and will now be content, will have a rude awakening if the nation returns to business as usual. There will be neither rest nor tranquility in America until the Negro is granted his citizenship rights. The whirlwinds of revolt will continue to shake the foundations of our nation until the bright day of justice emerges.

But there is something that I must say to my people, who stand on the worn threshold which leads into the palace of justice. In the process of gaining our rightful place, we must not be guilty of wrongful deeds. Let us not seek to satisfy our thirst for freedom by drinking from the cup of bitterness and hatred. We must forever conduct our struggle on the high plain of dignity and discipline. We must not allow our creative protests to degenerate into physical violence. Again and again we must rise to the majestic heights of meeting physical force with soul force. The marvelous new militancy, which has engulfed the Negro community, must not lead us to a distrust of all white people. For many of our white brothers, as evidenced by their presence here today, have come to realize that their destiny is tied up with our destiny. And they have come to realize that their freedom is inextricably bound to our freedom. We cannot walk alone. And as we walk, we must make the pledge that we shall always march ahead. We cannot turn back.

There are those who are asking the devotees of Civil Rights, "When will you be satisfied?" We can never be satisfied as long as the Negro is the victim of the unspeakable horrors of police brutality; we can never be satisfied as long as our bodies, heavy with the fatigue of travel, cannot gain lodging in the motels of the highways and the hotels of the cities; we cannot be satisfied as long as the Negro's basic mobility is from a smaller ghetto to a larger one; we can never be satisfied as long as our children are stripped of their selfhood and robbed of their dignity by signs stating "For Whites Only"; we cannot be satisfied as long as the Negro in Mississippi cannot vote and a Negro in New York believes he has nothing for which to vote. No! No, we are not satisfied, and we will not be satisfied until "justice rolls down like waters and righteousness like a mighty stream."

I am not unmindful that some of you have come here out of great trials and tribulations. Some of you have come fresh from narrow jail cells. Some of you have come from areas where your quest for freedom left you battered by the storms of persecution and staggered by the winds of police brutality. You have been the veterans of creative suffering. Continue to work with the faith that unearned suffering is redemptive. Go back to Mississippi. Go back to Alabama. Go back to South Carolina. Go back to Georgia. Go back to Louisiana. Go back to the slums and ghettos of our Northern cities, knowing that somehow this situation can and will be changed. Let us not wallow in the valley of despair.

I say to you today, my friends, so even though we face the difficulties of today and tomorrow, I still have a dream. It is a dream deeply rooted in the American dream. I have a dream that one day this nation will rise up and live out the true meaning of its creed, "We hold these truths to be self-evident, that all men are created equal." I have a dream that one day on the red hills of Georgia, sons of former slaves and the sons of former slaves owners will be able to sit down together at the table of brotherhood. I have a dream that one day even the state of Mississippi, a state

10

sweltering with the heat of injustice, sweltering with the heat of oppression, will be transformed into an oasis of freedom and justice. I have a dream that my four little children will one day live in a nation where they will not be judged by the color of their skin, but by the content of their character.

I HAVE A DREAM TODAY!

I have a dream that one day down in Alabama—with its vicious racists, with its Governor having his lips dripping with the words of interposition and nullification—one day right there in Alabama, little black boys and black girls will be able to join hands with little white boys and white girls as sisters and brothers.

I HAVE A DREAM TODAY!

15   I have a dream today that one day every valley shall be exalted, and every hill and mountain shall be made low. The rough places will be plain and the crooked places will be made straight, "and the glory of the Lord shall be revealed, and all flesh shall see it together."

This is our hope. This is the faith that I go back to the South with. With this faith we will be able to hew out of the mountain of despair a stone of hope. With this faith we will be able to transform the jangling discords of our nation into a beautiful symphony of brotherhood. With this faith we will be able to work together, to pray together, to struggle together, to go to jail together, to stand up for freedom together, knowing that we will be free one day. And this will be the day. This will be the day when all of God's children will be able to sing with new meaning, "My country 'tis of thee, sweet land of liberty, of thee I sing. Land where my fathers died, land of the pilgrims' pride, from every mountainside, let freedom ring." And if America is to be a great nation, this must become true.

So let freedom ring from the prodigious hilltops of New Hampshire; let freedom ring from the mighty mountains of New York; let freedom ring from the heightening Alleghenies of Pennsylvania; let freedom ring from the snow-capped Rockies of Colorado; let freedom ring from the curvaceous slopes of California. But not only that. Let freedom ring from Stone Mountain of Georgia; let freedom ring from Lookout Mountain of Tennessee; let freedom ring from every hill and mole hill of Mississippi. "From every mountainside, let freedom ring." And when this happens, and when we allow freedom to ring, when we let it ring from every village and every hamlet, from every state and every city, we will be able to speed up that day when all of God's children, black men and white men, Jews and Gentiles, Protestants and Catholics, will be able to join hands and sing in the words of the old Negro spiritual: "Free at last. Free at last. Thank God Almighty, we are free at last."

Questions for Discussion

1. What is the "dream" to which the title of the essay refers? What techniques or strategies does King use to define his dream? Is his definition effective? Why or why not?
2. What does King mean by his analogy of a "promissory note"? Why is this an effective metaphor?
3. Who is the primary audience of King's speech, the "we" to whom he refers in paragraph 4, and the "you" in paragraph 10? How does King try to appeal to the needs and concerns of this audience, as well as to stretch his message beyond the immediate needs and expectations of the present audience and to appeal to other audiences, including those who might see the speech on television or hear it on radio?
4. What does King mean by "creative suffering" in paragraph 10? How does this expression reflect different aspects of his vision of nonviolent resistance?

Ideas for Writing

1. Write a speech in the form of an essay and/or multimedia presentation that discusses a dream that you have for your society. Emphasize the role that citizens need to play in realizing the dream. Express your dream in emotional and persuasive language and imagery (including, if you desire, a description of slides, audio clips, or other multimedia features) in order to appeal to the specific audience that you understand well and want to persuade. Indicate your intended audience.
2. Based on your understanding and reading about the current state of civil rights in America, write an essay in which you reflect on whether King, if he were alive today, would feel that his dream for African-Americans, as well as all minorities in our nation, had come true. What aspects of his dream might King feel still remain to be accomplished?

Hispanics and the American Dream
LINDA CHAVEZ

Linda Chavez writes about Hispanic issues from a conservative perspective. She has been a columnist for *USA Today*, and has written for many publications including *The Washington Post*, *The Wall Street Journal*, and *The New Republic*. She regularly appears on the *McLaughlin Group*, *CNN & Co.*, and *The NewsHour with Jim Leherer*. Her books include *Out of the Barrio: Toward a New Politics of Hispanic Assimilation* (1992) and *From Sugar Daddies to Uncle Sam* (1999). Chavez has held public positions such as director of the U.S. Commission on Civil Rights and president of the Center for Equal Opportunity. The following essay, which appeared originally in *Imprimis* (1996), presents a positive picture of recent social and economic advances made by Hispanics in the United States.

———————— ✦ ————————

The more than twenty-one million Hispanics now living in the United States are fast becoming the nation's largest minority group. Some demographers can already see the day when one of three Americans will be of Hispanic descent. Will this mean a divided nation with millions of unassimilated, Spanish-speaking, poor, uneducated Hispanics living in the barrios? Well, here is one reply:

> Each decade offered us hope, but our hopes evaporated into smoke. We became the poorest of the poor, the most segregated minority in schools, the lowest paid group in America, and the least educated minority in this nation.

This pessimistic view of Hispanics' progress—offered in 1990 by the president of the National Council of La Raza, one of the country's leading Hispanic civil rights groups—is the prevalent one among Hispanic leaders and is shared by many outside the Hispanic community as well. Hispanics are widely perceived as the dregs of society with little hope of participating in the American Dream.

The trouble with this perception is that it is wrong. The success of Hispanics in the United States has been tremendous. They represent an emerging middle class that is a valuable addition to our culture and our economy. However, their story has been effectively suppressed by Hispanic advocates whose only apparent interest is in spreading the notion that Latinos cannot make it in this society. This has been an easy task since the Hispanic poor, who, although they only constitute about one-fourth of the Hispanic population, are visible to all. These are the Hispanics most likely to be studied, analyzed, and reported on, and certainly they are the ones most likely to be read about. A recent computer search of stories about Hispanics in major newspapers and magazines over a twelve-month period turned up more than eighteen hundred stories in which the words *Hispanic* or *Latino* occurred in close connection with the word *poverty*. In most people's minds, the expression "poor Hispanic" is almost redundant.

HAS HISPANICS' PROGRESS STALLED?

Most Hispanics, rather than being poor, lead solidly lower middle- or middle-class lives, but finding evidence to support this thesis is sometimes difficult. Of course, Hispanic groups vary one from another, as do individuals within any group. Most analysts acknowledge, for example, that Cubans are highly successful. Within one generation, they have virtually closed the earnings and education gap with other Americans. Although some analysts claim their success is due exclusively to their higher socioeconomic status when they arrived, many Cuban refugees—especially those who came after the first wave in the 1960s—were in fact skilled or semiskilled workers with relatively little education. Their accomplishments in the United States mainly are attributable to diligence and hard work.

Cubans have tended to establish enclave economies, in the   5
traditional immigrant mode, opening restaurants, stores, and other émigré-oriented services. Some Cubans have even formed banks, specializing in international transactions attuned to Latin American as well as local customers, and others have made major investments in real estate development in South Florida. These ventures have provided not only big profits for a few Cubans but jobs for many more. By 1980, there were eighteen thousand Cuban-owned businesses in Miami, and about 70 percent of all Cubans there owned their own homes.

But Cubans are, as a rule, dismissed as the exception among Hispanics. What about other Hispanic groups? Why has there been no "progress" among them? The largest and most important group is the Mexican American population. Its leaders have driven much of the policy agenda affecting all Hispanics, but the importance of Mexican Americans also stems from the fact that they have had a longer history in the United States than any other Hispanic group. If Mexican Americans whose families have lived in the United States for generations are not yet making it in this society, they may have a legitimate claim to consider themselves a more or less permanently disadvantaged group.

That is precisely what Mexican American leaders suggest is happening. Their "proof" is that statistical measures of Mexican American achievement in education, earnings, poverty rates, and other social and economic indicators have remained largely unchanged for decades. If Mexican Americans had made progress, it would show up in these areas, so the argument goes. Since it doesn't, progress must be stalled. In the post-civil rights era, it is also assumed that the failure of a minority to close the social and economic gap with whites is the result of persistent discrimination. Progress is perceived not in absolute but in relative terms. The poor may become less poor over time, but so long as those on the upper rungs of the economic ladder are climbing even faster, the poor are believed to have suffered some harm, even if they have made absolute gains and their lives are much improved. But in order for Hispanics (or any group on the lower rungs) to close the gap, they would have to progress at an even greater rate than non-Hispanic whites.

Is this a fair way to judge Hispanics' progress? No. It makes almost no sense to apply this test today (if it ever did) because the Hispanic population itself is changing so rapidly. In 1959, 85 percent of all persons of Mexican origin living in the United States were native-born. Today, only about two-thirds of the people of Mexican origin were born in the United States, and among adults barely one in two was born here. Increasingly, the Hispanic population, including that of Mexican origin, is made up of new immigrants, who, like immigrants of every era, start off at the bottom of the economic ladder. This infusion of new immigrants is bound to distort our image of progress in the Hispanic population if, each time we measure the group, we include people who have just arrived and have yet to make their way in this society.

In 1980, there were about 14.6 million Hispanics living in the United States; in 1990, there were nearly twenty-one million, representing an increase of 44 percent in one decade. At least one-half of this increase was the result of immigration, legal and illegal. Not surprisingly, when these Hispanics—often poorly educated with minimal or no ability to speak English—are added to the pool being measured, the achievement level of the whole group falls. Yet no major Hispanic organization will acknowledge the validity of this reasonable assumption. Instead, Hispanic leaders complain, "Hispanics are the population that has benefited least from the American economy."

In fact, a careful examination of the voluminous data on the Hispanic population gathered by the Census Bureau and other federal agencies shows that, as a group, Hispanics have made significant progress and that most of them have moved into the social and economic mainstream. In most respects, Hispanics—particularly those born here—are very much like other Americans: They work hard, support their own families without outside assistance, have more education and higher earnings than their parents, and own their own homes. In short, they are pursuing the American Dream with increasing success.

10

THE HISPANIC FAMILY

No institution is more important to the success of Hispanics (or any group) than the family. Studies published in the early 1990s reported that 73 percent of all Mexican-origin families and 77 percent of all Cuban-origin families consist of married couples. Only 20 percent of the Mexican-origin and 19 percent of the Cuban-origin families are headed by women with no husband present. While out-of-wedlock births to Mexican-origin women are higher than those to white women generally, they fall considerably short of the number of such births to black women, and Hispanic children born out of wedlock are still likely to grow up in families with two parents.

The babies of Mexican-origin women, even those who have received little or no prenatal care, are generally quite healthy. There is also a lower infant mortality rate and smaller incidence of low birth weight, a common predictor of health problems, than among blacks and whites. While researchers are not sure what accounts for the apparent health of even poor Mexican babies, one reason may be that their mothers are less likely to drink, smoke, or use drugs, and they place special emphasis on good nutrition while pregnant.

In general, Hispanic families are somewhat more traditional than non-Hispanic families: Men are expected to work to support their families and women to care for children. Hispanic families tend to be child-centered, which increases the importance of women's role as childbearers. Hispanics are also more likely than other Americans to believe that the demands and needs of the family should take precedence over those of the individual. In an earlier age this attitude was common among other ethnic groups—Italians, for example. Today, however, it runs counter to the dominant culture of individualism characteristic of American life and may even impede individual success. This perhaps explains why so many young Hispanics are starting to drop out of school to take jobs, a decision that has some immediate financial benefits for the family but is detrimental to the individual in the long run. Nonetheless, Hispanics' attachment to family is one of their most positive cultural attributes. Family members are expected to help each other in times of financial or other need, which some analysts believe explains why so many Mexican-origin families shun welfare even when their poverty makes them eligible for assistance.

HISPANICS AND PUBLIC POLICY

For most Hispanics, especially those born in the United States, the last few decades have brought greater economic opportunity and social mobility. They are building solid lower middle- and middle-class lives that include two-parent households, with a male head who works full-time and earns a wage commensurate with his education and training. Their educational level has been steadily rising, their earnings no longer reflect wide disparities with those of non-Hispanics, and their occupational distribution is coming to resemble more closely that of the general population. They are buying homes—42 percent of all Hispanics owned or were purchasing their homes in 1989, including 47 percent of all Mexican Americans—and moving away from inner cities. Even in areas with very high concentrations of Hispanics, like Los Angeles, the sociologist Douglas Massey reports, "segregation [is] low or moderate on all dimensions." And, in what is perhaps the ultimate test of assimilation, about one-third of all U.S.-born Hispanics under the age of thirty-five are marrying non-Hispanics.

In light of these facts, the policy prescriptions offered by many Hispanic advocacy organizations and by most politicians seem oddly out of sync. They rely too much on government programs of doubtful efficacy like affirmative action, welfare, and bilingual public education. And they perpetuate demeaning stereotypes of the very people they claim they are championing. What they should be doing instead is promoting tax reform, deregulation, enterprise zones, English instruction, and private education—all of which will help Hispanics help themselves.

Groups do not all advance at precisely the same rate in this society—sometimes because of discrimination, sometimes because of other factors. As Thomas Sowell and others have pointed out, no multiethnic society in the world exhibits utopian equality of income, education, and occupational status for every one of its ethnic groups. What is important is that opportunities be made available to all persons, regardless of race or ethnicity. Ultimately, however, it will be up to individuals to take advantage of those opportunities. Increasing numbers of Hispanics are doing just that. And no government action can replace the motivation and will to succeed that propels genuine individual achievement.

Questions for Discussion

1. According to Chavez, why does such a negative stereotype of the Hispanic or Latino exist in this culture? What has perpetuated this stereotype and why is it inaccurate?
2. Why have Cubans, seen as an exception, been successful, in Chavez's view?
3. Why does Chavez believe that the progress of Mexican-Americans has been misrepresented by the organizations that represent them?
4. How has the traditional Hispanic family structure supported the ability of Hispanics to succeed in America? What does Chavez believe is the key to furthering the success of Hispanics in the United States?

Ideas for Writing

1. Referring to Chavez's evidence and research that you do on your own, write an argument that supports or refutes her claim that Hispanics are inaccurately stereotyped as poor and

unable to progress as quickly as other minorities in the
United States.

2. Interview Hispanic families in your community or in a
nearby community to find out how they feel about the stereotypes of Hispanics that they encounter in their daily lives.
What do they value most about their family structure and
about their educational opportunities? Write up your interview in the form of an essay, quoting directly from your interviews when relevant.

Should English Be the Law?
ROBERT D. KING

Robert D. King (b. 1936) received an M.S. in mathematics from
Georgia Tech and a Ph.D. in German Linguistics from the University of Wisconsin in 1965. King is a professor at the University of
Texas at Austin, where he has taught since 1965 and served as
Chair of the Linguistics Department. He has published numerous
scholarly articles in linguistics and a book, *Nehru and the Language Politics of India* (1996). Currently he is working on a book
about language conflicts in America, titled, *Leave Language Alone,
Dammit!* In the following essay, written for the *Atlantic Monthly*
in 1997, King discusses the "English Only" movement and takes
an historical and international perspective on the failure of efforts to establish a single national language or to ban minority
languages and dialects.

◆

We have known race riots, draft riots, labor violence, secession, antiwar protests, and a whiskey rebellion, but one kind
of trouble we've never had: a language riot. Language riot? It
sounds like a joke. The very idea of language as a political force—
as something that might threaten to split a country wide apart—
is alien to our way of thinking and to our cultural traditions.

This may be changing. On August 1 of last year [1996] the
U.S. House of Representatives approved a bill that would make
English the official language of the United States. The vote was

259 to 169, with 223 Republicans and thirty-six Democrats voting in favor and eight Republicans, 160 Democrats, and one independent voting against. The debate was intense, acrid, and partisan. On March 25 of last year the Supreme Court agreed to review a case involving an Arizona law that would require public employees to conduct government business only in English. Arizona is one of several states that have passed "Official English" or "English Only" laws. The appeal to the Supreme Court followed a 6-to-5 ruling, in October of 1995, by a federal appeals court striking down the Arizona law. These events suggest how divisive a public issue language could become in America—even if it has until now scarcely been taken seriously.

Traditionally, the American way has been to make English the national language—but to do so quietly, locally, without fuss. The Constitution is silent on language: the Founding Fathers had no need to legislate that English be the official language of the country. It has always been taken for granted that English *is* the national language, and that one must learn English in order to make it in America. . . .

. . . That tradition began to change in the wake of the anything-goes attitudes and the celebration of cultural differences arising in the 1960s. A 1975 amendment to the Voting Rights Act of 1965 mandated the "bilingual ballot" under certain circumstances, notably when the voters of selected language groups reached five percent or more in a voting district. Bilingual education became a byword of educational thinking during the 1960s. By the 1970s linguists had demonstrated convincingly—at least to other academics—that black English (today called African-American vernacular English or Ebonics) was not "bad" English but a different kind of authentic English with its own rules. Predictably, there have been scattered demands that black English be included in bilingual-education programs.

It was against this background that the movement to make   5
English the official language of the country arose. In 1981 Senator S. I. Hayakawa, long a leading critic of bilingual education and bilingual ballots, introduced in the U.S. Senate a constitutional amendment that not only would have made English the official language but would have prohibited federal and state laws and regulations requiring the use of other languages. His English Language Amendment died in the Ninety-seventh Congress. . . .

. . . Many issues intersect in the controversy over Official English: immigration (above all), the rights of minorities (Spanish-speaking minorities in particular), the pros and cons of bilingual education, tolerance, how best to educate the children of immigrants, and the place of cultural diversity in school curricula and in the American society in general. The question that lies at the root of most of the uneasiness is this: Is America threatened by the preservation of languages other than English? Will America, if it continues on its traditional path of benign linguistic neglect, go the way of Belgium, Canada, and Sri Lanka—three countries among many whose unity is gravely imperiled by language and ethnic conflicts?

LANGUAGE AND NATIONALITY

. . . The marriage of language and nationalism goes back at least to Romanticism and specifically to Rousseau, who argued in his *Essay on the Origin of Languages* that language must develop before politics is possible and that language originally distinguished nations from one another. A little-remembered aim of the French Revolution—itself the legacy of Rousseau—was to impose a national language on France, where regional languages such as Provençal, Breton, and Basque were still strong competitors against standard French, the French of the Ile de France. As late as 1789, when the Revolution began, half the population of the south of France, which spoke Provençal, did not understand French. A century earlier the playwright Racine said that he had had to resort to Spanish and Italian to make himself understood in the southern French town of Uzès. After the Revolution nationhood itself became aligned with language. . . .

In much of the world, ethnic unity and cultural identification are routinely defined by language. To be Arab is to speak Arabic, Bengali identity is based on language in spite of the division of Bengali-speakers between Hindu India and Muslim Bangladesh. When eastern Pakistan seceded from greater Pakistan in 1971, it named itself Bangladesh: *desa* means "country"; *bangla* means not the Bengali people or the Bengali territory but the Bengali language.

Scratch most nationalist movements and you find a linguistic grievance. The demands for independence of the Baltic states (Latvia, Lithuania, and Estonia) were intimately bound up with fears for the loss of their respective languages and cultures in a sea of Russianness. In Belgium the war between French and Flemish threatens an already weakly fused country. The present atmosphere of Belgium is dark and anxious, costive; the metaphor of divorce is a staple of private and public discourse. The lines of terrorism in Sri Lanka are drawn between Tamil Hindus and Sinhalese Buddhists—and also between the Tamil and Sinhalese languages. Worship of the French language fortifies the movement for an independent Quebec. Whether a united Canada will survive into the twenty-first century is a question too close to call. Much of the anxiety about language in the United States is probably fueled by the "Quebec problem": unlike Belgium, which is a small European country, or Sri Lanka, which is halfway around the world, Canada is our close neighbor.

Language is a convenient surrogate for nonlinguistic claims   10
that are often awkward to articulate, for they amount to a demand for more political and economic power. Militant Sikhs in India call for a state of their own: Khalistan ("Land of the Pure" in Punjabi). They frequently couch this as a demand for a linguistic state, which has a certain simplicity about it, a clarity of motive—justice, even, because states in India are normally linguistic states. But the Sikh demands blend religion, economics, language, and retribution for sins both punished and unpunished in a country where old sins cast long shadows.

Language is an explosive issue in the countries of the former Soviet Union. The language conflict in Estonia has been especially bitter. Ethnic Russians make up almost a third of Estonia's population, and most of them do not speak or read Estonian, although Russians have lived in Estonia for more than a generation. Estonia has passed legislation requiring knowledge of the Estonian language as a condition of citizenship. Nationalist groups in independent Lithuania sought restrictions on the use of Polish—again, old sins, long shadows. . . .

. . . Slovakia, relieved now of the need to accommodate to Czech cosmopolitan sensibilities, has passed a law making Slovak its official language. (Czech is to Slovak pretty much as Croatian is to Serbian.) Doctors in state hospitals must speak to patients in Slovak, even if another language would aid diagnosis and treatment. Some 600,000 Slovaks—more than 10 percent of the population—are ethnically Hungarian. Even staff meetings in Hungarian-language schools must be in Slovak. (The government dropped a stipulation that church weddings be conducted in Slovak after heavy opposition from the Roman Catholic

Church.) Language inspectors are told to weed out "all sins per-petrated on the regular Slovak language." Tensions between Slo-vaks and Hungarians, who had been getting along, have begun to arise.

The twentieth century is ending as it began—with trouble in the Balkans and with nationalist tensions flaring up in other parts of the globe. (Toward the end of his life Bismarck predicted that "some damn fool thing in the Balkans" would ignite the next war.) Language isn't always part of the problem. But it usually is.

UNIQUE OTHERNESS

Is there no hope for language tolerance? Some countries manage to maintain their unity in the face of multilingualism. Examples are Finland, with a Swedish minority, and a number of African and Southeast Asian countries. Two others could not be more un-like as countries go: Switzerland and India.

15   German, French, Italian, and Romansh are the languages of Switzerland. The first three can be and are used for official pur-poses; all four are designated "national" languages. Switzerland is politically almost hyperstable. It has language problems (Ro-mansh is losing ground), but they are not major, and they are never allowed to threaten national unity.

Contrary to public perception, India gets along pretty well with a host of different languages. The Indian constitution offi-cially recognizes nineteen languages, English among them. Hindi is specified in the constitution as the national language of India, but that is a pious postcolonial fiction: outside the Hindi-speaking northern heartland of India, people don't want to learn it. English functions more nearly than Hindi as India's lingua franca.

From 1947, when India obtained its independence from the British, until the 1960s blood ran in the streets and people died because of language. Hindi absolutists wanted to force Hindi on the entire country, which would have split India between north and south and opened up other fracture lines as well. For as long as possible Jawaharlal Nehru, independent India's first Prime Minister, resisted nationalist demands to redraw the capricious state boundaries of British India according to language. By the time he capitulated, the country had gained a precious decade to prove its viability as a union.

Why is it that India preserves its unity with not just two languages to contend with, as Belgium, Canada, and Sri Lanka have, but nineteen? The answer is that India, like Switzerland, has a strong national identity. The two countries share something big and almost mystical that holds each together in a union transcending language. That something I call "unique otherness."

The Swiss have what the political scientist Karl Deutsch called "learned habits, preferences, symbols, memories, and patterns of landholding": customs, cultural traditions, and political institutions that bind them closer to one another than to people of France, Germany, or Italy living just across the border and speaking the same language. There is Switzerland's traditional neutrality, its system of universal military training (the "citizen army"), its consensual allegiance to a strong Swiss franc—and fondue, yodeling, skiing, and mountains. Set against all this, the fact that Switzerland has four languages doesn't even approach the threshold of becoming a threat.

As for India, what Vincent Smith, in the *Oxford History of India*, calls its "deep underlying fundamental unity" resides in institutions and beliefs such as caste, cow worship, sacred places, and much more. Consider *dharma*, *karma*, and *maya*, the three root convictions of Hinduism; India's historical epics; Gandhi; *ahimsa* (nonviolence); vegetarianism; a distinctive cuisine and way of eating; marriage customs; a shared past; and what the Indologist Ainslie Embree calls "Brahmanical ideology." In other words, "We are Indian; we are different." . . .

. . . We like to believe that to pass a law is to change behavior; but passing laws about language, in a free society, almost never changes attitudes or behavior. Gaelic (Irish) is living out a slow, inexorable decline in Ireland despite enormous government support of every possible kind since Ireland gained its independence from Britain. The Welsh language, in contrast, is alive today in Wales in spite of heavy discrimination during its history. Three out of four people in the northern and western counties of Gwynedd and Dyfed speak Welsh.

I said earlier that language is a convenient surrogate for other national problems. Official English obviously has a lot to do with concern about immigration, perhaps especially Hispanic immigration. America may be threatened by immigration; I don't know. But America is not threatened by language.

The usual arguments made by academics against Official English are commonsensical. Who needs a law when, according to the 1990 census, 94 percent of American residents speak English anyway? (Mauro E. Mujica, the chairman of U.S. English, cites a higher figure: 97 percent.) Not many of today's immigrants will see their first language survive into the second generation. This is in fact the common lament of first-generation immigrants: their children are not learning their language and are losing the culture of their parents. Spanish is hardly a threat to English, in spite of isolated (and easily visible) cases such as Miami, New York City, and pockets of the Southwest and southern California. The everyday language of south Texas is Spanish, and yet south Texas is not about to secede from America.

But empirical, calm arguments don't engage the real issue: language is a symbol, an icon. Nobody who favors a constitutional ban against flag burning will ever be persuaded by the argument that the flag is, after all, just a "piece of cloth." A draft card in the 1960s was never merely a piece of paper. Neither is a marriage license.

25   Language, as one linguist has said, is "not primarily a means of communication but a means of communion." Romanticism exalted language, made it mystical, sublime—a bond of national identity. At the same time, Romanticism created a monster: it made of language a means for destroying a country.

America has that unique otherness of which I spoke. In spite of all our racial divisions and economic unfairness, we have the frontier tradition, respect for the individual, and opportunity; we have our love affair with the automobile; we have in our history a civil war that freed the slaves and was fought with valor; and we have sports, hot dogs, hamburgers, and milk shakes—things big and small, noble and petty, important and trifling. "We are Americans; we are different."

If I'm wrong, then the great American experiment will fail—not because of language but because it no longer means anything to be an American; because we have forfeited that "willingness of the heart" that F. Scott Fitzgerald wrote was America; because we are no longer joined by Lincoln's "mystic chords of memory."

We are not even close to the danger point. I suggest that we relax and luxuriate in our linguistic richness and our traditional tolerance of language differences. Language does not threaten

American unity. Benign neglect is a good policy for any country when it comes to language, and it's a good policy for America.

Questions for Discussion

1. What negative consequences do those who advocate an "Official Language" policy see in the flourishing of numerous languages in the United States? What other issues, not directly related to language, does King believe "intersect" with the movement to establish an Official English? Do you think that any of these issues could be resolved by establishing an English Only policy?

2. What point does King make through his brief history of the efforts to establish national language in order to define the national culture and character? Have these efforts been successful?

3. King states that "language is a convenient surrogate for non-linguistic claims." What are some of these claims, and what examples does King give to support his claim and to clarify the negative effects of using language as a way of consolidating political power?

4. What does King mean by the expression, "unique otherness," and how does this quality in a country help to preserve its cohesion, regardless of linguistic differences? Does the United States seem to possess "unique otherness," and if so, what makes this country unique, in King's view? What will cause us to fail? Do you agree with King? Explain your point of view.

5. King presents several common arguments made against an Official English policy. What are these arguments, and why does he believe they "don't engage the real issue" of language?

Ideas for Writing

1. Write an essay that explores King's view of the importance of its "unique otherness" for America's survival. Do the examples of unique American concerns that he presents seem to you to be the sign of a coherent culture? Do you believe that the idea of America as "uniquely other" is consistent with the view that this is a country of immigrants, each bringing something unique to the American mix?

2. Argue either for or against King's central argument for benign neglect, that is, that we need no special laws or "official"

protections for English to make it our common language. Do you believe that America is in any way diminished by the fact that certain groups of people in the country don't speak English well or at all?

Viet-Kieu

ANDREW PHAM

Andrew Pham was born in Viet Nam in 1967, but fled to California with his family when he was ten. After graduating from the University of California at Los Angeles, Pham worked for a time as an engineer and technician at United Airlines. Against his parents' advice, he quit his job and sold all of his possessions to embark on a year-long bicycle journey that took him through Mexico, Japan, and finally to Viet Nam. He traveled 2,357 miles and ended his journey in Saigon. "Viet-Kieu" is excerpted from his memoir *Catfish and Mandala*, which documents Pham's search for his cultural identity and his mixed feelings about being a Vietnamese-American citizen.

———————————— ✦ ————————————

The closer I come to Nha Trang the more frequently I see group tours busing to local points of interest. The locals are familiar with the tourist traffic and don't shout "*Oy! Oy!*" at foreigners. The main road loops around a mountain and enters the outskirts of the city from the south side. There is a shortcut, some high school kids point out to me, up the mountain and along the cliff. It's a good sporting ride, they say. I'm about to bag 120 miles today and have no wish to climb a mountain. I come into the city the easy way.

Although the outlying area is a mirror image of all the other dusty little towns, the city center is far more developed than anything I've seen. I limp the battered bike through town, heading toward the water where the locals have told me there is lodging. Shady lanes unroll between banks of sprawling buildings set back behind brick fences. There's a nice flavor here predating the Liberation of '75. I was just a kid then, but I remember Mom being very hip with her bellbottoms and buggy sunglasses. She must have wasted scores of film rolls in Nha Trang, her favorite city. The breeze is fresh, sweet, not salty like Phan Thiet. Out on the beachfront boulevard, I am suddenly in Waikiki! Someone has ripped it out of Hawaii and dropped it in downtown Nha Trang. A colossal skeleton of the Outrigger Hotel is being framed on the beach practically in the surf line. Tall, gleaming towers of glass and steel are already taking residence a stone's throw from the water. The sandy stretch of beach is jammed with fancy restaurants, bars hopping with modern rock, jazz, and Vietnamese pop. Aromas of grilled food turn heads and sharpen appetites. Along the avenue, fat Europeans and Australians pad about in thong bikinis, sheer sarongs, and Lycra shorts, dropping wads of dollars for seashells, corals, lacquered jewelry boxes, and bad paintings, loot, mementos, evidence.

I take the cheapest room available to a Viet-kieu at a government-run hotel (for some reason, Danes and Germans get lower rates), jump through a cold shower, then get back on my bike to head to the Vietnamese part of Nha Trang, where the food is cheaper and better. I am ravenous. Diarrhea be damned. Tonight I'm going to eat anything I want. After nearly three months of sporadic intestinal troubles, I'm still hoping that my system will acclimatize. I'm Vietnamese after all, and these microorganisms once thrived in my gut as thoroughly as in any Vietnamese here.

I eat dinner at an alley diner, nine tables crammed between two buildings lit with a couple of bare light bulbs. The family running the place says they are happy to have me, although they generally don't like foreigners. Eat too little, drink too little, but talk too much, they complain. Foreigners like to sit and sit and talk. Vietnamese eat and get out. Lounging is done in coffeehouses and beer halls. No problem. I prove to them I'm Vietnamese. I down two large bottles of Chinese beer and gorge myself on a monstrous meal of grilled meat served with a soy-and-pork-fat gravy, wrapping the meat in rice paper, cucumber, mint, pickled daikon, sour carrot, fresh basil, lettuce, chili pepper, cilantro, and rice vermicelli. Then I clear out quickly. I go to a hotel to check on a friend who might be in town. As a tour guide, he is a regular at the hotel. The concierge confirms that my friend Cuong and his tour are in town. I leave him a note and wait for him at an ice-cream parlor down the street.

"Hello! Andrew!"   5

"Cuong!"

I met him a few weeks after I arrived in Saigon. We bummed around the city several times with his girlfriends. I like him. We both agreed to check on each other when in Nha Trang or Vung Tau, both major cities on his itinerary.

He skips across the street, penny-loafing around the dog shit as he dodges motorbikes. Cuong doesn't wear sandals. No more. Not ever again. He told me, You can tell a Vietnamese by the way he wears his sandals. Is the stem firmly held between the toes? Or does the ball of the heel drag beyond the sandal? Do the sandals flap like loose tongues when he walks? Does he know there is mud between his toes? All this from a man who—in his own words—*"dribbled away* [his] *youth as a roadside petrol-boy selling gasoline out of glass bottles, wiping down motorbikes, hustling for dimes, and playing barefoot soccer in the dirt."*

He smoothes his shirt, fingers the ironed pleats of his gray slacks, straightens his pin-striped blue tie with red polka dots. Then, grinning, he steps closer and pumps my hand enthusiastically. "Calvin," he corrects me. "I'm sticking with your suggestion: Calvin. It's easier for the foreigners to pronounce." I'd come up with the name at his request. He wanted something that started with a "C" and was short and sharp and American.

10   "You made it! You're not hurt? No?" he says, patting me on the arm and looking me over. "A little thinner and darker, yes. Incredible. You biked all that way? Yes, yes, of course you did."

"You got my message?"

"Of course. May I join you?" he queries, forever the Vietnamese gentleman. I fill him in on all that happened since I last saw him nearly two months ago. When a waitress brings him his chilled Coke—no ice, just like the way foreigners drink their soda—he thanks her. She looks at him, a little startled to hear a Vietnamese man uttering platitudes like Westerners. Calvin has picked up the habit because he finds it more genteel and civilized.

I first made his acquaintance at a sidewalk café. He took me for a Japanese and wanted to practice his English. When I told him I was a Vietnamese from California, he was very uncomfortable using the term Viet-kieu, explaining that people said it with too many connotations. Sometimes, it was just a word, other times an insult or a term of segregation. *"Vietnamese are Vietnamese if they believe they are,"* he had said by way of explanation, and I liked him on the instant.

By Saigon standards, Calvin is a yuppie who came into his own by the most romantic way possible—by the compulsion of a promise made to his mother on her deathbed. One afternoon, when we were touring the outer districts of Saigon on his motorbike, Calvin pointed to a pack of greyhound-lean young men, shirtless, volleying a plastic bird back and forth with their feet.

"That was me. That's how I was until I was twenty-two. Can you believe it? I threw away all my young years, working odd jobs and messing around. I just didn't care." His mother bequeathed him, her only child, a small sum, which he spent on English classes, not bothering to finish up high school. With what little remained, he bribed his way into a job as a hotel bellhop and worked his way up. He entered a special school for tour guides. After three years of intense training, he makes four hundred dollars a month plus two hundred in tips. Now, twenty-nine, single, and rich even by Saigon standards, he fares better than college grads who are blessed if they can command two hundred dollars a month. His biggest regret: *"I wish my mother could see me now."*

Calvin sips his Coke and plucks a pack of Marlboros from his   15
shirt pocket, the American cigarette one of his main props for marking himself one of the upwardly mobile. "I'm down to half a pack a day," he mumbles apologetically, offering me a smoke. I decline. He puts his cigarette down saying: "Dirty, dirty, Vietnamese habit." Calvin keeps a list of "dirty Vietnamese habits" and steels himself against them.

I tell him that Americans used to call cigarettes "white slavers." He considers that for a moment then smirks. *"That has a double meaning for us, doesn't it."* He counts the cigarettes remaining in the pack. *"Last one today,"* he announces. He seems to want my approval so I nod. Vindicated, he ignites the last of his daily nicotine allowance. He sighs the smoke downwind. *"Tell me. Tell me everything about your trip."*

As I recount the events since I last saw him, Calvin grows increasingly excited, digging me more for the details of Vietnam than for the actual mechanics of bike touring. How did the police treat you? Hanoi people are more formal than Southerners, aren't they? You think Uncle Ho's body is a hoax? What's the countryside like? Is it pretty like the Southern country? He flames another cigarette and orders us a round of beer. By our third round, he has chain-smoked into a second pack of Marlboros.

Late in the night, when I am sapped of tales from the road, Calvin, who is beer-fogged, leans back in his chair and asks, *"America is like a dream, isn't it?"*

After all I've seen, I agree. *"Sure."*

We contemplate the beer in our glasses. I ask him, *"Do you*   20
want to go there?" I don't know why I ask him this. Maybe, believing that he is my equivalent in Vietnam, I want him to say that he

really loves the country and that it is magical, wonderful in ways I have yet to imagine. More powerful, more potent than the West.

Calvin sounds annoyed. *"Of course. Who wouldn't?"* He pauses, taking long, pensive drags on his cigarette. *"But perhaps only to visit. To see, understand-no?"*

"Why?"

"Simple. Here. . .here, I am a king." He leans over the table, shaking the cigarette at me. *"In America you, I mean all you Viet-kieu, are guests. And guests don't have the same rights as hosts."* He sits back, legs crossed at the knees, and throws a proprietary arm over the city. *"At least, here, I am king. I belong. I am better than most Vietnamese."*

"No, we're not guests. We're citizens. Permanent. Ideally we are all equal. Equal rights," I insert lamely, the words, recalled from elementary school history lessons, sounding hollow.

25   *"Right, but do you FEEL like an American? Do you?"*

Yes! Yes! Yes, I do. I really do, I want to shout it in his face. Already, the urge leaves a bad taste in my mouth. *"Sometimes, I do. Sometimes, I feel like I am a real American."*

I wish I could tell him. I don't mind forgetting who I am, but I know he wouldn't understand. I don't mind being looked at or treated just like another American, a white American. No, I don't mind at all. I want it. I like it. Yet every so often when I become really good at tricking myself, there is always that inevitable slap that shocks me out of my shell and prompts me to reassess everything.

How could I tell him my shame? How could I tell him about the drive-bys where some red-faced white would stick his head out of his truck, giving me the finger and screaming, "Go home, Chink!" Could I tell him it chilled me to wonder what would happen if my protagonist knew I was Vietnamese? What if his father had died in Vietnam? What if he was a Vietnam vet? Could I tell Calvin about the time my Vietnamese friends and I dined in a posh restaurant in Laguna Beach in Southern California? A white man at the next table, glaring at us, grumbled to his wife, "They took over Santa Ana. And now they're here. This whole state is going to hell." They was us Vietnamese. Santa Ana was now America's Little Saigon.

Could I tell Calvin I was initiated into the American heaven during my first week Stateside by eight black kids who pulverized me in the restroom, calling me Viet Cong? No. I grew up fighting blacks, whites, and Chicanos. The whites beat up the blacks. The blacks beat up the Chicanos. And everybody beat up the Chinaman whether or not he was really an ethnic Chinese. These new Vietnamese kids were easy pickings, small, bookish, passive, and not fluent in English.

So, we congregate in Little Saigons, we hide out in China-   30
towns and Japantowns, blending in. We huddle together, surrounding ourselves with the material wealth of America, and wave our star-spangled banners, shouting: "We're Americans. We love America."

I cannot bring myself to confront my antagonists. Cannot always claim my rights as a naturalized citizen. Cannot, for the same reason, resist the veterans' pleas for money outside grocery stores. Cannot armor myself against the pangs of guilt at every homeless man wearing army fatigues. Sown deep in me is a seed of discomfort. Maybe shame. I see that we Vietnamese Americans don't talk about our history. Although we often pretend to be modest and humble as we preen our successful immigrants stories, we rarely admit even to ourselves the circumstances and the cost of our being here. We elude it all like a petty theft committed ages ago. When convenient, we take it as restitution for what happened to Vietnam.

Calvin senses my discomfort. It is his talent, a marked skill of his trade. He looks away, reaching for yet another cigarette to cover the silence I opened. He asks me the question that Vietnamese throughout Vietnam have tried to broach obliquely: *"Do they look down on Vietnamese in America? Do they hate you?"*

I don't want to dwell on that. Vietnamese believe that white Americans are to Viet-kieu as Viet-kieu are to Vietnamese, each one a level above the next, respectively. And, somehow, this shames me, maybe because I cannot convince myself that it is entirely true or false. I divert the thrust and ask him, *"You are Westernized. You know how different foreigners are from Vietnamese. How do you feel showing them around the country?"*

"I like the work. Many of them are very nice. Curious about our culture. I like the Australians most. Rowdy and lots of trouble, but they respect Vietnamese."

"But don't you see the reactions on their faces when they see our   35
squalor? Don't you hear the things they say about us? Don't tell me you've never heard it."

He looks uncomfortable, drawing deep from his nicotine stick, sighing the smoke to the stars. Then to his credit and my everlasting respect for him, he says quietly, facing the sky, *"I do. I can't help it but I do. I take them out on the Saigon streets, you*

know, the poor parts because they ask me. They want pictures. I see them flinch at the beggars, the poverty of Vietnamese. The chicken-shacks we live in."
A wordless lull falls between us. We're both drunk. I am irritated at having to delve into a subject I avoid, and feeling mean-spirited I have goaded him onto equally disconcerting ground.
"It's very hard being a tour guide. Sometimes I feel like a pimp."
He switches into his tour-guide English: "Here, look at this, sir. Yes, ma'am, these are the average Vietnamese. Yes, they are poor. Yes, sir. Here is our national monument. Very big. Very important to Vietnamese. You impressed? No, not so big?" He shrugs, saying, *"I know they've got bigger monuments in their countries. Older, more important. What do our little things mean to them?"*
The silence tells me we are moving too far into no-man's-land. One more cigarette. More beer. Tusking the smoke out of his nostrils, he seems to brace himself, gathering force like a wave, building before cresting white. As his beliefs come barreling out, I know the crushing impact of his words will stay with me, for in them I catch a glimpse of myself and of the true Cuong, the Cuong that came before and is deeper than the suave Calvin facing me. *"Vietnamese aren't ashamed of our own poverty. We're not ashamed of squatting in mud huts and sleeping on rags. There is no shame in being poor. We were born into it just as Westerners are born white. The Westerners are white as we are yellow. There is already a difference between us. Our poverty is minor in the chasm that already exists. A small detail. The real damning thing is the fact that there are Viet-kieu, our own brothers, skin of our skin, blood of our blood, who look better than us, more civilized, more educated, more wealthy, more genteel. Viet-kieu look kingly next to the average Vietnamese. Look at you, look at me. You're wearing old jeans and I'm wearing a suit, but it's obvious who. . .who is superior. Can't you see? We look like monkeys because you make us look like monkeys just by your existence."*
40 *"Is this truly how Vietnamese see us Viet-kieu?"*
"Some call you the lost brothers. Look at you. Living in America has lightened your skin, made you forget your language. You have tasted Western women and you're probably not as attracted to Vietnamese women anymore. You eat nutritious Western food and you are bigger and stronger than us. You know better than to smoke and drink like Vietnamese. You know exercise is good so you don't waste your time sitting in cafés and smoking your hard-earned money away. Someday,

your blood will mix so well with Western blood that there will be no difference between you and them. You are already lost to us."

I listened with dismay as his observations fall on me like a sentence, but I can tell in the back of his mind he is saying: And I want to be more like you because that's where the future is. He must suspect I am doubting what he has told me the first time our paths crossed: *"Vietnamese are Vietnamese if they believe they are."*

Calvin and I bid each other good night, each going his own way. He has to resolve a fracas of intoxicated Australians in his charge back at the hotel. In our drunkenness, our conversation crossed forbidden boundaries and we were both depressed. Maybe it is just the beer wearing off. I pedal down to the beach for some sea air. As I coast along the ocean boulevard, a gorgeous girl, unusually tall for a Vietnamese, dressed in the traditional *ao dai* like a college student, tails me on her expensive motorbike, a Honda Dream, the Vietnamese Cadillac. Hello, she says in English. Hello, I smile. She thinks I'm Japanese or Korean. How are you, she asks me. Good, I say—always glad to talk to students eager to practice their English. And you, I say to keep the conversation going, how are you? You are very pretty, she tells me. No, I chuckle, standing now with her on the dark sidewalk, you are pretty. Very pretty. Pretty enough, I fancy silently to myself, for me to fall madly in love with. My heart dances ahead of me with improbable possibilities. Wild schemes streak through my head ratting out ways for me to stay in Nha Trang longer to make her acquaintance. Maybe get a job here. There are so many foreign companies, it should be easy. And on and on. Hopeful. I am smiling.

Then she says, "You go with me?"

"Yes, sure. Where? Anywhere! Let's go!"

"You go with me very cheap. You go. Me very cheap, very good. You go with me very cheap. Very, very cheap. I make you happy."

My smile feels waxy. I turn away, looking at the surf rolling on the white sand, the moon pearling us all. She parrots it over and over.

No, yes, maybe, later, I must meet a friend now, see you soon, bye, I blurt for the sake of blurting and I ride away from the tourist boardwalk with my money, my opportunities, my privileges, my life. I look back once and see her glossy cherry lips mouthing those words to me, a red wound in the neon night of Nha Trang.

45

Questions for Discussion

1. What does the term Viet-kieu mean? How do Calvin and Andrew feel about those who are Viet-kieu?
2. How does meeting Calvin and learning about his job in Saigon affect Andrew's feelings about his decision to become a citizen of the United States? Is Andrew respected as a Vietnamese-American? Does this selection give you insights into the life of an immigrant citizen? What are they?
3. Why does Andrew see the pretty Vietnamese woman's "glossy cherry lips" like "a red wound in the neon night of Nha Trang?" What are the implications of his observation?
4. After reading and reflecting on this selection, do you think that Andrew feels clearer about his identity as a Vietnamese-American, or more confused? Explain your answer.

Ideas for Writing

1. Write an essay that discusses some of the major problems that a particular immigrant group in your community has had in adjusting to the experience of becoming American citizens and adjusting to American culture. If possible, interview at least one person in this group of immigrants to gather more information.
2. Write an essay that presents the process through which one becomes a citizen of this country. As part of your research, interview several immigrant citizens who came to the United States while still fairly young, as Andrew Pham did. Try to get a sense for how they managed to become citizens and how they feel about their decision. Do some of them miss their homeland or carry powerful images of their life there? Conclude with a summary of what you have learned from your interviews.

Extending the Theme

1. Compare the views on the relationships of minorities such as blacks, Asian-Americans and Hispanics to the American dream as presented in the essays by King, Chavez, and Pham. Which author's point of view seems most realistic and relevant? What conclusions can you draw about the future of minorities in the United States?

2. Discuss the issues raised by Lapham and Quindlen on the crucial issues of identity that minority Americans in particular, and all Americans by extension, face today. Which of the issues explored by the two authors seems of most immediate concern? What experiences have you had that have helped you to realize the significance of this issue, and what solutions do you hope for?

3. Write an essay on the future role of minorities as American citizens in this 21st century. To support your claims and conclusions, refer to the ideas of the authors in this chapter and to your own experiences and readings.

4. Choose a particular minority group profiled in this chapter. Read about the historical struggles that this group has had to overcome in order to be accepted as American citizens. Write an essay in which you discuss what you have learned and draw conclusions about the future of this minority group. Refer to the writers in the chapter and your own experiences to support your claims and conclusions.

5. Visit a community-based organization or a national group with a local organization in your community. Read the organization's promotional literature and visit the local chapter to observe how the organization functions. Interview workers and managers at the organization; if possible, participate in one of their functions such as a meeting or a rally, or help the organization complete some of its practical tasks. Write up your findings and evaluate the organization in terms of the impact it has had and continues to have on your community and nationally, especially on the minority group it is chartered to serve.

Education and Citizenship

Learned institutions ought to be favorite objects with free people. They throw that light over the public mind which is the best security against crafty and dangerous encroachments on the public liberty.

JAMES MADISON

Our progress as a nation can be no swifter than our progress in education.

JOHN FITZGERALD KENNEDY

The Congress declares it to be the policy of the United States that a high quality education for all individuals and a fair and equal opportunity to obtain that education are a societal good, are a moral imperative, and improve the life of every individual, because the quality of our individual lives ultimately depends on the quality of the lives of others.

HELPING DISADVANTAGED STUDENTS MEET HIGH STANDARDS, 1996

America was founded and continues to flourish because of the ideals expressed in the quotations that open this chapter. Democracy can only function when its citizens are informed and educated. However, a basic problem in achieving equal educational opportunities for all U.S. citizens is rooted in the fact that our Constitution does not provide any provisions for a federal role in educational leadership. Even today the national government only provides 10 percent of all funding for education, leaving the major decisions about curriculum and funding to the individual states, local communities, and private institutions.

Some educators, such as Linda Darling-Hammond in her essay "Unequal Opportunity: Race and Education," argue that the quality of education citizens receive varies greatly according to class and race. Despite civil rights legislation that mandated integration starting in the mid-1960s, two thirds of minority students are educated at schools where only a handful of white students attend. In contrast, the wealthiest 10 percent of schools spend ten times more money on the education of their students than the poorest 10 percent of schools spend on their students. To remedy this situation, Darling-Hammond calls for more funding to pay for better teachers with more knowledge and experience who can provide the guidance and inspiration necessary to motivate students through better curriculum, smaller class size, and individual attention.

In her essay "Keeping Close to Home: Class and Education," bell hooks speaks from her own experiences as a young black woman attending an elite college, where she comes to realize the vast cultural divide between white students from upper class families and minority students. Hooks argues that institutions of higher education should not become means for assimilation, but rather places where diversity can be embraced and respected.

Because of the difficulties involved in reforming entire school districts, innovative magnet, charter, and model schools that operate within larger school districts are becoming increasingly popular. This chapter's readings provide conflicting ideas about the ideal type of alternative school and reformist curriculum. Educator E. D. Hirsch in "The Common School and The Common Good" calls for a national curriculum with common standards and has developed testing models in a number of alternative schools that involve accountability in teaching and mastery of a uniform knowledge-base. In contrast to Hirsch's approach, Deborah Meier, who has devoted her career to setting up community-based schools, believes that the best schools have local standards and demand the committed engagement of teachers, parents, and students.

Another approach to improving the educational experience of minority students and the children of poverty involves community service. Psychiatrist and educator Robert Coles argues in his essay "Community Service" that our inner-city schools can be revitalized by encouraging idealistic college students and older adults to teach in such institutions, where they can experience the material and spiritual needs of the children while sharing a wealth of knowledge and enthusiasm for learning with inner-city youth.

Clearly, as teachers and as students, we need to think critically about the crucial issues in education today. Only when we have an educational system that serves the needs of all citizens, rich and poor, from every ethnic and cultural background, can we build a society that is truly democratic in the way that the framers of the Constitution intended it to be. In such a democracy, all citizens will benefit because more citizens will be educated and able to make informed judgments about local and national concern.

Unequal Opportunity: Race and Education

LINDA DARLING-HAMMOND

Linda Darling-Hammond earned her B.A. at Yale University in 1973 and her Ph.D. from Temple College in 1978. Currently she is the Charles C. Ducommun Professor of Education at Stanford University. Hammond began her career as a public school teacher and has always been deeply engaged in efforts to redesign schools so that they focus more effectively on teaching and learning. She is the author of many books, the most highly acclaimed of which is *The Right to Learn* (1997); it was awarded the American Educational Research Association's Outstanding Book Award in 1998. Hammond has also worked as an Advisor for Education Research at the White House. The essay that follows first appeared in the *Brookings Review*.

✦

W E. B. Du Bois was right about the problem of the 21st century. The color line divides us still. In recent years, the most visible evidence of this in the public policy arena has been the persistent attack on affirmative action in higher education and employment. From the perspective of many Americans who believe that the vestiges of discrimination have disappeared, affirmative action now provides an unfair advantage to minorities.

From the perspective of others who daily experience the consequences of ongoing discrimination affirmative action is needed to protect opportunities likely to evaporate if an affirmative obligation to act fairly does not exist. And for Americans of all backgrounds, the allocation of opportunity in a society that is becoming ever more dependent on knowledge and education is a source of great anxiety and concern.

At the center of these debates are interpretations of the gaps in educational achievement between white and non-Asian minority students as measured by standardized test scores. The presumption that guides much of the conversation is that equal opportunity now exists; therefore, continued low levels of achievement on the part of minority students must be a function of genes, culture, or a lack of effort and will (see, for example, Richard Herrnstein and Charles Murray's *The Bell Curve* and Stephan and Abigail Thernstrom's *America in Black and White*).

The assumptions that undergird this debate miss an important reality: educational outcomes for minority children are much more a function of their unequal access to key educational resources, including skilled teachers and quality curriculum, than they are a function of race. In fact, the U.S. educational system is one of the most unequal in the industrialized world, and students routinely receive dramatically different learning opportunities based on their social status. In contrast to European and Asian nations that fund schools centrally and equally, the wealthiest 10 percent of U.S. school districts spend nearly 10 times more than the poorest 10 percent, and spending ratios of 3 to 1 are common within states. Despite stark differences in funding, teacher quality, curriculum, and class sizes, the prevailing view is that if students do not achieve, it is their own fault. If we are ever to get beyond the problem of the color line, we must confront and address these inequalities.

THE NATURE OF EDUCATIONAL INEQUALITY

Americans often forget that as late as the 1960s most African-American, Latino, and Native American students were educated in wholly segregated schools funded at rates many times lower than those serving whites and were excluded from many higher education institutions entirely. The end of legal segregation followed by efforts to equalize spending since 1970 has made a substantial difference for student achievement. On every major national test, including the National Assessment of Educational Progress, the gap in minority and white students' test scores narrowed substantially between 1970 and 1990, especially for elementary school students. On the Scholastic Aptitude Test (SAT), the scores of African-American students climbed 54 points between 1976 and 1994, while those of white students remained stable.

Even so, educational experiences for minority students have continued to be substantially separate and unequal. Two-thirds of minority students still attend schools that are predominantly minority, most of them located in central cities and funded well below those in neighboring suburban districts. Recent analyses of data prepared for school finance cases in Alabama, New Jersey, New York, Louisiana, and Texas have found that on every tangible measure—from qualified teachers to curriculum offering—schools serving greater numbers of students of color had significantly fewer resources than schools serving mostly white students. As William L. Taylor and Dianne Piche noted in a 1991 report to Congress: 5

> Inequitable systems of school finance inflict disproportionate harm on minority and economically disadvantaged students. On an inter-state basis, such students are concentrated in states, primarily in the South, that have the lowest capacities to finance public education. On an intra-state basis, many of the states with the widest disparities in educational expenditures are large industrial states. In these states, many minorities and economically disadvantaged students are located in property-poor urban districts which fare the worst in educational expenditures . . . (or) in rural districts which suffer from fiscal inequity.

Jonathan Kozol's 1991 *Savage Inequalities* described the striking differences between public schools serving students of color in urban settings and their suburban counterparts, which typically spend twice as much per student for populations with many fewer special needs. Contrast MacKenzie High School in Detroit, where word processing courses are taught without word processors because the school cannot afford them, or East St. Louis Senior High School, whose biology lab has no laboratory tables or usable dissecting kits, with nearby suburban schools where children enjoy a computer hookup to Dow Jones to study stock transactions and science laboratories that rival those in some industries. Or contrast Paterson, New Jersey, which could not afford the qualified teachers needed to offer foreign language courses to most high school students, with Princeton, where foreign languages begin in elementary school.

Even within urban school districts, schools with high concentrations of low-income and minority students receive fewer instructional resources than others. And tracking systems exacerbate these inequalities by segregating many low-income and minority students within schools. In combination, these policies leave minority students with fewer and lower-quality books, curriculum materials, laboratories, and computers; significantly larger class sizes; less qualified and experienced teachers; and less access to high-quality curriculum. Many schools serving low-income and minority students do not even offer the math and science courses needed for college, and they provide lower-quality teaching in the classes they do offer. It all adds up.

WHAT DIFFERENCE DOES IT MAKE?

Since the 1966 Coleman report, *Equality of Educational Opportunity*, another debate has raged as to whether money makes a difference to educational outcomes. It is certainly possible to spend money ineffectively; however, studies that have developed more sophisticated measures of schooling show how money, properly spent, makes a difference. Over the past 30 years, a large body of research has shown that four factors consistently influence student achievement: all else equal. students perform better if they are educated in smaller schools where they are well known (300 to 500 students is optimal), have smaller class sizes (especially at the elementary level), receive a challenging curriculum, and have more highly qualified teachers.

Minority students are much less likely than white children to have any of these resources. In predominantly minority schools, which most students of color attend, schools are large (on average, more than twice as large as predominantly white schools and reaching 3,000 students or more in most cities); on average, class sizes are 15 percent larger overall (80 percent larger for nonspecial education classes); curriculum offerings and materials are lower in quality; and teachers are much less qualified in terms of levels of education, certification, and training in the fields they teach. And in integrated schools, as UCLA professor Jeannie

Oakes described in the 1980s and Harvard professor Gary Or-
field's research has recently confirmed, most minority students
are segregated in lower-track classes with larger class sizes, less
qualified teachers, and lower-quality curriculum.

Research shows that teachers' preparation makes a tremen-   10
dous difference to children's learning. In an analysis of 900 Texas
school districts, Harvard economist Ronald Ferguson found that
teachers' expertise—as measured by scores on a licensing examination, master's degrees, and experience—was the single most
important determinant of student achievement, accounting for
roughly 40 percent of the measured variance in students' reading
and math achievement gains in grades 1–12. After controlling for
socioeconomic status, the large disparities in achievement between black and white students were almost entirely due to differences in the qualifications of their teachers. In combination, differences in teacher expertise and class sizes accounted for as
much of the measured variance in achievement as did student
and family background.

Ferguson and Duke economist Helen Ladd repeated this
analysis in Alabama and again found sizable influences of teacher
qualifications and smaller class sizes on achievement gains in
math and reading. They found that more of the difference between the high- and low-scoring districts was explained by
teacher qualifications and class sizes than by poverty, race, and
parent education.

Meanwhile, a Tennessee study found that elementary school
students who are assigned to ineffective teachers for three years
in a row score nearly 50 percentile points lower on achievement
tests than those assigned to highly effective teachers over the
same period. Strikingly, minority students are about half as likely
to be assigned to the most effective teachers and twice as likely to
be assigned to the least effective.

Minority students are put at greatest risk by the American
tradition of allowing enormous variation in the qualifications of
teachers. The National Commission on Teaching and America's
Future found that new teachers hired without meeting certification standards (25 percent of all new teachers) are usually assigned to teach the most disadvantaged students in low-income
and high-minority schools, while the most highly educated new
teachers are hired largely by wealthier schools. Students in poor
or predominantly minority schools are much less likely to have

teachers who are fully qualified or hold higher-level degrees. In schools with the highest minority enrollments, for example, students have less than a 50 percent chance of getting a math or science teacher with a license and a degree in the field. In 1994, fully one-third of teachers in high-poverty schools taught without a minor in their main field and nearly 70 percent taught without a minor in their secondary teaching field.

Studies of underprepared teachers consistently find that they are less effective with students and that they have difficulty with curriculum development, classroom management, student motivation, and teaching strategies. With little knowledge about how children grow, learn, and develop, or about what to do to support their learning, these teachers are less likely to understand students' learning styles and differences, to anticipate students' knowledge and potential difficulties, or to plan and redirect instruction to meet students' needs. Nor are they likely to see it as their job to do so, often blaming the students if their teaching is not successful.

15   Teacher expertise and curriculum quality are interrelated, because a challenging curriculum requires an expert teacher. Research has found that both students and teachers are tracked: that is, the most expert teachers teach the most demanding courses to the most advantaged students, while lower-track students assigned to less able teachers receive lower-quality teaching and less demanding material. Assignment to tracks is also related to race: even when grades and test scores are comparable, black students are more likely to be assigned to lower-track, nonacademic classes.

WHEN OPPORTUNITY IS MORE EQUAL

What happens when students of color do get access to more equal opportunities? Studies find that curriculum quality and teacher skill make more difference to educational outcomes than the initial test scores or racial backgrounds of students. Analyses of national data from both the High School and Beyond Surveys and the National Educational Longitudinal Surveys have demonstrated that, while there are dramatic differences among students of various racial and ethnic groups in course-taking in such areas as math, science, and foreign language, for students with similar course-taking records, achievement test score differences by race or ethnicity narrow substantially.

Robert Dreeben and colleagues at the University of Chicago conducted a long line of studies documenting both the relationship between educational opportunities and student performance and minority students' access to those opportunities. In a comparative study of 300 Chicago first graders, for example, Dreeben found that African-American and white students who had comparable instruction achieved comparable levels of reading skill. But he also found that the quality of instruction given African-American students was, on average, much lower than that given white students, thus creating a racial gap in aggregate achievement at the end of first grade. In fact, the highest-ability group in Dreeben's sample was in a school in a low-income African-American neighborhood. These children, though, learned less during first grade than their white counterparts because their teacher was unable to provide the challenging instruction they deserved.

When schools have radically different teaching forces, the effects can be profound. For example, when Eleanor Armour-Thomas and colleagues compared a group of exceptionally effective elementary schools with a group of low-achieving schools with similar demographic characteristics in New York City, roughly 90 percent of the variance in student reading and mathematics scores at grades 3, 6, and 8 was a function of differences in teacher qualifications. The schools with highly qualified teachers serving large numbers of minority and low-income students performed as well as much more advantaged schools.

Most studies have estimated effects statistically. However, an experiment that randomly assigned seventh grade "at-risk" students to remedial, average, and honors mathematics classes found that the at-risk students who took the honors class offering a pre-algebra curriculum ultimately outperformed all other students of similar backgrounds. Another study compared African-American high school youth randomly placed in public housing in the Chicago suburbs with city-placed peers of equivalent income and initial academic attainment and found that the suburban students, who attended largely white and better-funded schools, were substantially more likely to take challenging courses, perform well academically, graduate on time, attend college, and find good jobs.

WHAT CAN BE DONE?

20   . . . Last year the National Commission on Teaching and America's Future issued a blueprint for a comprehensive set of policies to ensure a "caring, competent, and qualified teacher for every child," as well as schools organized to support student success. Twelve states are now working directly with the commission on this agenda, and others are set to join this year. Several pending bills to overhaul the federal Higher Education Act would ensure that highly qualified teachers are recruited and prepared for students in all schools. Federal policymakers can develop incentives, as they have in medicine, to guarantee well-prepared teachers in shortage fields and high-need locations. States can equalize education spending, enforce higher teaching standards, and reduce teacher shortages, as Connecticut, Kentucky, Minnesota, and North Carolina have already done. School districts can reallocate resources from administrative superstructures and special add-on programs to support better-educated teachers who offer a challenging curriculum in smaller schools and classes, as restructured schools as far apart as New York and San Diego have done. These schools, in communities where children are normally written off to lives of poverty, welfare dependency, or incarceration, already produce much higher levels of achievement for students of color, sending more than 90 percent of their students to college. Focusing on what matters most can make a real difference in what children have the opportunity to learn. This, in turn, makes a difference in what communities can accomplish.

AN ENTITLEMENT TO GOOD TEACHING

The common presumption about educational inequality—that it resides primarily in those students who come to school with inadequate capacities to benefit from what the school has to offer—continues to hold wide currency because the extent of inequality in opportunities to learn is largely unknown. We do not currently operate schools on the presumption that students might be entitled to decent teaching and schooling as a matter of course. In fact, some state and local defendants have countered school finance and desegregation cases with assertions that such remedies are not required unless it can be proven that they will produce equal outcomes. Such arguments against equalizing opportunities to learn have made good on Du Bois's prediction that the problem of the 21st century would be the problem of the color line.

But education resources do make a difference, particularly when funds are used to purchase well-qualified teachers and high-quality curriculum and to create personalized learning communities in which children are well known. In all of the current sturm und drang about affirmative action, "special treatment," and the other high-volatility buzzwords for race and class politics in this nation, I would offer a simple starting point for the next century's efforts: no special programs, just equal educational opportunity.

Questions for Discussion

1. Why does Darling-Hammond think that affirmative action is still needed in education? Explain why you agree or disagree with her.
2. What statistics does Darling-Hammond present to demonstrate that "access" rather than race is the principal cause of minority underachievement in schools today? Are her arguments convincing?
3. Darling-Hammond argues that four major factors influence student achievement. What are these factors, and how does she demonstrate their impact on student success?
4. What types of programs and funding does Darling-Hammond discuss that are being implemented to improve the quality of teaching in our country? Do these programs seem adequate to bridge the gap in minority achievement?

Ideas for Writing

1. Darling-Hammond makes the point that the quality of education in the United States is more linked to social status than it is in any of the European or Asian nations where funding for schools is centralized and equal. Write an essay in which you respond to this fact. You might decide to try to find out how this has come about and why the problem of unequal funding to rich and poor children has not yet been solved.

2. Darling-Hammond argues that teaching expertise is fundamental to educating children. Refer to her article and research this topic further. What do you think would be the best
   way to encourage highly qualified teachers to work in minority, inner-city school districts?

Keeping Close to Home: Class and Education

BELL HOOKS

Bell hooks (born Gloria Watkins, 1952) is one of America's leading cultural and educational theorists. Hooks received her B.A.
from the University of Wisconsin-Madison and her Ph.D. from
Stanford University. Her essay collections include *Black Looks:
Race and Representation* (1992) and *Killing Rage* (1995). In the following selection from *Talking Back, Thinking Feminist Thinking
Black* (1989), hooks writes about her struggle to become educated
without losing her sense of herself as an African-American
woman from a working-class background.

———————— ✦ ————————

To a southern black girl from a working-class background who
had never been on a city bus, who had never stepped on an
escalator, who had never travelled by plane, leaving the comfortable confines of a small town Kentucky life to attend Stanford
University was not just frightening; it was utterly painful. My parents had not been delighted that I had been accepted and
adamantly opposed my going so far from home. At the time, I did
not see their opposition as an expression of their fear that they
would lose me forever. Like many working-class folks, they feared
what college education might do to their children's minds even as
they unenthusiastically acknowledged its importance. They did
not understand why I could not attend a college nearby, an all-
black college. To them, any college would do. I would graduate,
become a school teacher, make a decent living and good marriage.
And even though they reluctantly and skeptically supported my
educational endeavors, they also subjected them to constant

harsh and bitter critique. It is difficult for me to talk about my parents and their impact on me because they have always felt wary, ambivalent, mistrusting of my intellectual aspirations even as they have been caring and supportive. I want to speak about these contradictions because sorting through them, seeking resolution and reconciliation has been important to me both as it affects my development as a writer, my effort to be fully self-realized, and my longing to remain close to the family and community that provided the groundwork for much of my thinking, writing, and being.

Studying at Stanford, I began to think seriously about class differences. To be materially underprivileged at a university where most folks (with the exceptions of workers) are materially privileged provokes such thought. Class differences were boundaries no one wanted to face or talk about. It was easier to downplay them, to act as though we were all from privileged backgrounds, to work around them, to confront them privately in the solitude of one's room, or to pretend that just being chosen to study at such an institution meant that those of us who did not come from privilege were already in transition toward privilege. To not long for such transition marked one as rebellious, as unlikely to succeed. It was a kind of treason not to believe that it was better to be identified with the world of material privilege than with the world of the working class, the poor. No wonder our working-class parents from poor backgrounds feared our entry into such a world, intuiting perhaps that we might learn to be ashamed of where we had come from, that we might never return home, or come back only to lord it over them.

Though I hung with students who were supposedly radical and chic, we did not discuss class. I talked to no one about the sources of my shame, how it hurt me to witness the contempt shown the brown-skinned Filipina maids who cleaned our rooms, or later my concern about the $100 a month I paid for a room off-campus which was more than half of what my parents paid for rent. I talked to no one about my efforts to save money, to send a little something home. Yet these class realities separated me from fellow students. We were moving in different directions. I did not intend to forget my class background or alter my class allegiance. And even though I received an education designed to provide me with a bourgeois sensibility, passive acquiescence was not my only option. I knew that I could resist. I could rebel. I could shape the direction and focus of the various forms of knowledge available to me. Even though I sometimes envied and longed for greater material advantages (particularly at vacation times when I would be one of few if any students remaining in the dormitory because there was no money for travel), I did not share the sensibility and values of my peers. That was important—class was not just about money; it was about values which showed and determined behavior. While I often needed more money, I never needed a new set of beliefs and values. For example, I was profoundly shocked and disturbed when my peers would talk about their parents without respect, or would even say that they hated their parents. This was especially troubling to me when it seemed that these parents were caring and concerned. It was often explained to me that such hatred was "healthy and normal." To my white, middle-class California roommate, I explained the way we were taught to value our parents and their care, to understand that they were obligated to give us care. She would always shake her head, laughing all the while, and say, "Missy, you will learn that it's different here, that we think differently." She was right. Soon, I lived alone, like the one Mormon student who kept to himself as he made a concentrated effort to remain true to his religious beliefs and values. Later in graduate school I found that classmates believed "lower class" people had no beliefs and values. I was silent in such discussions, disgusted by their ignorance.

Carol Stack's anthropological study, *All Our Kin*, was one of the first books I read which confirmed my experiential understanding that within black culture (especially among the working class and poor, particularly in southern states), a value system emerged that was counter-hegemonic, that challenged notions of individualism and private property so important to the maintenance of white-supremacist, capitalist patriarchy. Black folk created in marginal spaces a world of community and collectivity where resources were shared. In the preface to *Feminist Theory: from margin to center*, I talked about how the point of difference, this marginality, can be the space for the formulation of an oppositional world view. That world view must be articulated, named if it is to provide a sustained blueprint for change. Unfortunately, there has existed no consistent framework for such naming. Consequently both the experience of this difference and documentation of it (when it occurs) gradually loses presence and meaning.

5   Much of what Stack documented about the "culture of poverty," for example, would not describe interactions among most black poor today irrespective of geographical setting. Since the black people she described did not acknowledge (if they rec-

ognized it in theoretical terms) the oppositional value of their world view, apparently seeing it more as a survival strategy determined less by conscious efforts to oppose oppressive race and class biases than by circumstance, they did not attempt to establish a framework to transmit their beliefs and values from generation to generation. When circumstances changed, values altered. Efforts to assimilate the values and beliefs of privileged white people, presented through media like television, undermine and destroy potential structures of opposition.

Increasingly, young black people are encouraged by the dominant culture (and by those black people who internalize the values of this hegemony) to believe that assimilation is the only way to survive, to succeed. Without the framework of an organized civil rights or black resistance struggle, individual and collective efforts at black liberation that focus on the primacy of self-definition and self-determination often go unrecognized. It is crucial that those among us who resist and rebel, who survive and succeed, speak openly and honestly about our lives and the nature of our personal struggles, the means by which we resolve and reconcile contradictions. This is no easy task. Within the educational institutions where we learn to develop and strengthen our writing and analytical skills, we also learn to think, write, and talk in a manner that shifts attention away from personal experience. Yet if we are to reach our people and all people, if we are to remain connected (especially those of us whose familial backgrounds are poor and working-class), we must understand that the telling of one's personal story provides a meaningful example, a way for folks to identify and connect.

Combining personal with critical analysis and theoretical perspectives can engage listeners who might otherwise feel estranged, alienated. To speak simply with language that is accessible to as many folks as possible is also important. Speaking about one's personal experience or speaking with simple language is often considered by academics and/or intellectuals (irrespective of their political inclinations) to be a sign of intellectual weakness or even anti-intellectualism. Lately, when I speak, I do not stand in place—reading my paper, making little or no eye contact with audiences—but instead make eye contact, talk extemporaneously, digress, and address the audience directly. I have been told that people assume I am not prepared, that I am anti-intellectual, unprofessional (a concept that has everything to do with class as it determines actions and behaviors), or that I am reinforcing the stereotype of black as non-theoretical and gutsy.

Such criticism was raised recently by fellow feminist scholars after a talk I gave at Northwestern University at a conference on "Gender, Culture, Politics" to an audience that was mainly students and academics. I deliberately chose to speak in a very basic way, thinking especially about the few community folks that had come to hear me. Weeks later, KumKum Sangari, a fellow participant who shared with me what was said when I was no longer present, and I engaged in quite rigorous critical dialogue about the way my presentation had been perceived primarily by privileged white female academics. She was concerned that I not mask my knowledge of theory, that I not appear anti-intellectual. Her critique compelled me to articulate concerns that I am often silent about with colleagues. I spoke about class allegiance and revolutionary commitments, explaining that it was disturbing to me that intellectual radicals who speak about transforming society, ending the domination of race, sex, class, cannot break with behavior patterns that reinforce and perpetuate domination, or continue to use as their sole reference point how we might be or are perceived by those who dominate, whether or not we gain their acceptance and approval.

This is a primary contradiction which raises the issue of whether or not the academic setting is a place where one can be truly radical or subversive. Concurrently, the use of language and style of presentation that alienates most folks who are not academically trained reinforces the notion that the academic world is separate from real life, that everyday world where we constantly adjust our language and behavior to meet diverse needs. The academic setting is separate only when we work to make it so. It is a false dichotomy which suggests that academics and/or intellectuals can only speak to one another, that we cannot hope to speak with the masses. What is true is that we make choices, that we choose our audiences, that we choose voices to hear and voices to silence. If I do not speak in a language that can be understood, then there is little chance for dialogue. This issue of language and behavior is a central contradiction all radical intellectuals, particularly those who are members of oppressed groups, must continually confront and work to resolve. One of the clear and present dangers that exists when we move outside our class of origin, our collective ethnic experience, and enter hierarchical institutions which daily reinforce domination by race, sex, and class, is that we gradually assume a mindset similar to those who dominate and oppress, that we lose critical consciousness because it is not reinforced or affirmed by the environment. We must be ever vigilant. It is important that we know who we are speaking to, who we most want to hear us, who we most long to move, motivate, and touch with our words.

When I first came to New Haven to teach at Yale, I was truly surprised by the marked class divisions between black folks— students and professors—who identify with Yale and those black folks who work at Yale or in surrounding communities. Style of dress and self-presentation are most often the central markers of one's position. I soon learned that the black folks who spoke on the street were likely to be part of the black community and those who carefully shifted their glance were likely to be associated with Yale. Walking with a black female colleague one day, I spoke to practically every black person in sight (a gesture which reflects my upbringing), an action which disturbed my companion. Since I addressed black folk who were clearly not associated with Yale, she wanted to know whether or not I knew them. That was funny to me. "Of course not," I answered. Yet when I thought about it seriously, I realized that in a deep way, I knew them for they, and not my companion or most of my colleagues at Yale, resemble my family. Later that year, in a black women's support group I started for undergraduates, students from poor backgrounds spoke about the shame they sometimes feel when faced with the reality of their connection to working-class and poor black people. One student confessed that her father is a street person, addicted to drugs, someone who begs from passersby. She, like other Yale students, turns away from street people often, sometimes showing anger or contempt; she hasn't wanted anyone to know that she was related to this kind of person. She struggles with this, wanting to find a way to acknowledge and affirm this reality, to claim this connection. The group asked me and one another what we [should] do to remain connected, to honor the bonds we have with working-class and poor people even as our class experience alters.

Maintaining connections with family and community across class boundaries demands more than just summary recall of where one's roots are, where one comes from. It requires knowing, naming, and being ever-mindful of those aspects of one's past that have enabled and do enable one's self-development in the present, that sustain and support, that enrich. One must also honestly confront barriers that do exist, aspects of that past that do diminish. My parents' ambivalence about my love for reading led to intense conflict. They (especially my mother) would work to

10

ensure that I had access to books, but would threaten to burn the books or throw them away if I did not conform to other expectations. Or they would insist that reading too much would drive me insane. Their ambivalence nurtured in me a like uncertainty about the value and significance of intellectual endeavor which took years for me to unlearn. While this aspect of our class reality was one that wounded and diminished, their vigilant insistence that being smart did not make me a "better" or "superior" person (which often got on my nerves because I think I wanted to have that sense that it did indeed set me apart, make me better) made a profound impression. From them I learned to value and respect various skills and talents folk might have, not just to value people who read books and talk about ideas. They and my grandparents might say about somebody, "Now he don't read nor write a lick, but he can tell a story," or as my grandmother would say, "call out the hell in words."

Empty romanticization of poor or working-class backgrounds undermines the possibility of true connection. Such connection is based on understanding difference in experience and perspective and working to mediate and negotiate these terrains. Language is a crucial issue for folk whose movement outside the boundaries of poor and working-class backgrounds changes the nature and direction of their speech. Coming to Stanford with my own version of a Kentucky accent, which I think of always as a strong sound quite different from Tennessee or Georgia speech, I learned to speak differently while maintaining the speech of my region, the sound of my family and community. This was of course much easier to keep up when I returned home to stay often. In recent years, I have endeavored to use various speaking styles in the classroom as a teacher and find it disconcerts those who feel that the use of a particular patois excludes them as listeners, even if there is translation into the usual, acceptable mode of speech. Learning to listen to different voices, hearing different speech challenges the notion that we must all assimilate—share a single, similar talk—in educational institutions. Language reflects the culture from which we emerge. To deny ourselves daily use of speech patterns that are common and familiar, that embody a unique and distinctive aspect of our self is one of the ways we become estranged and alienated from our past. It is important for us to have as many languages on hand as we can know or learn. It is important for those of us who are black, who speak in particular patois as well as standard English, to express ourselves in both ways.

Often I tell students from poor and working-class backgrounds that if you believe what you have learned and are learning in schools and universities separates you from your past, this is precisely what will happen. It is important to stand firm in the conviction that nothing can truly separate us from our pasts when we nurture and enrich that connection. An important strategy for maintaining contact is ongoing acknowledgment of the primacy of one's past, of one's background, affirming the reality that such bonds are not severed automatically solely because one enters a new environment or moves toward a different class experience.

Again, I do not wish to romanticize this effort, to dismiss the reality of conflict and contradiction. During my time at Stanford, I did go through a period of more than a year when I did not return home. That period was one where I felt that it was simply too difficult to mesh my profoundly disparate realities. Critical reflection about the choice I was making, particularly about why I felt a choice had to be made, pulled me through this difficult time. Luckily I recognized that the insistence on choosing between the world of family and community and the new world of privileged white people and privileged ways of knowing was imposed upon me by the outside. It is as though a mythical contract had been signed somewhere which demanded of us black folks that once we entered these spheres we would immediately give up all vestiges of our underprivileged past. It was my responsibility to formulate a way of being that would allow me to participate fully in my new environment while integrating and maintaining aspects of the old.

One of the most tragic manifestations of the pressure black people feel to assimilate is expressed in the internalization of racist perspectives. I was shocked and saddened when I first heard black professors at Stanford downgrade and express contempt for black students, expecting us to do poorly, refusing to establish nurturing bonds. At every university I have attended as a student or worked at as a teacher, I have heard similar attitudes expressed with little or no understanding of factors that might prevent brilliant black students from performing to their full capability. Within universities, there are few educational and social spaces where students who wish to affirm positive ties to ethnicity—to blackness, to working-class backgrounds—can receive affirmation and support. Ideologically, the message is clear—assimilation is the way to gain acceptance and approval from those in power.

Many white people enthusiastically supported Richard Rodriguez's vehement contention in his autobiography, *Hunger of*

Memory, that attempts to maintain ties with his Chicano background impeded his progress, that he had to sever ties with community and kin to succeed at Stanford and in the larger world, that family language, in his case Spanish, had to be made secondary or discarded. If the terms of success as defined by the standards of ruling groups within white-supremacist, capitalist patriarchy are the only standards that exist, then assimilation is indeed necessary. But they are not. Even in the face of powerful structures of domination, it remains possible for each of us, especially those of us who are members of oppressed and/or exploited groups as well as those radical visionaries who may have race, class, and sex privilege, to define and determine alternative standards, to decide on the nature and extent of compromise. Standards by which one's success is measured, whether student or professor, are quite different from those of us who wish to resist reinforcing the domination of race, sex, and class, who work to maintain and strengthen our ties with the oppressed, with those who lack material privilege, with our families who are poor and working-class. . . .

. . . Always our first response when we are motivated to conform or compromise within structures that reinforce domination must be to engage in critical reflection. Only by challenging ourselves to push against oppressive boundaries do we make the radical alternative possible, expanding the realm and scope of critical inquiry. Unless we share radical strategies, ways of rethinking and revisioning with students, with kin and community, with a larger audience, we risk perpetuating the stereotype that we succeed because we are the exception, different from the rest of our people. Since I left home and entered college, I am often asked, usually by white people, if my sisters and brothers are also high achievers. At the root of this question is the longing for reinforcement of the belief in "the exception" which enables race, sex, and class biases to remain intact. I am careful to separate what it means to be exceptional from a notion of "the exception." . . .

. . . Open, honest communication is the most important way we maintain relationships with kin and community as our class experience and backgrounds change. It is as vital as the sharing of resources. Often financial assistance is given in circumstances where there is no meaningful contact. However helpful, this can also be an expression of estrangement and alienation. Communication between black folks from various experiences of material privilege was much easier when we were all in segregated sharing common experiences in relation to social institutions. Without this grounding, we must work to maintain ties, connection. We must assume greater responsibility for making and maintaining contact, connections that can shape our intellectual visions and inform our radical commitments.

The most powerful resource any of us can have as we study and teach in university settings is full understanding and appreciation of the richness, beauty, and primacy of our familial and community backgrounds. Maintaining awareness of class differences, nurturing ties with the poor and working-class people who are our most intimate kin, our comrades in struggle, transforms and enriches our intellectual experience. Education as the practice of freedom becomes not a force which fragments or separates, but one that brings us closer, expanding our definitions of home and community.

Questions for Discussion

1. What ideas on class differences and education did hooks focus on during her time at Stanford? How did class realities separate her both from her fellow students and from her parents? Why did she "talk to no one" about her class shame and guilt?
2. Why does academic language and expression (both written and oral) alienate people who are not academically trained? What personal examples does hooks present of her own efforts to bridge the gap between the language of the academy and the language of minorities, as well as others from non-mainstream cultural traditions?
3. According to hooks, how does "romanticization" of lower-class backgrounds "undermine the possibility of true connection"?
4. What advice does hooks have for students from such backgrounds who fear that university learning will separate them from their pasts? How does her advice differ from that of Richard Rodriguez? What seems helpful about her advice?

Ideas for Writing

1. Hooks argues against the assumption that "assimilation is the way to gain acceptance . . . from those in power." Write an essay in support of or in opposition to her position.
2. Write about what have you learned from this essay about issues of class, higher education, and citizenship. For example,

does hooks' essay suggest that academic education helps or hinders people from being good citizens and making useful contributions to their communities?

The Common School and The Common Good

E. D. HIRSCH, JR.

E. D. Hirsch, Jr. (b. 1928) earned his Ph.D. from Yale in 1957. While a Professor of English, Education, and Humanities at the University of Virginia and as a Fellow of the Institute for Advanced Study in the Social Sciences at Stanford, Hirsch developed a belief that a core body of knowledge should be taught in a systematic way to children around the country as a way of strengthening the role of the citizen in our democracy. In support of his philosophy of education and democracy, Hirsch founded the Core Knowledge Foundation in 1986, which serves as the hub of a growing network of Core Knowledge schools. His ideas are most concisely expressed in the controversial national bestseller *Cultural Literacy: What Every American Needs to Know* (1987). In the selection that follows, which is excerpted from his book, *The Schools We Need and Why We Don't Have Them* (1996), Hirsch makes his argument for the necessity of implementing a national core curriculum.

———————— ✦ ————————

Every nation that manages to achieve universal readiness in the early grades for all its children—a few examples are France, Hungary, Norway, Japan, Korea, Sweden, and Denmark—does so by following grade-by-grade standards. In large, diverse nations as well as small, homogenous ones, a common core curriculum appears to be the only practical means for achieving universal readiness at each grade level. Universal readiness, in turn, is the only means for achieving universal competence and for combining excellence with fairness. In contrast, no nation that *dispenses* with grade-by-grade standards has managed to achieve universal readiness, excellence, and fairness. The Netherlands, for example, is a non-core-curriculum nation that has managed to attain a high average level of excellence because of very high achievement among the top half of its students, but it has failed to achieve universal competence and fairness. Indeed, the Netherlands, the only non-core-curriculum nation of Northern Europe, exhibits the lowest degree of educational fairness in that region, with some 16 percent of its schools falling below minimum competency, as contrasted with about 2.5 percent among its core-curriculum neighbors. (The United States figure is 30 percent of schools below minimum competency.)

An informative exception to this correlation is found in Switzerland, which lacks a national core curriculum but achieves the best combination of excellence and fairness in the world, having the highest average level of achievement coupled with the smallest standard deviation. But on closer inspection, we find that in fact Switzerland has one of the most detailed and demanding core curriculums in the world, with each canton specifying in detail the minimum knowledge and skill that each child achieve in each grade, and an accountability system that ensures the attainment of those universal standards. There is some commonality in standards among the cantons, but equally important, Swiss children rarely move from one canton to another in the course of their schooling. Each child therefore receives a highly coherent, carefully monitored sequence of early learnings such as children receive in countries that have grade-by-grade standards nationwide.

To the reader who may feel that these international data have little relevance to the United States, with its anticentralized educational traditions and its diversity, the Swiss example, in which each state fixes its own core curriculum, may appear to have the greatest affinity with our own tradition of state and local control. That would be the case, however, only if our children did not move so frequently from one school to another, and stayed put as the Swiss do. In the 1930s, William Bagley summarized the problem of American nomadism (which has grown more acute since he wrote):

> The notion that each community must have a curriculum all its own is not only silly, but tragic. It neglects two important needs. The first, as we have already seen, is the need of a democracy for many common elements in the culture of all people, to the end that the people may discuss collective problems in terms that will convey common meanings. The second need is extremely practical. It is the need of recognizing the fact that American people simply

will not "stay put." They are the most mobile people in the world.
. . . Under these conditions, failure to have a goodly measure of
uniformity in school subjects and grade placement is a gross injustice to at least ten million school children at the present time.

The injustice that Bagley identified has intensified for many
reasons, and it now extends to many more than ten million children. The average inner-city mobility rates (the percentage of
children in a school who transfer in or out during the school year)
lie routinely between 45 and 80 percent. Some inner-city school
have mobility rates of over 100 percent. A recent analysis from
the United States General Accounting Office reported that one
sixth of all third graders attend at least three schools between
first and third grade. Given the curricular incoherence of schooling even for those who stay at the same school, the fragmentation
and incoherence of the education provided to frequently moving
students are heartbreaking.

5   In sum, the high mobility of our children, especially of those
who can least afford educational disruption, makes common
learnings *more* needed in the United States than in most other nations. The argument that we are different from others and require
different educational arrangements points to more, not less, commonality in our educational standards. It is certainly true that we
cannot reasonably be compared to Switzerland, but our children's
high mobility rates are all the more reason why we cannot reasonably follow the Swiss principle of isolated localism. Our diversity, size, and nomadism are arguments in favor of, not against,
common, grade-by-grade standards. Until very recently, of
course, the idea of common standards in the United States has
been unthinkable among American educational experts. Localism
remains a quasi-sacred principle, despite the fact that few localities actually impose explicit content standards. But many people
are coming to feel that, considering the glaring knowledge gaps
and boring repetitions that children experience even when they
stay at the same school, continuing our educational incoherence,
nonaccountability, and inequity would be even more unthinkable.

Bagley's other point, that common learnings are necessary to
a functioning democracy, is an educational principle that has
been accepted in most democracies of the world, including our
own in its earlier years. The institution of the common school,
proposed by Jefferson and fostered by Horace Mann, had the goal
of giving all children the shared intellectual and social capital

that would enable them to participate as autonomous citizens in the economy and policy of the nation. When Jefferson said that if he had to choose between newspapers and the government, he would choose newspapers, he went on to say that his remark was premised on each citizen's being able to read and understand the newspapers. It was a prescient addendum. A citizenry cannot read and understand newspapers, much less participate effectively in a modern economy, without sharing the common intellectual capital that makes understanding and communication possible. In a large, diverse nation, the common school is the only institution available for creating a school-based culture that, like a common language, enables everyone to communicate in the public sphere.

The principle that children should enter a new grade already sharing the background knowledge required to understand the teacher and each other is at bottom the principle that enables the functioning of an entire community or nation. People cannot effectively meet in the classroom or in the marketplace unless they can communicate with and learn from each another. It is the duty of a nation's educational system to create this domain of public communicability. It cannot do so without the common school, and the common school cannot be truly such without providing each child the shared intellectual capital that will be needed in each early grade, and needed ultimately in society after graduation. A shared public culture that enables public communicability is essential to an effective community at every age and stage of life, and most emphatically in the early grades, when deficits can be made up. Once out of school, a citizen must continue to share the common intellectual capital of the nation in order to communicate and learn.

The need to develop and nurture this cultural commons was implicitly understood by the founders, and is consistent with their motivation for having a First Amendment clause that forbids the establishment of a state religion. Divisiveness was to be excluded from the cultural commons. Guided by the principle of public toleration enunciated by John Locke and others after the bloody seventeenth-century wars of religion, the founders desired that the laws and customs of the public sphere should favor no single sect but should promote the general welfare. Customs divisive and dangerous to the internal peace of the nation, chiefly sectarian religions, were to be relegated to the private sphere, enabling all to meet in the public sphere as fellow citizens and equals. The deliberately artificial wall of separation helped create and nurture a public domain of toleration and civility, while leaving everyone as free as possible in their private lives. It was a brilliant Enlightenment political innovation for encouraging internal peace and solidarity in a large nation, and it led to the development of a uniquely American public culture. The development of this cosmopolitan culture was thus no accident. It had been openly discussed in the later Enlightenment, notably in the writings of Immanuel Kant. In the minds of Jefferson, Mann, and other democratic theorists in France and elsewhere, the common school was to be not just the instrument of knowledge, literacy, and equality of opportunity but also the agent of a cosmopolitan culture that would promote universal respect and civility.

In our own day, the chief danger to this ecumenical, cosmopolitan public culture is not a religious but an ethnic sectarianism. The two kinds of sect, religious and ethnic, are highly similar in their divisiveness and their danger to the shared public sphere. Had the idea of ethnic strife been as present in the minds of the Founding Fathers as the idea of religious strife, our founding laws might have included a clause forbidding the establishment of a narrow ethnic culture. Just as the invocations of the Divinity in our public ceremonies are deliberately nonsectarian, hybrid affairs, engaged in by rabbis as well as priests, so our public culture is a hybrid construct that contains heterogeneous elements from various ethnic groups. Recently, Orlando Patterson has spoken of "cross-pollinating our multi-ethnic communities" in order to "promote that precious overarching national culture—the envy of the world—which I call ecumenical America." But Patterson sees a serious danger to that overarching culture in

> balkanizing America both intellectually and culturally. One has only to walk for a few minutes on any large campus (the unfortunate coalescence of the left separatists and the right republican anti-communitarian individualists/separatists!) to witness the pervasiveness of ethnic separatism, marked by periodic outbursts of other chauvinisms and hostilities.

10   Patterson urges instead a return to the cosmopolitan ideal of the commons:

> Universities and businesses should return to the principle of integration, to the notion that diversity is not something to be cele-

brated and promoted in its own right, but an opportunity for mutual understanding and the furtherance of an ecumenical national culture.

Patterson and others, notably Arthur Schlesinger, Jr., have been urging that the principle of multiculturalism should be guided into this ecumenical, cosmopolitan direction for the good of the nation rather than fostering its all-too-prevalent tendency toward angry separatism and mutual hostility. This book strongly supports that view. Whether multiculturalism should be given a Romantic, separatist form (in the tradition of Fichte) or an Enlightenment, cosmopolitan form (in the tradition of Kant) has an obvious bearing on the educational question of common learnings in the early grades. In my view, the Romantic version of ethnicity is as deleterious to public education as the Romantic conception of pedagogy. The common learnings taught in school should promote a cosmopolitan, ecumenical, hybrid public culture in which all meet on an equal footing—a culture that is as deliberately artificial and nonsectarian as our public invocations of the Divinity. This school-based culture belongs to everyone and to no one. Its function is analogous to that of the hybrid lingua francas of the medieval marketplace, which were the antecedents of the major national languages—themselves hybrid, artificially constructed affairs, mostly codified by committees.

In the United States, the process of reaching agreement about a sequence of common learnings in the early grades is likely to be lengthy, conflict-ridden, and, at the start, unofficial. A highly specific common core of content is still repellent to many Americans. Gradually, however, general agreement on such a core might be developed if the public and the educational community became fully persuaded that some degree of grade-by-grade commonality is necessary to educational excellence and equity. (A 50 percent common core has proved to be acceptable to parents in Core Knowledge schools.) The public will be all the more likely to reach this conclusion when it becomes more fully aware that the educational formalism has turned the jealously guarded principle of local curriculum control into a myth. As far as specific content is concerned, the local curriculum, with few exceptions, does not exist. One cannot reasonably endorse something that does not exist, though one can demand that it come into existence. If the public simply insisted upon a true common core of learnings at the local level, that would mark a huge advance in our educational arrangements, and might in time lead to still broader commonalities.

Because this book has been focused mainly on kindergarten through grade eight—decisive grades for determining the excellence and equity of schooling—I have paid scant attention to high school. That is a conscious omission. If the principles of early education advanced here were to be followed, American high schools would change perforce for the better. Their incoming students would have already received the foundational knowledge and skill needed for good citizenship. (In earlier eras, many exemplary citizens-to-be were compelled to leave school by the end of grade eight.) Students would not need to be shepherded into so many elementary courses; they could follow more varied and intensive strands of academic or vocational study according to their interests and abilities. As a consequence, the American high school would become a more interesting and effective place for all types of students.

Beyond urging agreement at the local level, I have not made any suggestions regarding the large-scale policies needed to create more demanding elementary schools. I haven't answered questions like What shall we do tomorrow? and Who shall be in charge? The possible administrative means for accomplishing the task are many, but there can be no substitute for the main elements of the task itself. Schools need to have a coherent, cumulative core curriculum which instills consensus values such as civic duty, honesty, diligence, perseverance, respect, kindness, and independent-mindedness; which gives students step-by-step mastery of *procedural knowledge* in language arts and mathematics; which gives them step-by-step mastery of *content knowledge* in civics, science, the arts, and the humanities; and which holds students, teachers, schools, and parents accountable for acceptable progress in achieving these specific year-by-year goals. Every school, in short, should have the basic characteristics described in an earlier chapter:

> All teachers at our school have not only pedagogical training but also a detailed knowledge of the subject matter that they teach. We instill in all children an ethic of toleration, civility, orderliness, responsibility, and hard work. Our staff has agreed on a definite core of knowledge and skill that all children will attain *in each grade*. We make sure that every child learns this core, and gains the specific knowledge and skill needed to prosper at the

next grade level, thus enabling knowledge to build upon knowledge. Our teachers continually confer with their colleagues about effective ways of stimulating children to learn and integrate this specific knowledge and skill. The specificity of our goals enables us to monitor children, and give focused attention where necessary. To this end, we provide parents with a detailed outline of the *specific* knowledge and skill goals for each grade, and we stay in constant touch with them regarding the child's progress. Through this knowledge-based approach, we make sure that *all* normal children perform at grade level, while, in addition, the most talented children are challenged to excel. Attaining this specific and well-integrated knowledge and skill gives our students pleasure in learning, as well as self-respect, and it ensures that they will enter the next grade ready and eager to learn more.

Since this emphasis on content and coherence requires a structuring of ideas, and because ideas are slow to change, my colleagues and I have been pursuing a school-by-school grassroots effort in which the leadership of one group of parents or teachers, or of a single principal or superintendent, can revolutionize the ideas and practices of an individual school. That school's success then sometimes encourages other schools to rethink their assumptions. This school-by-school effort is slow, but it is at least an avenue that can be taken now, without delay—the kind of initiative greatly facilitated by large-scale policies that consciously liberate individual initiative, policies such as "parental choice" and "charter schools," which give parents and teachers the power to change their own individual schools, so long as their students are trained to high standards of skill and knowledge.

It has taken nearly seventy years for Romantic progressivism to exercise virtually totalitarian intellectual dominion over not just schools of education but a large percentage of policymakers and the general public as well. Nothing truly effective in the way of large-scale policy change—through federal, state, or local mechanisms—can be accomplished, no new power relationships can be forged, until there is a change of mind by the general public—among whom I include two and a half million teachers. Once that occurs, many different public policies could be successful.

The strongest resistance to commonality in schooling may come from a widespread fear of uniformity—the last bastion of

15

misguided Romanticism. It is said that common elements in the curriculum would destroy our American essence, which is diversity. There is no evidence whatever that this fear of uniformity, which is widespread and often expressed, has any real-world foundation, or that a moiety of commonality in the school curriculum will turn everyone into interchangeable automatons. To the extent that this antisameness sentiment has any concrete implication for the curriculum, it would seem to be the current laissez-faire idea that if all schools and teachers do their own thing, then the invisible hand of nature will cause our children to be educated effectively, and thus ensure their individuality and diversity. The foundation for this curricular confidence (which has in fact resulted in huge knowledge gaps, boring repetitions, and glaring inequalities) would seem to be a Romantic faith in the watchful beneficence of nature, which "never did betray the heart that loved her." It is an expression of the same optimistic naturalism which supposes that the pace and quality of each child's scholarly attainments are determined naturally, and will follow an innate course of development which should not be interfered with by external impositions of drills and hard work.

Improving the effectiveness and fairness of education through enhancing both its content and its commonality has a more than educational significance. The improvement would, as everyone knows, diminish the economic inequities within the nation. Nothing could be more important to our national well-being than overcoming those inequities, which have grown ever greater in recent decades. But something equally significant is at stake. Many observers have deplored the decline in civility in our public life, and with it the decline in our sense of community. The interethnic hostilities that have intensified among us recently, the development of an us-versus-them mentality in political life, the astonishing indifference to the condition of our children—all bespeak a decline in the communitarian spirit, which used to be a hallmark of what Patterson calls our "ecumenical national culture." Bringing our children closer to universal competence is important. But an equally important contribution of the truly common school would be the strengthening of universal communicability and a sense of community within the public sphere. In the long run, that could be the common school's most important contribution to preserving the fragile fabric of our democracy.

Questions for Discussion

1. How does Hirsch apply Bagley's research and Jefferson's ideas to support his argument for a core curriculum?
2. Why does Hirsch think that a common curriculum is necessary to the functioning of a unified democratic nation? What evidence from foreign schools does he present to support his point of view?
3. Although Hirsch argues for a unified core curriculum in elementary school, he feels that high schools should be freer to develop alternative courses and cultural perspectives. What is the basis for this belief? Do you agree with him?
4. How does Hirsch believe that a common core curriculum could be established? Do you think his plan is realistic enough to be implemented?

Ideas for Writing

1. Do some research into the efforts of state and local public school district efforts to develop uniform curricula. Have any of these been successful? What has caused many of these efforts to fail? Write an essay that discusses your findings and draws conclusions about the viability of Hirsch's ideas.
2. Argue for or against Hirsch's underlying belief in the importance of a shared public culture. Do you believe that is necessary for a country as large and diverse as the United States to have a shared public culture? Do you believe we already have one or that the public schools should be involved in creating one?

Educating a Democracy
Deborah Meier

Born in 1931, Deborah Meier has worked for over 30 years in public education as a teacher, school principal, writer, and public advocate. She was the founder and teacher-director of a network of highly successful public elementary and secondary schools in East Harlem, New York. Serving primarily low-income black and

Latino students, these schools are considered exemplars of reform. Meier is currently vice-chair of the coalition of Essential Schools and Principal of Boston's Mission Hill Elementary School. She is the author of the books *The Power of Their Ideas: Lessons from a Small School in Harlem* (1995) and *In School We Trust: Creating Communities of Learning in an Era of Testing and Standardization* (2002). The selection that follows is from her book *Will Standards Save Public Education?* (2000).

———————— ✦ ————————

The current standards-based reform movement took off in 1983 in response to the widely held view that America was at extreme economic risk, largely because of bad schools. The battle cry, called out first in *A Nation at Risk*, launched an attack on dumb teachers, uncaring mothers, social promotion, and general academic permissiveness. Teachers and a new group labeled "educationists" were declared the main enemy, which undermined their credibility, and set the stage for cutting them and their concerns out of the cure. According to critics, American education needed to be reimagined, made more rigorous, and, above all, brought under the control of experts who, unlike educators and parents, understood the new demands of our economy and culture. The cure might curtail the work of some star teachers and star schools, and it might lead, as the education chief of Massachusetts recently noted, to a lot of crying fourth graders. But the gravity of the long-range risks to the nation demanded strong medicine.

Two claims were thus made: that our once-great public system was no longer performing well, and that its weaknesses were undermining America's economy. . . .

THE REAL CRISIS

. . . The coalition of experts who produced *A Nation at Risk* were wrong when they announced the failure of American public education and its critical role in our economic decline. Constructive debate about reform should begin by acknowledging this misjudgment. It should then also acknowledge the even bigger crisis that schools have played a major part in deepening, if not actually creating, and could play a big part in curing. This crisis requires quite a different set of responses, often in direct conflict with standardization.

An understanding of this other crisis begins by noting that we have the lowest voter turnout by far of any modern industrial country; we are exceptional for the absence of responsible care for our most vulnerable citizens (we spend less on child welfare—baby care, medical care, family leave—than almost every foreign counterpart); we don't come close to other advanced industrial countries in income equity; and our high rate of (and investment in) incarceration places us in a class by ourselves. All of these, of course, affect some citizens far more than others: and the heaviest burdens fall on the poor, the young, and people of color.

These social and political indicators are suggestive of a crisis 5 in human relationships. Virtually all discussions, right or left, about what's wrong in our otherwise successful society acknowledge the absence of any sense of responsibility for one's community and of decency in personal relationships. An important cause of this subtler crisis, I submit, is that the closer our youth come to adulthood the less they belong to communities that include responsible adults, and the more stuck they are in peer-only subcultures. We've created two parallel cultures, and it's no wonder the ones on the other side live and act: seemingly footloose and fancy-free but in truth often lost, confused, and knit together for temporary self-protection. The consequences are critical for all our youngsters, but obviously more severe—often disastrous—for those less identified with the larger culture of success.

Many changes in our society aided and abetted the shifts that have produced this alienation. But one important change has been in the nature of schooling. Our schools have grown too distant, too big, too standardized, too uniform, too divorced from their communities, too alienating of young from old and old from young. Few youngsters and few teachers have an opportunity to know each other by more than name (if that); and schools are organized such that "knowing each other" is nearly impossible. In these settings it's hard to teach young people how to be responsible to others, or to concern themselves with their community. At best they develop loyalties to the members of their immediate circle of friends (and perhaps their own nuclear family). Even when teens take jobs their fellow workers and their customers are likely to be peers. Apprenticeship as a way to learn to be an adult is disappearing. The public and its schools, the "real" world and the schoolhouse, young people and adults, have become disconnected, and until they are reconnected no list of particular bits of knowledge will be of much use.

In my youth there were over 200,000 school boards. Today there are fewer than 20,000 and the average school, which in my youth had only a few hundred students, now holds thousands. At this writing, Miami and Los Angeles are in the process of building the two largest high schools ever. The largest districts and the largest and most anonymous schools are again those that serve our least-advantaged children.

Because of the disconnection between the public and its schools, the power to protect or support them now lies increasingly in the hands of public or private bodies that have no immediate stake in the daily life of the students. CEOs, federal and state legislators, university experts, presidential think tanks, make more and more of the daily decisions about schools. For example, the details of the school day and year are determined by state legislators—often down to minutes per day for each subject taught, and whether Johnny gets promoted from third to fourth grade. The school's budget depends on it. Site-based school councils are increasingly the "in" thing, just as the scope of their responsibility narrows.

Public schools, after a romance with local power, beginning in the late 1960s and ending in the early 1990s, are increasingly organized as interchangeable units of a larger state organism, each expected to conform to the intelligence of some central agency or expert authority. The locus of authority in young people's lives has shifted away from the adults kids know well and who know the kids well—at a cost. Home schooling or private schooling seems more and more the natural next step for those with the means and the desire to remain in authority.

10   Our school troubles are not primarily the result of too easy course work or too much tolerance for violence. The big trouble lies instead in the company our children keep—or, more precisely, don't keep. They no longer keep company with us, the grown-ups they are about to become. And the grown-ups they do encounter seem less and less worthy of their respect. What kid, after all, wants to be seen emulating people he's been told are too dumb to exercise power, and are simply implementing the commands of the real experts?

Alternative Assumptions

Just as the conventional policy assumptions emerge naturally from a falsely diagnosed crisis, so does the crisis I have sketched suggest an alternative set of assumptions.

1. *Goals:* In a democracy, there are multiple, legitimate definitions of "a good education" and "well-educated," and it is desirable to acknowledge that plurality. Openly differing viewpoints constitute a healthy tension in a democratic, pluralistic society. Even where a mainstream view (consensus) exists, alternate views that challenge the consensus are critical to the society's health. Young people need to be exposed to competing views, and to adults debating choices about what's most important. As John Stuart Mill said, "It is not the mind of heretics that are deteriorated most, by the ban placed on all inquiry which does not end in the orthodox conclusions. The greatest harm is done to those who are not heretics, and whose whole mental development is cramped, and their reason cowed, by the fear of heresy."

2. *Authority:* In fundamental questions of education, experts should be subservient to citizens. Experts and laymen alike have an essential role in shaping both ends and means, the what and the how. While it is wise to involve experts from both business and the academy, they provide only one set of opinions, and are themselves rarely of a single mind. Moreover, it is educationally important for young people to be in the company of adults—teachers, family members, and other adults in their own communities—powerful enough to decide important things. They need to witness the exercise of judgment, the weighing of means and ends by people they can imagine becoming; and they need to see how responsible adults handle disagreement. If we think the adults in children's lives are, in Jefferson's words, "not enlightened enough to exercise their control with a wholesome discretion, the remedy is not to take it from them, but to inform their discretion by education."

3. *Assessment:* Standardized tests are too simple and simpleminded for high-stakes assessment of children and schools. Important decisions regarding kids and teachers should always be based on multiple sources of evidence that seem appropriate and credible to those most concerned. These are old testing truisms, backed even by the testing industry, which has never claimed the level of omniscience many standards advocates assume of it. The state should require only the forms of assessment be public, constitutionally sound, and subject to a variety of "second opinions" by experts representing other interested parties. Where states feel obliged to

set norms—for example, in granting state diplomas or access to state universities—these should be flexible, allowing schools maximum autonomy to demonstrate the ways they have reached such norms through other forms of assessment.

4. *Enforcement:* Sanctions should remain in the hands of the local community, to be determined by people who know the particulars of each child and each situation. The power of both business and the academy are already substantial; their access to the means of persuasion (television, the press, and so forth) and their power to determine access to jobs and higher education already impinge on the freedom of local communities. Families and their communities should not be required to make decisions about their own students and their own work based on such external measures. It is sufficient that they are obliged to take them into account in their deliberations about their children's future options.

5. *Equity:* A fairer distribution of resources is the principal means for achieving educational equity. The primary national responsibility is to narrow the resource gap between the most and least advantaged, both between 9 A.M. and 3 P.M. and during the other five sixths of their waking lives when rich and poor students are also learning—but very different things. To this end publicly accessible comparisons of educational achievement should always include information regarding the relative resources that the families of students, schools, and communities bring to the schooling enterprise.

6. *Effective Learning:* Improved learning is best achieved by improving teaching and learning relationships, by enlisting the energies of both teachers and learners. The kinds of learning required of citizens cannot be accomplished by standardized and centrally imposed systems of learning, even if we desired it for other reasons. Human learning, to be efficient, effective, and long-lasting, requires the engagement of learners on their own behalf, and rests on the relationships that develop between schools and their communities, between teachers and their students, and between the individual learner and what is to be learned.

No "scientific" argument can conclusively determine whether this set of assumptions or the set sketched earlier is true. Although some research suggests that human learning is less efficient when motivated by rewards and punishments, and that fear is a poor motivator, I doubt that further research will settle the issue. But because of the crisis of human relationships, I urge that we consider the contrary claims rather more seriously than we have. We may even find that in the absence of strong human relationships rigorous intellectual training in the most fundamental academic subjects cannot flourish. In a world shaped by powerful centralized media, restoring a greater balance of power between local communities and central authorities, between institutions subject to democratic control and those beyond their control, may be vastly more important than educational reformers bent on increased centralization acknowledge.

AN ALTERNATIVE MODEL

Suppose, then, we think about school reform in light of these alternative assumptions. What practical model of schools and learning do they support? In brief, our hope lies in schools that are more personal, compelling, and attractive than the Internet or TV, where youngsters can keep company with interesting and powerful adults who are in turn in alliance with the students' families and local institutions. We need to surround kids with adults who know and care for our children, who have opinions and are accustomed to expressing them publicly, and who know how to reach reasonable collective decisions in the face of disagreement. That means increasing local decision making, and simultaneously decreasing the size and bureaucratic complexity of schools. Correspondingly, the worst thing we can do is to turn teachers and schools into the vehicles for implementing externally imposed standards.

Is such an alternative practical? Are the assumptions behind it mere sentiment?

At the Mission Hill in Boston, one of ten new Boston public 15 schools initiated by the Boston Public Schools and the Boston Teachers Union, we designed a school to support such alternative practices. The families who come to Mission Hill are chosen by lottery and represent a cross section of Boston's population. We intentionally keep the school small with fewer than two hundred students ages five to thirteen—so that the adults can meet regularly, take responsibility for each other's work, and confer and argue over how best to get things right. Parents join the staff not only for formal governance meetings, but for monthly informal suppers, conversations, good times. Our oldest kids, the eighth graders, will graduate only when they can show us all that they meet our graduation standards, which are the result of lots of parent, staff, and community dialogue over several years.

All our students study—once when they are little, once when they are older—a schoolwide interdisciplinary curriculum. Last fall they all became experts on Boston and Mission Hill, learning its history (and their own), geography, architecture, distinct neighborhoods, and figures of importance. Last winter they all re-created ancient Egypt at 67 Allegheny Street. This coming winter they will re-create ancient China. Each spring they dig into a science-focused curriculum theme. The common curriculum allowed us, for example, to afford professional and amateur Egyptologists, who joined us from time to time as lively witnesses to a lifelong passion. We have a big central corridor that serves as our public mall, where kids paint murals and mix together to read and talk across ages. High school youngsters who share the building with us read with little ones, take them on trips, and generally model what it can mean to be a more responsible and well-educated person.

We invented our own standards, not out of whole cloth but with an eye to what the world out there expects and what we deem valuable and important. And we assess them through the work the kids do and the commentary of others about that work. Our standards are intended to deepen and broaden young people's habits of mind, their craftsmanship, and their work habits. Other schools may select quite a different way of describing and exhibiting their standards. But they too need to consciously construct their standards in ways that give schooling purpose and coherence, and then commit themselves to achieving them. And the kids need to understand the standards and their rationale. They must see school as not just a place to get a certificate, but a place that lives by the same standards it sets for them. Thus the Mission Hill school not only sets standards but has considerable freedom and flexibility with regard to how it spends its public funds and organizes its time to attain them. All ten pilot schools offer examples of different ways this might play out, ways that could be replicated in all Boston schools.

Standard setting and assessment are not once-and-for-all issues. We reexamine our school constantly to see that it remains a place that engages all of us in tough but interesting learning tasks, nourishes and encourages the development of reasonable and judicious trust, and nurtures a passion for making sense of things and the skills needed to do so. We expect disagreements—sometimes painful ones. We know that even well-intentioned, reasonable people cross swords over deeply held beliefs. And we know, too, that these differences can be sources of valuable education when the school itself can negotiate the needed compromises.

What is impressive at Mission Hill, at the other pilot schools, at the Central Park East School in New York's east Harlem, where I worked for twenty-five years, and the thousands of other small schools like them, is that over time the kids buy in. These schools receive the same per capita public funding as other schools receive, are subject to city and state testing, and must obey the same basic health, safety, and civil rights regulations. But because these schools are small, the families and faculties are together by choice, and all concerned can exercise substantial power over staffing, scheduling, curriculum, and assessment, the schools' cultural norms and expectations are very different than those of most other public schools.

The evidence suggests that most youngsters have a sufficiently deep hunger for the relationships these schools offer them—among kids and between adults and kids—that they choose school over the alternative cultures on the Net, tube, and street. Over 90 percent of Central Park East's very typical students stuck it out, graduated, and went on to college. And most persevered through higher education. Did they ever rebel, get mad at us, reassert their contrary values and adolescent preferences? Of course. Did we fail with some? Yes. But it turns out that the hunger for grown-up connections is strong enough to make a difference if we give it a chance. Studies launched in New York between 1975 and 1995 conducted on the other similar schools show the same pattern of success.

Standards, yes. Absolutely. But as Thedore Sizer, who put the idea of standards on the school map in the early 1980s, also told us then: we need standards held by real people who matter in the lives of our young. School, family, and community must forge their own, in dialogue with and in response to the larger world of which they are a part. There will always be tensions; but if the decisive, authoritative voice always comes from anonymous outsiders, then kids cannot learn what it takes to develop their own voice.

I know this "can be" because I've been there. The flowering of so many new public schools of choice over the past two decades proves that under widely different circumstances, very different kinds of leadership and different auspices, a powerful alternative to externally imposed standards is available.

And I also know the powerful reasons why it "can't be"— because I've witnessed firsthand the resistance even to allowing others to follow suit, much less encouraging or mandating them to do so. The resistance comes not simply from bad bureaucrats or fearful unions (the usual bogeymen), but from legislators and mayors and voters, from citizens who think that if an institution is public it has to be all things to all constituents (characterless and mediocre by definition), and from various elites who see teachers and private citizens as too dumb to engage in making important decisions. That's a heady list of resisters.

But small self-governing schools of choice, operating with considerable flexibility and freedom, also resonate with large numbers of people, including many of those who are gathering around charter schools, and even some supporters of privatization and home schooling. They too come from a wide political spectrum and could be mobilized.

ACCOUNTABILITY

25 And yet doubts about accountability will linger. In a world of smaller, more autonomous schools not responsible to centralized standardization, how will we know who is doing a good job and who isn't? How can we prevent schools from claiming they're doing just fine, and having those claims believed, when they may not be true? Are we simply forced to trust them, with no independent evidence?

What lies behind these worries? For those who buy into the conventional assumptions, anything but top-down standardization seems pointless. But for those whose concern is more practical there are some straightforward and practical answers to the issue of accountability that do not require standardization.

To begin with, I am not advocating the elimination of all systems for taking account of how schools and students are doing. In any case, that is hardly a danger.

Americans invented the modern, standardized, norm-referenced test. Our students have been taking more tests more often than any nation on the face of the earth, and schools and districts have been going public with test scores starting almost from the moment children enter school. For the third-or fourth-grade level (long before any of our international counterparts bother to test children) we have test data for virtually all schools, by race, class, and gender. We know exactly how many kids did better or worse in every subcategory. We have test data for almost every grade thereafter in reading and math, and to some degree in all other subjects. This has been the case for nearly half a century. Large numbers of our eighteen-year-olds now take standardized college entry tests (SATs and ACTs). In addition, the national government now offers us its own tests—the NAEP—which are given to an uncontaminated sample of students from across the United States and now reported by grade and state. And all of the above is very public.

In addition, public schools have been required to produce statements attesting to their financial integrity—how they spend their money—at least as rigorously as any business enterprise. They are held accountable for regularly reporting who works for them and what their salaries are. In most systems there are tightly prescribed rules and regulations; schools are obliged to fill out innumerable forms regarding almost every aspect of their work: how many kids are receiving special education, how many incidents of violence, how many suspensions, how many graduates, what grades students have received, how many hours and minutes they study each and every subject, and the credentials of their faculties. This information, and much more, is public. And the hiring and firing of superintendents has become a very common phenomenon.

In a nation in which textbooks are the primary vehicle for distributing knowledge in schools, a few major textbook publishers, because of a few major state textbook laws, dominate the field, offering most teachers and schools (and students) very standardized accounts of what is to be learned, and when and how to deliver this knowledge. Moreover, most textbooks have always come armed with their own end-of-chapter tests, increasingly designed to look like the real thing; indeed, test makers also are the publishers of many of the major standardized tests.

In short, we have been awash in accountability and standardization for a very long time, but we are missing precisely the qualities that the last big wave of reform was intended to respond to: teachers, kids, and families who know each other or each other's work and take responsibility for it; we are missing communities built around their own articulated and public standards and ready to show them off to others.

The schools I have worked in and support have shown how much more powerful accountability becomes when one takes this latter path. The work produced by Central Park East students, for example, is collected regularly in portfolios, and it is examined (and in the case of high school students, judged) by tough internal and external reviewers, in a process that closely resembles a doctoral oral exam. The standards by which a student is evaluated are easily accessible to families, clear to kids, and capable of being judged by other parties. In addition schools such as this undergo schoolwide external assessments that take into account the quality of their curriculum, instruction, staff development, and culture as well as the impact of the school on students' future success (in college, work, and so forth).

Are the approaches designed by Central Park East or Mission Hill the best way? That's probably the wrong question. We never intended to suggest that everyone should follow our system. It would be nice if it were easier for others to adopt our approach; it would be even better if it were easier—in fact required—for others to adopt alternatives to it, including the use of standardized tests if they so choose. My argument is for more local control, not for one true way.

I opt for more local control not because I think the larger society has no common interests at stake in how we educate all children, or because local people are smarter or intrinsically more honorable. The interests of wider publics are important in my way of thinking. I know that pressure exists at Mission Hill to not accept or push out students who are difficult to educate, who will make us look worse on any test, or whose families are a nuisance. It's a good thing that others are watching us to prevent such exclusion.

35 But the United States is now hardly in danger of too much localized power. (The only local powers we seem to be interested in expanding are those that allow us to resegregate our schools by race or gender.) What is missing is balance—some power in the hands of those whose agenda is first and foremost the feelings of particular kids, their particular families, their perceived local values and needs. (Without this balance, my knowledge that holding David over in third grade will not produce the desired effects is useless knowledge.) So is my knowledge of different ways to reach him through literature or history. This absence of local power is bad for David's education and bad for democracy. A backseat driver may be more expert than the actual driver, but there are limits to what can be accomplished from the rear seat.

In short, the argument is not about the need for standards or accountability, but what kind serves us best. I believe standardization will make it harder to hold people accountable and harder to develop sound and useful standards. The intellectual demands of the twenty-first century, as well as the demands of democratic life, are best met by preserving plural definitions of a good education, local decision making, and respect for ordinary human judgments.

Education and Democracy

If we are to make use of what we knew in Dewey's day (and know even better today) about how the human species best learns, we will have to start by throwing away the dystopia of the ant colony, the smoothly functioning (and quietly humming) factory where everything goes according to plan, and replace it with a messy, often rambunctious, community, with its multiple demands and complicated trade-offs. The new schools that might better serve democracy and the economy will have to be capable of constantly remaking themselves and still provide for sufficient stability, routine, ritual, and shared ethos. Impossible? Of course. So these schools will veer too far one way or the other at different times in their history, will learn from each other, shift focus, and find a new balance. There will always be a party of order and a party of messiness.

If schools are not all required to follow all the same fads, maybe they will learn something from their separate experiments. And that will help to nurture the two indispensable traits of a democratic society: a high degree of tolerance for others, indeed genuine empathy for them, as well as a high degree of tolerance for uncertainty, ambiguity, and puzzlement, indeed enjoyment of them.

A vibrant and nurturing community, with clear and regular guideposts—its own set of understandings, its people with a commitment to one another that feels something rather like love and affection—can sustain such rapid change without losing its humanity. Such a community must relish its disagreements, its oddballs, its misfits. Not quite families, but closer to our definition of family than of factory, such schools will make high demands on their members and have a sustaining and relentless sense of purpose and coherence, but will be ready also to always (at least sometimes) even reconsider their own core beliefs. Their members will come home exhausted, but not burned out.

Everything that moves us toward these qualities will be good 40 for the ideal of democracy. A democracy in which less than half its members see themselves as "making enough difference" to bother to vote in any election is surely endangered—far more endangered, at risk, than our economy. It's for the loss of belief in the capacity to influence the world, not our economic ups and downs, that we educators should accept some responsibility. What I have learned from thirty years in small powerful schools is that it is here above all that schools can make a difference, can alter the odds.

We can't beat the statistical advantage on the next round of tests that being advantaged has over being disadvantaged; we can, however, substantially affect the gap between rich and poor where it will count, in the long haul of life. Even there it's hard to see how schools by themselves can eliminate the gap, but we can stop enlarging it. The factory-like schools we invented a century ago to handle the masses were bound to enlarge the gap. But trained mindlessness at least fit the world of work so many young people were destined for. We seem now to be reinventing a twenty-first-century version of the factory-like school—for the mind-workers of tomorrow.

It is a matter of choice; such a future does not roll in on the wheels of inevitability. We have the resources, the knowledge, and plenty of living examples of the many different kinds of schools that might serve our needs better. All we need is a little more patient confidence in the good sense of "the people"—in short, a little more commitment to democracy.

Questions for Discussion

1. Why does Meier believe the experts who produced the book *A Nation at Risk* were wrong? According to Meier, what is the real crisis confronting our schools and the larger society?
2. What assumptions about public school difficulties does Meier provide in the six problem areas that she identifies? How do these assumptions challenge the way most public schools today are run?
3. How does Meier's example of the Mission Hill School help to clarify her six stated principles of education?
4. Why does Meier believe that the absence of "local power" in schools has a negative impact on our democracy? Were you convinced by her arguments? Explain your point of view.

Ideas for Writing

1. Write an essay in which you argue whether or not it is valuable for schools to put as much emphasis on local control as Meier proposes. What are some possible disadvantages of local control?

2. Write up a proposal for a change to a school in your community that would make it more closely resemble the Mission Hill School. Use the six reforms Meier proposes as your guide. What difficulties would you find in making such a change, and how could the reforms be implemented?

Community Service
Robert Coles

Robert Coles (b. 1929) is a child psychiatrist and a professor of psychiatry and medical humanities at Harvard. He is best known for his work with the lives of children, where he explores their moral, political, and spiritual sensibilities. The author of more than fifty books, Robert Coles won the Pulitzer Prize for his *Children of Crisis* series. He is also known as an eloquent spokesman for voluntary and community service, which is the subject of his book, *The Call of Service: A Witness to Idealism* (1993). In the following selection excerpted from *The Call of Service*, Coles profiles the idealism of today's youth, who often choose to volunteer or do community service through their high schools or colleges.

———————— ✦ ————————

Today's students are likely to express their lofty political and social impulses and practical desires to change the world through community service, even if in limited or modest ways. I have spent many years—since 1978—working with college students engaged in community service; they tutor the young, keep company with the elderly, visit the sick, run summer camps, design and implement educational programs in prisons, help the medically needy and indigent get hospital care, and argue in the courts on behalf of tenants or workers. Often those students experience the same conflicts or misgivings that deeply troubled the activists of the civil rights era and that now trouble older people working full-time as community organizers.

"I want to help the kids I know," a college junior told me, but he had his eye on what he called "the larger picture." When I asked him to fill me in on the details of that picture, he was both voluble and impassioned. "This entire ghetto is a breeding ground of crime, and someday it has to go! Don't ask me how we'll do it, but until the nation addresses the problems here in this ghetto neighborhood, we'll keep having the troubles, the riots, the problems with drugs and violence. I tutor the kids, and I try to tell them there's a better life for them to lead if they'll only study and do well in school. But they only half-believe me when they're young, and when they become teenagers, they're cynical—boy, are they cynical. I guess I'd be if I was living where they are. It's hard for someone like me to argue against that cynicism, so I try to undermine it. I try to be as thoughtful and helpful as I can. I try to keep teaching, and I try to show these kids that there's another world out there, and it's not a totally bad one or a totally callous one. I take them to Cambridge, and I show them that world, and I hope it rubs off on them."

His words spoke of an earnest dedication to children, even those whose prospects seemed poor. This dedication was enabled not by a fatuous refusal to look at a grim social reality, or by a romanticism that proposed salvation through tutoring and friendship. That young man had taken a close, hard look at the obstacles and had told himself (as his work showed) that one person could give direction to another in a classroom, on a playground.

On the other hand, doubts and misgivings asserted themselves again and again. "Sometimes I think I'm just kidding myself. I think I should forget tutoring and mentoring, and field trips and summer camps, and just go to work as a political organizer, something like that—try to change the whole system. If I was a lawyer—I say that a lot out loud to myself: 'If you were a lawyer . . .' But I never really finish the sentence, because I've seen the law students come here and take on cases, and what they do seems exciting for a while: fighting against lead poisoning, or dangerous stairways, or rats all over the place, or not enough heat in the winter. But you know, it's like a drop in the bucket: this is a neighborhood of thousands of people, and they're locked in—they just don't seem to be able to break out, and the world I belong to, the white world of affluence and power, that world doesn't really want these folks. Maybe it has no use for them, no jobs for them, though there's prejudice, too, plenty of it. "My dad says, If a black boy really works hard he can make it, he can go to a good school. He's a trustee of one [a fine New England private school], and he says the school goes begging for black kids, but they're hard to come by. I don't think Dad realizes what those kids have been through by the time they're thirteen or fourteen and old enough to go to high school. A lot of them, they've just surrendered. I've taught them; they're smart, plenty of them are, but they're not 'into' school: it's not their idea of something that will lead to anything. That's what they tell me, and then I talk myself blue in the face, but in the middle I can see they're tuning out on me. That's when I tune out on myself and think of politics or the law—but I'll never go into either."

Nevertheless, he persisted. Twice a week he went to a ghetto school, in spite of an extremely busy academic schedule, to teach math to some fifth-graders; sometimes he would bring several of them back to his college dorm for a meal. The commitment was exhilarating as well as exhausting; he took pride in a child's thank you, a child's declaration that she was doing better in school, a child's wide-eyed awe at the sight of a well-known university, followed by questions about how one gets there and where one goes as a graduate.

Soon we will take a sustained look at the emotional ups and downs of those rendering service, but here I want to describe the efforts of one young woman in college who hadn't considered what community service might be until her boyfriend, a seemingly single-minded premed student, mentioned that he was going to be a Big Brother and do some tutoring.

She said, "We were having coffee at the beginning of school, and he told me he was going to be doing community service. I thought it had something to do with politics, maybe, or some charity, like the Community Fund. I remember looking at him in a different way. I'd never seen that side of him.

"Anyway, the more he told me about community service, the more I wanted to do it. So I volunteered—and here I am. I go to the school one afternoon a week. I sit with kids who are having trouble with their schoolwork. I teach reading and spelling. I try to connect with them—that's the first thing you have to do. If you don't, then you might as well go back home and call it quits. I tell

5

them what's happened to me during the week, and I bring good-
ies, and I've promised the kids that one of these days I'll teach
them how to make these oatmeal raisin cookies I make. I bring in
some books I used to read when I was their age—well, younger. I
can remember Mom or Dad reading the stories to me. It's so sad,
though—these kids have never owned a book, never seen a book
in their house, never had anyone read to them. They ask me why
my parents read to me. I tell them [it was] because they liked to—
and they believed reading is important, and it will make a big difference in your life. They aren't convinced, some of them. Others
seem convinced, but I'm not convinced that they're really convinced. A few—they break my heart—they're really eager, and
they're aching, that's the word, *aching* to get out of the ghetto and
live someplace else. This girl said to me she wanted to find 'someplace that's safe, where you can wake up and think you're really
going to go to bed that night in your house, and not in the hospital or in a funeral parlor!'

10   "I really work at the spelling. The kids will ask why—what's
such a big deal about spelling the word 'commit' with two *m's* and
one *t*? Why not one *m* and two *t's*? Why not two *m's* and two *t's*?
Stop being so uptight, they say to me. I sure don't want to be
someone who corrects someone else's spelling, a kid said. How
did I answer him? I wasn't sure what to say! I tried the 'rules'
strategy: we have to go by the rules, so everyone speaks the same
way and reads the same words and spells them the same way.

"The kids really pushed me. They said, So long as you can understand what someone writes—understand the words, then
that's all that counts! I gave them a speech about order and pre-
dictability, but I remembered my uncle saying that George
Bernard Shaw wanted to change the spelling of a lot of words, because spelling is so arbitrary and irrational, and I remembered
that Flannery O'Connor hated spelling and deliberately didn't
spell a lot of words right. I wouldn't want *her* there when I was
teaching the word 'commit' or 'commitment'! She'd probably
have spoken up, said, 'Hey, I don't have to take this, the way
you're spelling that word; I can spell it any which way I want!'"

Yet the young teacher knew that her students needed to learn
how to read and write and count and spell; they needed the same
educational competence she herself had long ago acquired. She
kept working against her students' indifference and surly distrust—and her own sophisticated qualms, her temptation to join
those boys and girls, to stoop rebelliously to their cynicism. She

kept reminding them and herself that jobs would eventually be at stake, and a distinctly improved standard of living.

"That's what community service is for me, if you want to know: the nitty-gritty of it is getting right in there with the kids, and not only teaching them how to spell 'commit,' and what it means, and 'commitment,' and how to use the word, but getting down in the pit with the kids, and trying to show them you're not some snotty white creep who's loaded with money and wants to make them feel dumb, and then get them to improve, so *she* can feel even smarter than she did before, and be even snottier!

"I'm being vague, I know. What I mean is, you've got to stand up for what you believe in. You've got to tell those kids, Look, this is the English language, and this is how you spell 'commit,' and if you want to be part of our society, our country, then when you see a red light, you stop your car, and when you see someone who is smiling and saying hello, you say hello back, and when you pick up a book, you read it in such a way that you stop if there's a period, and when you write, you begin a sentence with a capital letter, and you spell the word 'sentence' and not 'sentance,' the way my kids there told me they'd like to spell it, and 'commit,' not 'committ.'

"I think they get the message. They may not agree with me, but they realize that I'm putting myself on the line, and trying to reach them and give them some connection to the world of literacy. I really scored when I told the kids that if they knew how to spell 'commit' right, they'd do well in a job if they had to type for someone—and if the person writing misspelled the word, they could say, Hey, that's not spelled right! They got a big kick out of that—the boss-man falling flat on his face. They're used to hearing their parents talk about the know-it-all whites, and how you can't cross them, no matter what. I think they really took to the idea of learning how to spell so you can trip up some honky!"

She was doing her best to enjoy her community service work while at the same time taking it very seriously. That work eventually led to the end of her friendship with her premed classmate. Once, talking about the teaching they did in ghetto schools, he mentioned that this would help him get into medical school. She was appalled—and he was enraged by her dismay and disapproval, her naiveté. Their falling-out affected her work.

"I had more time for the kids. I stopped and asked myself: what do you want to do—jump fast into another relationship or stop for a while and try to figure out what kind of a relationship you want, and meanwhile spend a lot of time with these kids?

That way you're becoming *yourself*, not just defining yourself as a college student, or a field hockey player, or someone's girlfriend.

"It was then [after the breakup] that I figured out a way to teach reading better, and spelling. I took a course, and I put more energy and imagination into the class, and there was a big change in the kids: they could see that I was there with them, heart and soul, and they quieted down. When they started making noise, I spoke right up; my voice got tense, and I leveled with them and told them I wasn't there so we could waste time—I had too much respect for them. I really don't think it was *what* I said; I think it was my attitude—my *commitment* (with one *t!*). I *told them* I thought of them a lot *when I read something or saw* something on television or heard something over there, back in college, and so they began to pay more and more attention. And then I started making home visits, and did *that* make a big, big difference!"

At first, it made much more difference to her than to the children she was teaching. Her visits to homes were a measure of a new resolution, a step into territory she had only imagined or heard described by the children themselves or by sociologists. Now she was seeing their world firsthand, and now that world lived in her, even when she left it.

20 "I'd never seen where these kids live, how they live. I'd driven by, but it's another thing to go and walk up those stairs and be in the apartments. I don't want to be overly dramatic; it's not that I had any trouble, or that what I saw was so surprising or shocking. It's just that I finally began to see, right before my eyes, what separated those kids from me. At first, when I started teaching, I thought that if I could just go back a little to my own childhood and draw on it, then I'd make the connections I needed to make, and things would go well. But once I'd started going to the homes, it sunk in that these kids had to cross lots of bridges to get to me and my childhood, never mind me now. You can read a lot in books about 'the culturally deprived child,' but when you're sitting on a couch in a ghetto apartment building, looking and listening and wondering and worrying, then it's another story."

By her senior year she was a leader in her college community service program. She helped other volunteers settle in, helped them as they stumbled and sometimes thought of quitting. She was not interested in the political struggles of the ghetto where she worked, nor did she ever become an "activist," as some of her friends did.

"I'm a teacher here, and it's enough for me to do the best job I can. I have a friend who now wants to go to law school and fight with the school people and fight with the welfare department and fight with the store people and the real estate people. I guess I'm not a fighter. I wish I were sometimes. I'd like to go into court and sue somebody—anybody—for the sake of those kids I teach. But there's room for everybody, I guess. That's what one of the mothers told me when I said I wish I could go and change the world. She said, 'That's all right, you *are* changing the world!' Hearing her say that was like getting all A's on a report card."

I began to realize that she was telling me of more than a shift in activity. To be sure, she had learned how to become more effective, more knowledgeable about the children she intended to inform and even inspire. Yet she herself was being informed and inspired. It was an awakening of sorts, a change of moral direction.

The phrase "community service" these days commonly refers to the work done by young volunteers: high school and college students working in schools, hospitals, soup kitchens, nursing homes, or prisons. They help at camps and on playgrounds, visit homes and neighborhoods with books and instruction manuals, with basketballs and footballs and baseballs. Older people render community service in those same places and in other ways, too. When I talked with men and women at a General Motors factory in Framingham, Massachusetts, I got to know blue-collar and white-collar workers who proudly mentioned their community service. They described work with Boy Scouts, Girl Scouts, Little Leaguers; they talked about their visits to hospitals and nursing homes; they mentioned cleanup drives, weekend efforts to make streets, parks, and playgrounds clean and attractive.

A thirty-year-old assembly-line worker spoke with great feeling of his weekly visit to a nursing home two miles from his home. "I got into it by a fluke; a buddy of mine had to put his dad away in one of them, and he got all upset. He didn't have much money, and the place wasn't good. The only good thing about it, some people came and read to the old folks, and brought them cookies and cake, and just sat with them and watched TV with them and talked with them. They'd play checkers or cards, nothing fancy, and show them pictures of their family—shoot the breeze. Then my buddy's dad just suddenly died one day, and that was it. But for my friend it was hard to get that nursing home out of his mind. He talked with the priest; he told him he'd wake up in the middle of the night, and he'd be thinking of his dad—that's normal, that's grieving for you—but he'd be thinking of that nursing home, all those folks. It was sad. So the

25

priest said, Maybe the thing to do is go and visit one of those homes, and see if you can be of help, and that way you'll feel you're doing something good, something worthwhile—and it could be a kind of memorial to the old man. And my friend, he really liked that idea.

"So that was how it got started. He talked to me, and I said yes, and he and I went to this nursing home, and we told them we aren't anyone special, but we like to have fun, and we could try to give the folks in there a good time. We could bring them some cookies, and we can sing—I can sing a lot of songs, and my friend plays the piano (no big deal, but the tune gets across!) and we could always read from the papers, if someone was blind or had the shakes and couldn't hold the paper steady. They were glad we came—they said visitors really help the people, and the staff, too. So we started, and we weren't sure at first what we were going to do, and we were nervous, to start, but we just decided we'd be ourselves and try to be as friendly as we knew how, and my wife made these cookies, and I just went and offered them around, and they all told us to come back, and we did, and now we're regulars and we love it—it's part of our lives. You give something, and believe me, you get something back."

He was too modest to mention that he had urged others to work with the elderly or with young people in trouble with the law, with drugs and drinking. In fact, he always pointed to the initiatives, activities, and good ideas of friends of his, working men who made it their business to give time and energy to others. When a local paper wanted to highlight his volunteer efforts, he insisted that he be mentioned only as part of a group. And he urged that their work *not* be called community service.

"It's more a person-to-person thing, and it's us trying to be friendly to people who aren't having the best of times. I know, it does help everyone—the community—when you go and visit the old folks, but I don't think of it as service. To me, service means, like, the military, or you're doing something you've *got* to do, or you've been *told* to do it, or you've been *sentenced* to it, because you got in trouble with the law. To me, what we do is—well, it's us trying to offer something from our hearts, only we all got together, and we're organized about it."

He could have been speaking for many of the college students and older people who have the impulse to engage themselves in a broken world and find a place for their moral energy.

Questions for Discussion

1. What troubles Coles's students who go to tutor in the ghetto near Cambridge? What kind of help do they find most rewarding for those they help and for themselves?
2. What must a young teacher in the ghetto do in order to reach his or her student? What does community service mean to the young teacher about whom Coles is writing?
3. What does the young student teacher learn about "the culturally deprived child" when she visits her student's family in the ghetto? Why does she decide to remain a teacher rather than to become a political organizer? Why does Coles describe her decision as "an awakening of sorts, a change of moral direction"?
4. What definition of community service emerges from the conversation between Coles and the thirty-year-old assembly line worker?

Ideas for Writing

1. Drawing on your own experiences doing volunteer work or community service, write an essay in which you compare and/or contrast what Coles's students and the assembly line worker learned with what you learned.

2. Community service courses and projects have become requirements at many elementary, secondary schools, and colleges. Write an essay in which you argue whether or not the schools should require such courses and projects, and, if so, at what level they should begin and what their primary focus should be.

Extending the Theme

1. Hirsch and Meier present strikingly different ideas on how to develop school systems and curriculum to educate youth to become effective citizens in a democracy. Contrast the problems that each author perceives to be at the root of the current crisis in American education. Which author do you think has the better solution and why? Support your thesis, claims, and evidence through reference to the writer's text, your own experiences, and research that you have done on the solution.

2. Darling-Hammond and Meier focus on the effects of the education that minorities receive in American communities. Contrast the views of these writers and the solutions that each proposes. Which author presents the most relevant analysis of the situation and offers the most effective solutions? To support your discussion, use evidence from the essay you have chosen, your own experiences, and results of from your further research on the issue.

3. Coles argues for the importance of the role of interaction between the school and the larger community. Write an essay in which you contrast Coles's ideas on the need to reach out into the community to educate youth and to help solve problems within the educational curriculum to the views of Meier and hooks. Refer to the relevant authors' texts in presenting your response to the importance of interactions between the schools and the larger community. When relevant, refer to your own experiences to support your argument.

4. Observe what goes on in the classrooms of two schools at the same level (college, high school, middle school, or elementary) in different social, economic, or ethnic areas of your community. Write an essay in which you develop a comparative analysis, argument, and conclusions about which of these schools is best serving the needs of the students and which is most involved in encouraging active parent and community involvement with the school.

Citizenship and Civil Liberties

"We hold these Truths to be self-evident, that all Men are created equal, that they are endowed by their Creator with certain unalienable Rights, that among these are Life, Liberty, and the Pursuit of Happiness."

DECLARATION OF INDEPENDENCE

"Congress shall make no law respecting an establishment of religion, or prohibiting the free exercise thereof; or abridging the freedom of speech, or of the press, or the right of the people peaceably to assemble, and to petition the Government for a redress of grievances."

FIRST AMENDMENT TO THE CONSTITUTION

"The right of the people to be secure in their persons, houses, papers, and effects, against unreasonable searches and seizures, shall not be violated, and no Warrants shall issue, but upon probable cause, supported by Oath or affirmation, and particularly describing the place to be searched, and the persons or things to be seized."

FOURTH AMENDMENT TO THE CONSTITUTION

"Censorship reflects a society's lack of confidence in itself."

SUPREME COURT JUSTICE POTTER STEWART (1915–1985)

The first amendments to the Constitution were added to prevent the kinds of tyranny and exploitation that Americans had been subject to at the hands of Great Britain in the period before the Revolutionary War. As in the case of Amendments I and IV, the emphasis in almost all of the original and subsequent Constitutional amendments has been placed on broadening the protection of the individual rights of citizens and allowing citizens previously excluded from franchise (such as former slaves and women) to have more say in the democracy.

Until recently, the tendency in American jurisprudence has been to extend citizen rights even further than those enumerated in the Amendments to the Constitution. As Alan Dershowitz points out in his essay, "Rights as a Check on Democracy," court decisions concerning civil rights continue to redefine our communities. For example, Roe versus Wade, a controversial court decision, is based legally on a view of privacy rights that the framers of the Constitution did not specify. Even in times of political reaction and conservative courts, the civil rights guaranteed in the Amendments to the Constitution have helped to put a brake on "the process of tyranny."

Today, however, new forces have emerged in our communities that want to place limits on many of the rights that we have long taken for granted. These challenges to civil rights come from both conservative as well as liberal citizen groups and legislators. For example, Charles Lawrence III in his essay "On Racist Speech" argues for a limit to the right to free speech in cases of racist speech that intrude into the personal privacy of individuals, such as students in a college dorm. Going further than Lawrence, those who argue for removing "offensive books" from libraries usually claim that they are doing so in order to protect children and the community at large from pornography and obscenity that can infiltrate their lives. Sallie Tisdale in "The Myth of Social Consensus" argues that many of the social consensus laws today that have been passed by libraries and school boards go too far and represent a "tyranny of the majority."

Another area where we see conflicts over rights is in issues related to privacy. While there is no clear language in the Constitution about issues of privacy, the Fourth Amendment does guarantee people "to be secure in their persons, houses, papers, and effects against unreasonable searches and seizures." However, Amitai Etzioni in his essay, "Less Privacy is Good for Us (and You)," argues that the assumed right to privacy cherished by most Americans creates areas of conflict with the public's need to be secure from public diseases and epidemics, as in the case of

HIV testing, as well as the need to protect citizens from identity theft and fraud perpetrated by required IDs and biometric identification technology.

Richard Posner's recent essay "Security versus Civil Liberties" argues that civil libertarians are in conflict with the need for protection of citizens since 9/11 because of the continuing threat of terrorist attacks. Because we no longer feel safe as a nation, the government is willing to give less weight to liberty and privacy rights in cases where national security could be at risk. However, the American Civil Liberties Union continues to take a very strong stance for civil liberties for all citizens, even after 9/11. In her speech about the Patriot Act made before Congressman John Conyers' Forum on national security and the Constitution, ACLU President Nadine Strossen argues that the words of Dr. Martin Luther King, Jr., "Injustice anywhere is a threat to justice everywhere," could be applied as a critique of many provisions of the Patriot Act, including its acceptance of long-term detention without official charges, of relaxed guide lines related to spying on unaccused citizens, and of the suspension of normal attorney-client privacy rights.

As our country enters a new period of turmoil, many people disagree about whether we need to extend rights and protections to individual citizens and minority groups or curtail rights in the name of community consensus and national security. As Justice Potter Stewart says in the quotation at the beginning of this chapter, "Censorship reflects a society's lack of confidence in itself." Perhaps we need to look more deeply at our declining sense of self-confidence and security as a nation to consider whether our fears are justified.

Rights as a Check on Democracy
ALAN DERSHOWITZ

Alan Dershowitz graduated from Brooklyn College and Yale Law School. A civil-liberties lawyer, his outspoken opinions have put him at odds with liberals and conservatives alike. He has taught for many years at Harvard and has lectured around the country and abroad. He has written many articles on civil liberties issues as well as many books, including *The Abuse Excuse* (1997) and *Supreme Injustice: How the High Court Hijacked Election 2000*

(2001). In the following essay, taken from *Shouting Fire: Civil Liberties in a Turbulent Age* (2002), Dershowitz describes how civil rights and liberties evolve through experience and history within a democratic society.

---- ◆ ----

The effect of entrenching rights in a democracy is to eliminate certain issues from majoritarian control. Put another way, it is to take certain entrenched rights and place them outside the sphere of pure democracy. But if one believes, as I do, that rights are not divine, natural, or eternal, and that they are a product of the experiences and history of a people, then there is some burden to justify the antidemocratic character of rights. I do not see rights, properly limited, as antithetical to democracy properly defined. I see rights as the most important check and balance within a democracy.

Rights should not prevent all change, especially if rights themselves are subject to constant reevaluation based on the changing experiences of the people. Rights do slow down certain kinds of change, under certain circumstances. Spiro Agnew, in criticizing liberals who insisted on exercising their rights, once characterized individual rights as a "head-wind blowing in the face of the ship of state." It is an apt metaphor, though Agnew did not understand it in its positive sense. It is the function of rights in a democracy to put pressure on government to change course, to move cautiously, to protect important and enduring values from precipitous abrogation. Learned Hand once observed that when liberty dies in the hearts of men and women, "no court can save it; . . . no court can even do much to help it." He was right about the first part of his observation: courts alone cannot save liberty. But he was wrong about the second part: courts can, by properly enforcing rights, slow down the process of tyranny—at least sometimes, as they did during the McCarthy period. Rights work, in part, by taking certain powers away from temporary majorities and vesting the ability to constrain these powers in those who lack traditional political influence or who are otherwise subject to discrimination or marginalization. One genre of rights actually opens up the channels of democracy: free speech, equality in voting, and protection against the establishment of religion. Other genres of rights, while not opening up the channels of democracy as directly as these core rights do, allow democracy to operate more fairly. If Winston Churchill was right when he said that a democracy should be judged by the manner in which it treats its most despised, then the rights of accused criminals, aliens, the mentally ill and other marginalized people, are an important part of the democratic process.

In a democratic system, the unelected judiciary must have only limited power to overrule current majority preferences on the basis of entrenched rights. When the Constitution is clear about a particular right trumping a preference—as with the right against compelled self-incrimination overriding our preference for swift conviction of the guilty—then positivism prevails, with little or no need to debate about the source or legitimacy of the right. The plain language of the Constitution governs. The only way to change a clearly expressed constitutional right is by the cumbersome and rarely used process of formal amendment. When the claimed right is not explicitly in the Constitution—as with the rights of parents to forbid grandparents from visiting a child—then process should prevail, accompanied by inevitable conflict over the source and legitimacy of the claimed right and counterright. In the latter instances—when claimed rights are not explicit in the Constitution—which are far more common than the former, those who claim that a right should trump a majoritarian preference have the burden of establishing why their preference deserves to be treated as a right.

The burden rests on them, because in the absence of a compelling claim of right, democracy demands that majoritarian preferences prevail over minority preferences. In seeking to satisfy this burden, the rights claimant can properly point to history and experience in an effort to persuade decision makers that his claim should be treated as a right. As history and experience change, the persuasiveness of a particular claim for status as a right may also change. But history and experience change more gradually than shifting majoritarian preferences. In this respect, rights that are not clearly entrenched are always subject to reevaluation over time. The judiciary, under this approach, is generally limited to slowing down change rather than preventing it. The New Deal is a perfect example of this process at work. The Supreme Court repeatedly ruled that progressive social legislation made necessary by the Depression violated the Constitution's broad requirement of due process. But changing history and experience eventually made it abundantly clear that the high court's conception of property rights (based on substantive due process) was anachronistic and unsuited to the changing realities of American life. It required a change of personnel to finalize the

Supreme Court's institutional about-face. Changing personnel—
the appointing process—is also part of the mechanism for
change, just as the doctrine of stare decisis (deference to precedent) is part of the mechanism for slowing down change and
making it more gradual.

5   Many other examples could be cited to demonstrate the wisdom of Holmes's observation that the life of the law has been experience rather than logic—or God, or nature, or any other universal and immutable truth or external source.

The relatively new concept of environmental rights is obviously a response to the relatively new assaults on the environment growing out of industrialism. Though environmentalist
concerns trace their origins to the biblical prohibition against destroying the fruit-bearing trees of a conquered people, the more
recent experiences of industrialized nations have turned this concern into a nascent "right." I recall visiting a preindustrial country with high unemployment and low productivity and being told,
"What this country needs is a little more pollution!" The history
and experiences of *that* nation did not yet reflect the need for environmental rights.

Lesser-developed nations, on the other hand, may have a
heightened experiential need for positive economic rights. The
Nobel Prize–winning economist Amartya Sen has made a compelling case for the inexorability of the relationship between political and economic rights. He points to the startling fact that no
functioning democracy with political rights has ever experienced
a famine, and argues that the most basic rights should include a
mix of traditional negative political rights (i.e., the government
may not restrict freedom of speech, religion, and so on) and positive economic rights (i.e., economic facilities, social opportunities, and protective security).

In the United States, we generally limit our concept of rights
to those negative restrictions on governmental power that have
their sources in the Constitution. "Congress shall make no law
abridging . . . ," is the paradigm. But there are movements from
all sides of the political spectrum for a more expansive, positive
view of rights. Many on the right, and even the center, favor a
constitutional amendment establishing victims' rights. Some on
the left advocate a right to affirmative action based on race or
gender. Some see health care, education, and safety as rights.
Others advocate welfare, or at least a minimum subsistence, as a
right.

The difficult question is whether to "constitutionalize" so many areas of what have traditionally been deemed matters of politics and policy. To constitutionalize a preference into a right is to remove it from majoritarian determination and to turn it over to unelected judges (at least in the federal system) for judicial review.

The power of judicial review has itself derived its legitimacy from the experiences of our people over time. It has become an important component of liberty, though—like other components—it is subject to abuse and misuse. 10

The Supreme Court decision in the 2000 presidential election case is a prime example of the abuse and misuse of judicial review. Invoking the "equal protection" clause of the Constitution, five Republican justices—none of whom had been sympathetic to an expansive view of that clause in previous cases—stopped the hand recount that could have changed the result of the election. In doing so, they have indirectly influenced who will be nominated to serve as their successors on the high court, thereby eliminating an important component of our system of checks and balances. This decision, which has been widely criticized by the experts, neither opened the channels of democracy nor protected the rights of the disenfranchised.

Questions for Discussion

1. According to Dershowitz, in what sense are rights "the most important check and balance" within a democracy? How do rights slow down certain kinds of change? How do they take power away from the majority?

2. What distinction does Dershowitz draw between "clearly expressed constitutional rights" and "claimed rights"? What sort of evidence is needed for claimed rights to be successfully argued and accepted by the majority?

3. What does Dershowitz see as the proper role of the judiciary in relation to claimed rights and social change? Why does Dershowitz agree with Holmes that "the life of the law is experience rather than logic"? What examples of "experiential need" for changes in rights does he provide? Do you find his examples convincing?

4. What does Dershowitz see as the danger involved in "constitutionalize[ing] a preference into a right"? How does he use the Presidential election of 2000 as an example of the abuse

of judicial review? Does this example seem relevant to his overall discussion?

Ideas for Writing

1. Do some research into recent efforts to create Constitutional amendments guaranteeing various rights; then write an essay in which you discuss why these efforts have failed and whether you agree with Dershowitz that it is not a good idea to constitutionalize by amendment many of the ideas that people consider to be part of their "rights" at a particular moment in history.

2. Write an essay in which you argue for something you believe should be your "right" to do or believe, even though the majority in your community, state, or nation objects to it and has passed laws against it. What evidence and experiences would you provide to persuade those who don't agree that this act or idea should be a right?

On Racist Speech
Charles R. Lawrence III

Charles R. Lawrence III (b. 1943) received his B.A. from Haverford College and his J.D. from Yale University. Since 1992, he has been a Professor of Law at the Georgetown University Law Center. His books include *Words That Wound: Critical Race Theory, Assaultive Speech, and the First Amendment* (with Mari J. Matsuda; 1993) and *We Won't Go Back: Making the Case for Affirmative Action* (with Mari J. Matsuda; 1997). He has also served on the District of Columbia Board of Education. Lawrence specializes in issues such as hate-speech protections, anti-discrimination law, and equal protection. In the following article, he contrasts ordinary free speech protections with the limits of speech in cases of racist speech.

――――――― ✦ ―――――――

I have spent the better part of my life as a dissenter. As a high school student, I was threatened with suspension for my refusal to participate in a civil defense drill, and I have been a conspicuous consumer of my First Amendment liberties ever since. There are very strong reasons for protecting even racist speech. Perhaps the most important of these is that such protection reinforces our society's commitment to tolerance as a value, and that by protecting bad speech from government regulation, we will be forced to combat it as a community.

But I also have a deeply felt apprehension about the resurgence of racial violence and the corresponding rise in the incidence of verbal and symbolic assault and harassment to which blacks and other traditionally subjugated and excluded groups are subjected. I am troubled by the way the debate has been framed in response to the recent surge of racist incidents on college and university campuses and in response to some universities' attempts to regulate harassing speech. The problem has been framed as one in which the liberty of free speech is in conflict with the elimination of racism. I believe this has placed the bigot on the moral high ground and fanned the rising flames of racism.

Above all, I am troubled that we have not listened to the real victims, that we have shown so little understanding of their injury, and that we have abandoned those whose race, gender, or sexual preference continues to make them second-class citizens. It seems to me a very sad irony that the first instinct of civil libertarians has been to challenge even the smallest, most narrowly framed efforts by universities to provide black and other minority students with the protection the Constitution guarantees them.

The landmark case of *Brown v. Board of Education* is not a case that we normally think of as a case about speech. But *Brown* can be broadly read as articulating the principle of equal citizenship. *Brown* held that segregated schools were inherently unequal because of the *message* that segregation conveyed—that black children were an untouchable caste, unfit to go to school with white children. If we understand the necessity of eliminating the system of signs and symbols that signal the inferiority of blacks, then we should hesitate before proclaiming that all racist speech that stops short of physical violence must be defended.

University officials who have formulated policies to respond to incidents of racial harassment have been characterized in the press as "thought police," but such policies generally do nothing more than impose sanctions against intentional face-to-face insults. When racist speech takes the form of face-to-face insults, catcalls, or other assaultive speech aimed at an individual or small group of persons, it falls directly within the "fighting words" exception to First Amendment protection. The Supreme Court has held that words which "by their very utterance inflict injury or tend to incite an immediate breach of the peace" are not protected by the First Amendment.

If the purpose of the First Amendment is to foster the greatest amount of speech, racial insults disserve that purpose. Assaultive racist speech functions as as a preemptive strike. The invective is experienced as a blow, not as a proffered idea, and once the blow is struck, it is unlikely that a dialogue will follow. Racial insults are particularly undeserving of First Amendment protection because the perpetrator's intention is not to discover truth or initiate dialogue but to injure the victim. In most situations, members of minority groups realize that they are likely to lose if they respond to epithets by fighting and are forced to remain silent and submissive.

Courts have held that offensive speech may not be regulated in public forums such as streets where the listener may avoid the speech by moving on, but the regulation of otherwise protected speech has been permitted when the speech invades the privacy of the unwilling listener's home or when the unwilling listener cannot avoid the speech. Racist posters, fliers, and graffiti in dormitories, bathrooms, and other common living spaces would seem to clearly fall within the reasoning of these cases. Minority students should not be required to remain in their rooms in order to avoid racial assault. Minimally, they should find a safe haven in their dorms and in all other common rooms that are a part of their daily routine.

I would also argue that the university's responsibility for ensuring that these students receive an equal educational opportunity provides a compelling justification for regulations that ensure them safe passage in all common areas. A minority student should not have to risk becoming the target of racially assaulting speech every time he or she chooses to walk across campus. Regulating vilifying speech that cannot be anticipated or avoided would not preclude announced speeches and rallies—situations that would give minority-group members and their allies the chance to organize counterdemonstrations or avoid the speech altogether.

The most commonly advanced argument against the regulation of racist speech proceeds something like this: We recognize that minority groups suffer pain and injury as the result of racist speech, but we must allow this hate mongering for the benefit of society as a whole. Freedom of speech is the lifeblood of our democratic system. It is especially important for minorities because often it is their only vehicle for rallying support for the redress of their grievances. It will be impossible to formulate a prohibition so precise that it will prevent the racist speech you want to suppress without catching in the same net all kinds of speech that it would be unconscionable for a democratic society to suppress.

Whenever we make such arguments, we are striking a balance on the one hand between our concern for the continued free flow of ideas and the democratic process dependent on that flow, and, on the other, our desire to further the cause of equality. There can be no meaningful discussion of how we should reconcile our commitment to equality and our commitment to free speech until it is acknowledged that there is real harm inflicted by racist speech and that this harm is far from trivial. 10

To engage in a debate about the First Amendment and racist speech without a full understanding of the nature and extent of that harm is to risk making the First Amendment an instrument of domination rather than a vehicle of liberation. We have not known the experience of victimization by racist, misogynist, and homophobic speech, nor do we equally share the burden of the societal harm it inflicts. We are often quick to say that we have heard the cry of the victims when we have not.

The *Brown* case is again instructive because it speaks directly to the psychic injury inflicted by racist speech by noting that the symbolic message of segregation affected "the hearts and minds" of Negro children "in a way unlikely ever to be undone." Racial epithets and harassment often cause deep emotional scarring and feelings of anxiety and fear that pervade every aspect of a victim's life.

Brown also recognized that black children did not have an equal opportunity to learn and participate in the school community if they bore the additional burden of being subjected to the humiliation and psychic assault contained in the message of segregation. University students bear an analogous burden when they are forced to live and work in an environment where at any moment they may be subjected to denigrating verbal harassment and assault. The same injury was addressed by the Supreme Court when it held that sexual harassment that creates a hostile or abusive work environment violates the ban on sex discrimination in employment of Title VII of the Civil Rights Act of 1964.

Carefully drafted university regulations would bar the use of words as assault weapons and leave unregulated even the most heinous of ideas when those ideas are presented at times and places and in manners that provide an opportunity for reasoned rebuttal or escape from immediate injury. The history of the development of the right to free speech has been one of carefully evaluating the importance of free expression and its effects on other important societal interests. We have drawn the line between protected and unprotected speech before without dire results. (Courts have, for example, exempted from the protection of the First Amendment obscene speech and speech that disseminates official secrets, that defames or libels another person, or that is used to form a conspiracy or monopoly.)

15   Blacks and other people of color are skeptical about the argument that even the most injurious speech must remain unregulated because, in an unregulated marketplace of ideas, the best ones will rise to the top and gain acceptance. Our experience tells us quite the opposite. We have seen too many good liberal politicians shy away from the issues that might brand them as being too closely allied with us.

Whenever we decide that racist speech must be tolerated because of the importance of maintaining societal tolerance for all unpopular speech, we are asking blacks and other subordinated groups to bear the burden for the good of all. We must be careful that the ease with which we strike the balance against the regulation of racist speech is in no way influenced by the fact that the cost will be borne by others. We must be certain that those who will pay that price are fairly represented in our deliberations and that they are heard.

At the core of the argument that we should resist all government regulation of speech is the ideal that the best cure for bad speech is good, that ideas that affirm equality and the worth of all individuals will ultimately prevail. This is an empty ideal unless those of us who would fight racism are vigilant and unequivocal in that fight. We must look for ways to offer assistance and support to students whose speech and political participation are chilled in a climate of racial harassment.

Civil rights lawyers might consider suing on behalf of blacks whose right to an equal education is denied by a university's failure to ensure a nondiscriminatory educational climate or conditions of employment. We must embark upon the development of a First Amendment jurisprudence grounded in the reality of our history and our contemporary experience. We must think hard about how best to launch legal attacks against the most indefensible forms of hate speech. Good lawyers can create exceptions and narrow interpretations that limit the harm of hate speech without opening the floodgates of censorship.

Everyone concerned with these issues must find ways to engage actively in actions that resist and counter the racist ideas that we would have the First Amendment protect. If we fail in this, the victims of hate speech must rightly assume that we are on the oppressors' side.

Questions for Discussion

1. Why does Lawrence believe that bigots have been placed "on the moral high ground" in the recent debate over racist speech and incidents on campuses and the attempts at regulation by universities? Why does he believe it would be helpful to "listen to the real victims"?

2. How does the *Brown v. Board of Education* case pertain to speech on campus, according to Lawrence? What does the Supreme Court say about exceptions to the First Amendment in the case of hate speech? Why does Lawrence believe that Supreme Court decisions about sexual harassment in the workplace also support limiting of hate speech in campus settings?

3. How does Lawrence attempt to refute the argument that it is impossible to frame an exception to the First Amendment for hate speech so narrow that it avoids "catching in the net all kinds of speech that it would be unconscionable for a democratic society to suppress"? Is his argument convincing? Explain your point of view.

4. How does Lawrence refute the argument for absolute free speech that holds that "in an unregulated marketplace of ideas, the best will rise to the top," and "the best cure for bad speech is good [speech]"? Is his refutation successful here?

Ideas for Writing

1. Write an essay in response to Lawrence's recommendation of lawsuits against hate speech that would help to "limit the harm of hate speech without opening the floodgates of censorship." Would lawsuits be any more effective than university regulations at curbing hate speech? Is it possible to prohibit certain kinds of speech without opening the door to more dangerous possibilities of censorship?

2. Write an argument in favor of a solution for the problem of hate speech that is different from Lawrence's legalistic approach. You might consider his comments on the importance of "hearing from the victims."

The Myth of Social Consensus
SALLIE TISDALE

Sallie Tisdale is an author who drew on her experiences of working as a registered nurse in her first book, *Harvest Moon* (1987), a portrait of a nursing home. She has taught at Northwestern, Antioch, New York University, and the University of California, and has published in many national magazines and newspapers. Tisdale's recent books include *Talk Dirty to Me: An Intimate Philosophy of Sex* (1994) and *The Best Thing I Ever Tasted: The Secret of Food* (2001). In the selection below, a speech she delivered at a Reed College Alumni program, Tisdale discusses her ideas on censorship and free speech.

———————— ✦ ————————

I was the kind of child who loved libraries; they seemed radical places, dreams almost. I began going alone to the little Carnegie Library down the street from my house when I was about six years old. The library was a free place in which to roam, to be left alone, to think and imagine without constraint. My mother was a school-teacher and a great reader, and she believed in letting me have whatever I wanted to read. Her rule was that if I could figure out how to find it, I could read it. Then one day, when I was about thirteen, I found *The Joy of Sex*. When I tried to check it out, the librarian—who knew me and my mother, as everyone knew just about everyone else in that little town—called my mother at home and asked if it was all right.

Almost 25 years later, in Napa, California, a children's book by Norma Klein called *Naomi in the Middle* was challenged by a city councilor. It was inappropriate for schoolchildren, he said. The book, he explained, "could spark some thoughts and some creative adventures that they shouldn't have at this point in their lives."

I waited impatiently by that long-ago librarian's desk until my mother said I could have my book. I took it home and read it with no apparent harm. That was one more day in my lifelong affair with writing and books and libraries, with the idea of books and libraries, with the act of reading itself. Walt Whitman called reading "an exercise, a gymnast's struggle." To me it is creation, a lovemaking made of small discoveries, hidden treasures, big dreams. I've just finished a book that took me three years to write. The book is about sex—gender, desire, sexual acts, the importance of sexuality to human experience. And in the course of these three years I've been forced to examine my own writerly commitment to honesty. I've had to think long and carefully about the way a writer chooses what to say and what not to say, and how the world influences a writer's choices. I can't separate my external experience in this society, as an American of a certain age and a certain time, from my internal experience as a writer and reader. I've had to think about my role as a parent, and I've become—not coincidentally—actively involved in the politics of free expression and censorship. I am saddened almost beyond words when I think of what's being lost—what's already been destroyed—by people who are afraid of books. I want to address what happens to us as readers and as writers when we face the kind of censure so common today, and why it counts.

There are many legitimate questions to be asked about the 5 limits of free expression, the role of education, and individual responsibility. Unfortunately, very few of these questions are being asked in public discourse, and little genuine dialogue is taking place. Instead I see people of all political and social stripes engaged in a battle over books and words, a war that takes place in a kind of no-man's-land devoid of irony.

Louis Brandeis once said, "It is the function of speech to free men from the bondage of irrational fears." But those irrational fears are what drive people to silence certain kinds of speech. I consider prudery—and I don't specifically mean sexual prudishness at all—to be a great insult against life. The kind of prudishness I mean, the kind of prudishness that leads to the banning of a book, is a squeamishness about everything Other, everything different, disturbing, new. Of course, those people who spend hours and weeks trying to ban a book they fear will incite teen suicide—a book like *Romeo and Juliet*—could spend those hours and weeks volunteering as tutors or suicide hotline counselors or foster parents. But prevention of teen suicide itself is not really their point. Their point is to prevent a polyglot and free-ranging society, and teen suicide is just the convenient hook to hang that fear upon.

Books are potent things; I could never honestly calm a person's fear of a book by telling him or her that books don't matter. Just look what Martin Luther accomplished with a list tacked up on a door. Books and stories and reading are the meat of revolution and change; they can be dangerous and unpredictable. But no matter how repugnant or grotesque, or how apparently unimportant a book may be, to remove it from examination is to take a position against change, against the possibility of change. So Aristophanes' classic play, *Lysistrata*, was banned from a Florida school because it "promotes women's lib." A book called *Myths and Their Meanings* was challenged in Colorado because, one citizen believed, stories about Zeus and Apollo might undermine teachings on Western civilization. To ban any one book is to ban, in essence, the idea of books themselves—it means to close the marketplace of imagination, the free exchange of ourselves.

We sometimes delude ourselves into thinking we live in a wildly free society. Again and again in the last few years, I've been asked to respond to a person's concern about the rampant promiscuity of 1990s America. Isn't this a terribly sexual time? I am asked. But I don't think so. I think it's a terribly *lewd* time; I think we live in a world awash with shallow sexual images precisely because we *are* so prudish about sex. And in the same way, I think we are so bombarded with information itself, with a proliferation of all kinds of media, data, pictures, plots, statistics, stories, and consumer campaigns that we can be lulled into thinking this is a time of free information and Socratic conversation.

Sometimes I read book-banning anecdotes and laugh; a few do seem to illustrate an epidemic of nuttiness. But I have to remind myself that it's *real*, that it happens, that these are real books and writers and real readers being hurt.

10   There are more formal challenges against books in schools and public libraries than ever before. They have occurred in almost every state. Oregon has repeatedly been in the top five states in terms of the number of challenges; in 1992 and 1993, Oregon was second only behind California. That's not necessarily bad; I think the number of challenges reflects the heterogeneous nature of these states, and the fact that we read a lot of books around here. And people have as much right to complain about a book as they do to read one. But almost half of the attempts nationwide to remove or restrict school and library materials are successful.

What has been challenged, placed on a restricted shelf, or simply banned in recent years? *Snow White. Hansel and Gretel. Sleep-*

ing Beauty. The Clan of the Cave Bear. The Adventures of Huckle-berry Finn. Tom Sawyer. In Sandy, Oregon, *All Quiet on the Western Front.* Pearl Buck's *The Good Earth. Tarzan of the Apes. Of Mice and Men. A Wrinkle in Time. Little House on the Prairie. The Bible. Newsweek.* This is a most incomplete short list, and please bear in mind that most of these books have been challenged not once in one place, but again and again, in one town after the other.

The most common reason given in objection to a book is religion. The second most common reason is that the work is sexually offensive or immoral. The third is simply that it contains profanity. The explanations given often seem illogical and confused. The single most challenged school material in the country is a self-esteem program called Pumsy, which uses puppets to help children act out socially problematic events. Pumsy has been accused of fomenting everything from New Age humanism, group therapy, hypnosis and mental illness to hallucinations. In one case, the objector complained that Pumsy was a kind of "mind control." Another said it was a form of Hinduism.

But with a careful reading, an agenda is frequently clear. Religious objection or sexual offense often reveals itself to be at one and the same time religious and sexual propaganda; the objection is not just that something is contained in the book, but that something opposite is not. Almost every year the Multnomah County Library receives challenges to its books about the heretic religion of Roman Catholicism.

Jerry Falwell, in the same essay and almost in the same paragraph, bemoans the loss of active Christian teaching in the public schools—"We were taught," he writes, "to reverence God, the Bible, and prayer"—and then accuses secular humanists of taking over the schools in order to indoctrinate children. Stephen King, who has seen every one of his novels banned in one place or another, said it best when he said, "What censorship is at bottom is about who's on top."

Many of the books banned, challenged, or restricted are guilty only of being original. They are attacked for being too gruesome or dark, too occult, too questioning of Christianity or too respectful of other religions. Some books are banned simply because they have information *about* other religions—again here in Oregon, a book on stress management was banned from the Eagle Point high school library because it discussed yoga and meditation. These books are "unpatriotic" or "unconventional" or they "promote critical thinking." Some books are too honest about the

15

angst of the modern teenager, about depression, suicide, drug use; they are seen to be disrespectful of the status quo, the elderly, wealth, power, or authority. Others speak to ordinary life in an uncomfortably realistic way, with profanity and intense emotion.

A certain amount of censorship is about protecting children from a painful history and the painful realities of the present day. It is about trying to fix the real world to fit one's ideal, and this is one of the easiest kinds of censorship for me as a parent to practice. It is remarkably easy to rationalize not telling a child something, to not answer a question directly, and to go from there to making sure the child doesn't get hold of the information somewhere else. But where do we stop? *Night*, a memoir of living in a Nazi concentration camp, was challenged in Illinois for being too "negative." In Waukesha, Wisconsin, a novel by Tim O'Brien about Vietnam was banned, when the school board decided that the Vietnam War was too sensitive a topic for high school students to study. In Columbus, Indiana, a challenge has not yet been resolved that would restrict any text which used the word "nigger" in any context. In Auburn, Washington, the use of the word "Halloween" is no longer allowed. Trying to cover all the possible bases of discomfort, the Arts Council of Fairfax County, Virginia, refuses to allow the depiction of anything showing "nudes, weaponry, drug paraphernalia . . . violence, religious scenes, political expression or unpatriotic subjects."

Even when we are ostensibly trying to protect children, this kind of censorship acts largely to protect each other and ultimately, ourselves, from the facts of life. There are people who would have us rewrite Homer, Shakespeare, and other works of history to fix the politically incorrect errors of the past. *Huckleberry Finn, The Learning Tree, Tom Sawyer*, and *Little House on the Prairie* have all been banned because of their purportedly racist content. In California, a local NAACP chapter challenged the book *The Cay*. The book is now being reviewed statewide. One NAACP official involved said, "Any book that offends any group should be taken out of the public libraries and schools."

His remark illustrates precisely the kind of limited vision censorship requires. Surely he doesn't mean that if a biography of Martin Luther King, Jr. offended a member of the Aryan Nation, that book should be removed from circulation? But that is what he said. Physical censorship and physical repression leads to a psychic censorship, a repression of thought. Anyone who has ever written a memoir knows what it means to practice hindsight about our individual pasts. To practice hindsight about our communal history is to perform a frontal lobotomy on the culture.

To deny people, especially children, any reflection of their ordinary lives, is to dislocate them. What happens to a child's sense of intellectual curiosity and social identity when every question is met with a stark glare? Or, worse, the black marker blotting out the answer, the example, the illustration? Dian Fossey's book, *Gorillas in the Mist*, was allowed in a Pennsylvania high school class only after the passages describing gorilla mating habits were deleted. Quite recently, the California State Board of Education banned a short story by Alice Walker from an English-language competency test because it was "anti-meat eating." At the same time, they removed an excerpt from Annie Dillard's *An American Childhood*, because the scene of a snowball fight was "too violent." In Wellsville, Kansas, a student production of *Dracula* was allowed to continue only after most references to blood were removed.

Part of the problem we are facing now is the confusion between whether books are or are not effective tools at transmitting ideas. When this confusion collides with the myth of a social consensus— with the idea that we actually agree in this country on what is good and not good—all hell breaks loose. Then the *Webster's Ninth Collegiate Dictionary* is banned because it contains a definition of the word "fuck." Perhaps we would all agree on the idea that *dictionaries*, as a concept, are good. But could we ever all agree on what a dictionary should do, what it should be, what it is for? 20

The idea that books should *not* be powerful, should not change the reader, is a new idea. Thoreau said, "How many a man has dated a new era in his life from the reading of a book." Throughout history, literacy was considered a weapon. That's one reason it was withheld from the masses, from the poor, from women, and kept as an almost-exclusive tool of the wealthy and powerful men who ran society. They claimed that reading and writing distracted and bewildered these supposedly weak-minded members of society, who, anyway, had better things to do. But those in charge also knew what could happen. A few hundred years ago, anyone caught in England with written material criticizing the crown could have their hands amputated, and in some cases, their heads.

What happens today? A library aide in Kalispell, Montana, helped two students research a project on witchcraft. The project was approved, but the school library lacked enough information, so the aide loaned the students two of her own books. For this she was fired.

.

In Riverside, California, members of the Eagle Forum, founded by Phyllis Schlafly, protested a work about Rosa Parks because it "questions authority."

In Lake County, Florida, a newly elected school board began their tenure by refusing to allow a Head Start program to open. They then tried, without success, to ban federally funded breakfasts for poor students. The head of the school board, who identifies herself as a conservative Christian, speaks no foreign languages and has never traveled outside of the United States, managed to pass a new policy requiring school teachers to identify the United States as an inherently superior culture to that of any other country or period in history.

25   Such acts are little more than a kind of magical thinking. If we believe certain books will cause men to commit rape, then by banning the books, we can bring rape to an end. And we all know rapists stop at the library first. If we believe certain books and stories and ideas cause people to criticize authority, then by banning the ideas a utopian state of respect for authority will appear. If that hasn't happened yet, it's just a sign of how much more needs to be done, that not enough books have been banned yet.

It hardly seems fair to move into the really juicy territory of nudity and sexual material now, but move I must. I've spent several years now talking to people about sex, and it took time for me to learn how to do so frankly. I know how difficult a confrontation with sexuality can be for people. But nudity? Sometimes I despair. In Oshkosh, Wisconsin, a formal challenge was made against the high school yearbook because of its "disgusting" nudity. The cover showed a detail from Michelangelo's Sistine Chapel—that of God creating Adam. Said one upset parent, "It surprises me what passes in the name of culture."

One of the most pervasive modern American fears is that of the ordinary human body. We suffer a kind of physical dysphoria in this country. The "breast" and the "penis" evoke shame. The fact that just about every one in the world either has a penis or breasts is irrelevant. The very idea of penises and breasts haunts people. We fear their loss, we count the loss of either as unadulterated tragedy, but the depiction of a healthy breast or penis is condemned.

A desperate effort is made to protect childhood innocence by sparing children the sight of the naked human body as long as possible. The sadness is that such efforts destroy their real innocence—the simple belief children have that their bodies are good. What do children learn from having the book *Where's Waldo?*

snatched from the classroom shelves? This hugely popular book has been banned repeatedly because, in one crowded beach scene, the tiny profile of a woman's breast is visible. In Columbus, Ohio, the school librarian took it upon herself to paint clothes on the naked babies in Maurice Sendak's *In the Night Kitchen* and *Outside Over There*.

Again, the breast, with irony. *A Woman's Worth*, a book by Marianne Williamson about the painfully low self-esteem many American women experience, was refused distribution by wholesalers in the Midwest and the South because the woman on the cover has half a breast exposed. Since we women have breasts, what does this tell us about self-esteem? About shame? And about what we do and don't agree upon?

This "sex panic," like everything else, is really about being   30
right, presuming consensus instead of working toward it. The conservative feminist lawyer, Catharine MacKinnon, is fond of calling women like me "Uncle Toms." Because Catharine MacKinnon believes that pornography hurts women, she flatly states that any woman who disagrees is a traitor and cannot be considered a feminist. I have found myself over the last few years in the position of defending pornography as a feminist. As far as MacKinnon is concerned, I need only refuse to fight pornography—I need only defend free speech—to be one of her enemies. She calls us "Oreos." MacKinnon's colleagues, Andrea Dworkin and John Stoltenberg, call feminists who oppose censorship "pimps."

In October of 1992, law students at the University of Michigan, where Catharine MacKinnon teaches, sponsored a conference on prostitution. As part of the conference, a local artist named Carol Jacobsen was hired to curate an art show.

Jacobsen's approach was to present art made by prostitutes about their lives. Before the conference opened, a part of the show, an autobiographical videotape by a woman named Veronica Vera, was removed by John Stoltenberg, one of the conference speakers. He said it was "dangerous to women." When Carol Jacobsen found out, she chose to shut down her entire exhibit rather than show only parts of it.

I know Veronica Vera, and I've seen her videotape. I believe that Vera's offense was that she doesn't bemoan her varied sexual experience. She celebrates it. She tells her story with humor and intelligence and a sensual joy in life. She credits her Catholic upbringing with turning her kinky, and credits her brief experiences as a sex worker with improving her self-esteem, her social life, and her savings account. This is not the vision of prostitution that MacKinnon's theories describe. There is no doubt in my mind that if the art show had featured tragic stories by miserable ex-prostitutes, no censorship would have taken place; the show would instead have been applauded for its honesty and raw power.

There is a particular irony here that almost escapes view. Jacobsen's show was deliberately created as a forum for an almost completely silent and repressed class of women. That forum was shut down—silenced by a kind of scorched-earth politics. In the name of promoting one point of view, another point of view (and all debate between the points of view) was cut off. MacKinnon herself, speaking to journalists about the ensuing controversy, dismissed the removal of the art as "a made-up sort of nothing incident." It wasn't to Carol Jacobsen, and it wasn't to Veronica Vera, and it wasn't to me. Such things should never be dismissed by anyone with an investment in social dialogue. In 1970, the English novelist Brigid Brophy said it quite neatly: "To defend society from sex is no one's business. To defend it from officiousness is the duty of everyone who values freedom—or sex."

35   I belong to something called the Working Group, a committee of women formed by the National Coalition Against Censorship specifically to work on pornography issues. A lot of my time defending pornography's right to exist, and the right of any consenting adult to buy and make pornography without interference, has in the last few years centered around a proposed law called the Pornography Victim's Compensation Act. This bill came very close to passing into federal law last year, and was defeated only after a lengthy and expensive campaign by a coalition of writers, publishers, and anti-censorship groups. The Act would have created a "private right of action," that is, a civil law, in which the "producers, distributors, exhibitors, and sellers" of a work judged "obscene" could be sued by the victim of an act influenced by the work. (I will only mention in passing that such cause-and-effect relationships are extraordinarily hard to prove, and that if we were to look at the literary influences on violence and sexual crimes, the Bible would have to be considered carefully.)

The act as written is a masterpiece of circular thinking. The victim in question needs to prove that the work in question is "obscene"—also an extraordinarily difficult thing to prove, and by Supreme Court definition, a local and therefore relative concept—and that the writer or bookseller involved should have "foreseen" that the violent act would occur. So if a nut reads a book which describes rape, and then rapes someone, the author and publisher and distributor and independent bookseller could all be sued for damages—that is, if the book was proven to be obscene rather than artistic in nature, and if the author *et al.* could have known that someone would imitate the rape. Of course, this is very bad law, and probably unusable in a court, but a great deal of money and time was spent promoting and fighting its tenets. It has already risen again in different forms. The Violence Against Women Act was written with a provision that judges would have to be trained in the causal relationship between violence and pornography, though such a relationship has never been proven to exist. And what happens to women who live with violence, if rape is never described, if they are taught not to tell the story, not to explain?

I've come to believe that it isn't enough to respond to sexual censorship by saying something like, "Well, pornography is bad, but censorship is worse." We have to go a step further into our world of differences, and admit that plenty of thoughtful and good-hearted people think pornography is a good thing. Just like art, we *don't* know it when we see it. What's bread-and-butter to you might be poison to me, or a big yawn. And vice versa.

Don Wildmon scares me; Jesse Helms scares me. But I'm also genuinely worried by my liberal acquaintance who wants to eliminate "brutality" from Hollywood films. I'm worried by my poet friend who believes artists have a duty to produce only "positive and nourishing" art. I'm worried just as much by all the socially involved, politically concerned people who want to restrict—and punish—racist slang or images of violence against women. Each of these people has a specific example, a particular word or image, one book or movie, one incident or picture, that exemplifies what they think goes too far.

If we agree—and I know we don't—that images "subordinating women" should be illegal, what happens next? Using language adopted from the works of Catharine MacKinnon and Andrea Dworkin, the Canadian Supreme Court passed *Regina* v. *Butler* in 1992. Butler states that "protecting" women against "harm" and "degradation" is a higher value than protecting the freedom of speech.

I wish Andrea Dworkin and Catharine MacKinnon would just   40
wise up. I wish they could see how quaint and Victorian their rhetoric is, how dangerously allied they are with a conservative position that is no friend to female equality. Dworkin is, like me, a

member of PEN, which has a venerable reputation for protecting freedom of speech. She fails to see to the dark heart of book banning. Only those who already have power have an interest in censorship. Those who have trouble being heard and seen in the first place, whose voices are quietest, have the most to lose. Minorities, all women, the poor, the disenfranchised and politically incorrect—these are the people censorship hurts first.

Since the Butler decision, more than a fourth of all Canadian feminist bookstores have had material seized, and books by people such as David Leavitt, Kathy Acker, and bell hooks have not been allowed past the border. Andrea Dworkin's own book, titled *Woman Hating*, was seized at the Canadian border because of its title alone.

All these things weaken us—as a society, as a nation. They weaken the body of our culture. By bringing our children up in isolation—isolation from history, new ideas, their own experiences—and by keeping ourselves in isolation, we are like people without antibodies, vulnerable to the slightest germ. We lose touch with the ground on which this country was built; we become afraid of freedom.

The Bill of Rights almost didn't get written, partly because the leaders of the time—far-thinking men like Noah Webster and Alexander Hamilton—thought the rights in question were so obviously natural and worthy they would never be restricted. (Just as an aside, I have to point that they were also writing laws to protect the world they had made. A less rights-laden group, like Jefferson's personal slaves, or the wives and daughters of any one of them, would likely have suggested the Bill of Rights seemed like a good idea.) In the end it was James Madison who prevailed, reciting again and again his fear of the tyranny of the majority, his desire to protect the rights of a minority even if it consisted of a single person. Words and pictures and ideas that don't bother anyone don't need protection.

Now there is a ballot proposal in Anchorage that would create a new tyranny of the majority—by allowing local citizens to vote, case by case, on whether any given book in the elementary school library should be available to students.

45   In Oklahoma, a program of environmental education was repeatedly challenged for being Satanic, "eastern," "psychological," and "anti-Christian." One woman objecting explained that all environmental education is "Satanic," because the Bible says that the Earth will burn. Do we want to go to the polls on this?

In Bloomington, Indiana, the book *The Bridge to Terabithia* by Katherine Patterson was challenged by a group of fifth-graders' parents because, the parents explained, the book teaches that people are innately good. And "God's word teaches us that we are all sinners," they explained. How do we vote on that?

Catcher in the Rye by J.D. Salinger is perhaps the most publicly and repeatedly challenged novel for young people. When it was challenged in Illinois not long ago for its "underlying hostility toward Christianity," the complainant added that "respect for God's name overrides the separation of church and state." To some, it also overrides the Bill of Rights. The social scientist Marcia Pally called democracy "a contact sport," and she was right.

When Ray Bradbury's classic work on censorship, *Fahrenheit 451*, was taught in an Irvine, California public school not long ago, the students were given copies with all the obscenities blacked out. In a recent essay, Bradbury described his dismay over the years as teachers and school librarians had committed similar crimes against his work. But he had only just then found out that his own publisher had done the same: over the years since *Fahrenheit 451* was first published, one editor after the other had snipped offensive passages out of the work when new editions were being printed, until 75 separate sections of Bradbury's original writing were gone.

Such patronizing behavior makes us not only weak, but infantile. In Georgia, the Heritage Education and Review Organization, which calls itself HERO, circulated a test for parents to use to determine if their children have been infected by "humanism." One of the questions on the test was, "Do your teachers ask you to make decisions about what is right and wrong?" Do these parents prefer their children to go out into the world unfinished—*untried?* This is what we get from censored thinking. This is what happens when people don't read books.

My good friend Karen Karbo wrote an essay last year about her experiences with a publisher's lawyer. She had written a novel, *The Diamond Lane*, in which a character is injured by a falling ceiling fan in a fancy Los Angeles restaurant. This accident is a minor but critical turning point in the plot. The publisher's lawyer worried that any of the dozens of trendy restaurants in that neighborhood of L.A. might sue, though for what was not clear. Karen was reminded that her book contract, as do almost all book contracts, stipulates that if she is sued, and wins, she splits court costs 50:50 with her publisher. If she is sued and loses, she pays all the court costs herself. In Karen's words, "A cop sitting on your back bumper can make you nervous. He may only be on his way to Dunkin' Donuts, but the knowledge that he is sitting back there, watching, makes you slow down even if you aren't speeding."

Of course, we who work against censorship have our own agendas. I have my reader's agenda, and I have my parent's agenda, and I have my writer's agenda, which is two-fold: I want, of course, to be able to write what I want, without interference. I want to decide for myself, for better and for worse, what to say and how to say it. But deeper, and with more of a chill, I worry about what happens to me as a writer when I am faced with censure of any kind.

When I finished my new book, my publishers decided to have the company lawyer read it. She had a number of questions, most of them about whether or not I was quoting people with their permission, and so on. It was the usual stuff, except for my reference to one of Andrea Dworkin's books. Though my comment was nothing more than a bit of literary criticism, the lawyer wanted me to edit it out. Why? Because Dworkin and MacKinnon are litigious, because they have sued my publisher before, because, as the lawyer pointed out, the "opinion defense" isn't as strong as it used to be. And, she added, even an obvious nuisance suit could cost me a bundle.

A lot of harm has been done in this world and to this world by do-gooders, people who are, above all else, sure of themselves. We live in what is arguably the most heterogeneous society of all time, and we live here with an unfinished and immature ethic, without a whole foundation. Such a foundation may be impossible. And for all this, each of us has to act, has to choose how to act, every day.

Creativity is fundamentally amoral. In the making of creative work, anything goes, everything is material. Then the mature artist decides what works and what doesn't, what serves the story and what distracts. I write for a lot of reasons, to express ideas, to challenge ideas, to tell stories, but mostly I write because of an irrational addiction to language. I love prosody, the sound of words, their layered uses, the feel of a good sentence in my mouth. Does some writing cause harm? Of course it does. Writing couldn't cause good if it didn't cause harm. But I don't write to cause harm or to create good particularly. I write just to write, for writing's sake. To do so wholeheartedly means coming to terms with ambivalence. It means sometimes being a little pushy, a little demanding, if the story needs it. In my work, my duty is to the work. Maturity, I believe, means not only tolerating ambivalence and discomfort, but to some extent encouraging it.

This talk is supposed to be on the limits of expression. I cannot tell you what I think the limits are. I can tell you what my limits are, but they are just for me. The idea of defining it, finding words to describe and write into law what should not be allowed to be written—I can't. As for social consensus, there never has been much that was black and white in the world. There are few issues in which a thoughtful person couldn't find more than one side, see the wisdom or at least the motivation for the conflict. The most useful, important and difficult practice for us as citizens is to practice that—practice not just solving problems, but understanding why social problems are so hard to solve, why so many good people, reasonable people, fail to agree. I can't find five like-minded people, in this room, on this campus, this city, five people who seem to think about the world in similar ways, and gather them around a table and get them to agree on a definition of almost anything. Pluralism is one of this country's great conundrums, but it's also one of our glories. I want to keep slugging away, digging out a position of tolerance toward the intolerant. I want to make clear my willingness to put up with people who don't want to put up with me, because that is all I ask from them.

Courage is required. It's that simple. In Grand Saline, Texas, a group of parents accused a teacher of Satanic practices. She was seen to have committed several sins. She had used a reader which contained a story about Islam. She had discussed African folk tales. She had a picture of Santa Claus on the wall. The protesters pointed out that the letters in Santa can be arranged to spell Satan. After an extensive hate campaign, the teacher resigned.

Where, in all this, was the school principal? Why was the district superintendent so craven as to allow such a campaign to destroy a woman? Where were the other teachers, the other parents? Why such cowardice in the face of argument? Where is the courage of those who, above and beyond all of us, should be vigorously defending our right, and our children's right, to critical thinking?

It's only by going a little way toward another person, toward the confusing beliefs of another person, that we can go a little way into another, and find compassion. Nancy Garden's young adult book, *Annie On My Mind*, won an American Library Association Best Book award in 1982. In 1993 it was burned on the steps of the Kansas City School District, by a group of citizens led by two ministers. In writing about her experience this spring, Garden chose to quote her own fictional character: "Don't let ignorance win. Let love."

Questions for Discussion

1. How are Tisdale's ideas related to the quotation she provides from Justice Brandeis? According to Tisdale, what kind of fears drive book censorship? Why does she believe our society is not really free?
2. How does Tisdale refute the ideas of "religious objection . . . sexual offense . . . protecting children from a painful history and . . . painful realities" as grounds for book banning? Which examples are most helpful in supporting her position?
3. How does Tisdale attempt to refute Cathleen MacKinnon's views on censorship of pornography and the provisions of the Pornography Victim's Compensation Act? Is she successful? How does the example of ex-prostitute Veronica Vera help her to make her case?
4. Tisdale cites James Madison's fear of the "tyranny of the majority" concept, a major reason behind the passage of the Bill of Rights, as a justification for avoiding book censorship. After considering Madison's reasoning, do you agree with Tisdale that local citizens should not have the right to vote on whether certain books should be banned from school libraries in their communities?

Ideas for Writing

1. Write an argumentative essay in response to discussion question number four. In preparing your response, do some reading into the debate behind the passage of the original Bill of Rights. You should also consider the ambiguity of the terms "majority" and "minority" rights in voting and censorship issues.
2. The issue of censorship of pornography that is deemed violent and degrading to women is particularly divisive among feminists and civil libertarians today. Do some research into the debate over this issue and develop an argument either for or against such censorship.

Less Privacy Is Good for Us (and You)

AMITAI ETZIONI

Amitai Etzioni was born in Koln, Germany, in 1929. He received his
Ph.D. from the University of California, Berkeley (1958). Etzioni began his teaching career at Columbia University and has taught at
George Washington University (1980–1987). He is the editor of *The
Responsive Community: Rights and Responsibilities*, a communitarian quarterly, and is the author of twenty-one books, including *The
New Golden Rule: Community and Morality in a Democratic Society*
(1996) and *Next: The Road to the Good Society* (2001). The following
selection is excerpted from *The Limits of Privacy* (1999).

---------------- ✦ ----------------

Despite the fact that privacy is not so much as mentioned in the
Constitution and that it was only shoehorned in some thirty-
four years ago, it is viewed by most Americans as a profound,
inalienable right.

The media is loaded with horror stories about the ways privacy is not so much nibbled away as it is stripped away by bosses
who read your e-mail, neighbors who listen in on your cell
phones, and E-Z passes that allow tollbooth operators to keep
track of your movements. A typical headline decries the "End of
Privacy" (Richard A. Spinello, in an issue of *America*, a Catholic
weekly) or "The Death of Privacy" (Joshua Quittner, in *Time*).

It is time to pay attention to the other half of the equation
that defines a good society: concerns for public health and safety
that entail some rather justifiable diminution of privacy.

Take the HIV testing of infants. New medical data—for instance, evidence recently published by the prestigious *New England Journal of Medicine*—show that a significant proportion of
children born to mothers who have HIV can ward off this horrible disease but only on two conditions: that their mothers not
breast-feed them and that they immediately be given AZT. For
this to happen, mothers must be informed that they have HIV. An
estimated two-thirds of infected mothers are unaware. However,
various civil libertarians and some gay activists vehemently oppose such disclosure on the grounds that when infants are tested

for HIV, in effect one finds out if the mother is a carrier, and thus her privacy is violated. While New York State in 1996, after a very acrimonious debate, enacted a law that requires infant testing and disclosure of the findings to the mother, most other states have so far avoided dealing with this issue.

5   Congress passed the buck by asking the Institute of Medicine (IOM) to conduct a study of the matter. The IOM committee, dominated by politically correct people, just reported its recommendations. It suggested that all pregnant women be asked to consent to HIV testing as part of routine prenatal care. There is little wrong with such a recommendation other than it does not deal with many of the mothers who are drug addicts or otherwise live at society's margins. Many of these women do not show up for prenatal care, and they are particularly prone to HIV, according to a study published in the American Health Association's *Journal of School Health*. To save the lives of their children, they must be tested at delivery and treated even if this entails a violation of mothers' privacy.

Recently a suggestion to use driver's licenses to curb illegal immigration has sent the Coalition for Constitutional Liberties, a large group of libertarians, civil libertarians, and privacy advocates, into higher orbit than John Glenn ever traversed. The coalition wrote:

> This plan pushes us to the brink of tyranny, where citizens will not be allowed to travel, open bank accounts, obtain health care, get a job, or purchase firearms without first presenting the proper government papers.
>
> The authorizing section of the law . . . is reminiscent of the totalitarian dictates by Politburo members in the former Soviet Union, not the Congress of the United States of America.

Meanwhile, Wells Fargo is introducing a new device that allows a person to cash checks at its ATM machines because the machines recognize faces. Rapidly coming is a whole new industry of so-called biometrics that uses natural features such as voice, hand design, and eye pattern to recognize a person with the same extremely high reliability provided by the new DNA tests.

It's true that as biometrics catches on, it will practically strip Americans of anonymity, an important part of privacy. In the near future, a person who acquired a poor reputation in one part of the country will find it much more difficult to move to another part, change his name, and gain a whole fresh start. Biometrics see right through such assumed identities. One may hope that future communities will become more tolerant of such people, especially if they openly acknowledge the mistakes of their past and truly seek to lead a more prosocial life. But they will no longer be able to hide their pasts.

Above all, while biometrics clearly undermines privacy, the social benefits it promises are very substantial. Specifically, each year at least half a million criminals become fugitives, avoiding trial, incarceration, or serving their full sentences, often committing additional crimes while on the lam. People who fraudulently file for multiple income tax refunds using fake identities and multiple Social Security numbers cost the nation between $1 billion and $5 billion per year. Numerous divorced parents escape their financial obligations to their children by avoiding detection when they move or change jobs. (The sums owed to children are variously estimated as running between $18 billion to $23 billion a year.) Professional and amateur criminals, employing fraudulent identification documentation to make phony credit card purchases, cost credit card companies and retail businesses an indeterminate number of billions of dollars each year. The United States loses an estimated $18 billion a year to benefit fraud committed by illegal aliens using false IDs. A 1998 General Accounting Office report estimates identity fraud to cost $10 billion annually in entitlement programs alone.

People hired to work in child care centers, kindergartens, and schools cannot be effectively screened to keep out child abusers and sex offenders, largely because when background checks are conducted, convicted criminals escape detection by using false identification and aliases. Biometrics would sharply curtail all these crimes, although far from wipe them out singlehandedly.

The courts have recognized that privacy must be weighed against considerations of public interest but have tended to privilege privacy and make claims for public health or safety clear several high hurdles. In recent years these barriers have been somewhat lowered as courts have become more concerned with public safety and health. Given that these often are matters of state law and that neither legislatures nor courts act in unison, the details are complex and far from all pointing in one direction. But, by and large, courts have allowed mandatory drug testing of those who directly have the lives of others in their hands, including pilots, train engineers, drivers of school buses, and air traffic controllers, even though such testing violates their privacy. In case after case, the courts have disregarded objections to such tests by civil libertarians who argue that such tests constitute "suspicionless" searches, grossly violate privacy, and—as the ACLU puts it—"condition Americans to a police state."

All this points to a need to recast privacy in our civic culture, public policies, and legal doctrines. We should cease to treat it as unmitigated good, a sacred right (the way Warren and Brandeis referred to it in their famous article and many since) or one that courts automatically privilege.

Instead, privacy should rely squarely on the Fourth Amendment, the only one that has a balance built right into its text. It recognizes both searches that wantonly violate privacy ("unreasonable" ones) and those that enhance the common good to such an extent that they are justified, even if they intrude into one's privacy. Moreover, it provides a mechanism to sort out which searches are in the public interest and which violate privacy without sufficient cause, by introducing the concept of warrants issued by a "neutral magistrate" presented with "probable cause." Warrants also limit the invasion of privacy "by specification of the person to be seized, the place to be searched, and the evidence to be sought." The Fourth may have become the Constitutional Foundation of privacy a long time ago if it was not for the fact that *Roe v. Wade* is construed as a privacy right, and touching it provokes fierce opposition. The good news, though, is that even the advocates of choice in this area are now looking to base their position on some other legal grounds, especially the Fourteenth Amendment.

We might be ready to treat privacy for what it is: one very important right but not one that trumps most other considerations, especially of public safety and health.

Questions for Discussion

1. Make a list of the situations in which Etzioni believes that there are issues of public health and safety that justify the invasion of one's privacy. In each situation that Etzioni discusses, indicate whether you agree or disagree with his point of view.
2. How does Etzioni's article help readers to see the complexity of privacy issues? Provide examples from the text.
3. Why does Etzioni believe that privacy issues should be examined under the Fourth Amendment rather than the First Amendment? Do you agree or disagree with his point of view? Explain.

4. Clearly there is a gap between lawmakers and lawyers who understand the complex applications of the First and Fourth amendments and the typical American whose basic knowledge of law is minimal. What can be done to help people to understand and make a reasoned decision on the issues of privacy without having a comprehensive legal background?

Ideas for Writing

1. Write an essay that argues either in favor of Etzioni's point of view on privacy issues, against it, or for a different perspective on the issue.

2. Analyze the problems and contradictions in one of the privacy issues that Etzioni brings up in his article. Refer to research that you do on the issue as well as personal experiences that you have had or read about or have heard about from friends.

Security Versus Civil Liberties
RICHARD A. POSNER

Richard A. Posner (1939) was born in New York City. He graduated with a B.A. from Yale in 1959 and obtained his law degree from Harvard Law School in 1962. Posner worked in Washington, D.C., under the Johnson and Kennedy administrations; he accepted a full professorship at the University of Chicago in 1969. In 1981, Posner was appointed to be a judge in the U.S. Court of Appeals for the seventh circuit and was Chief Judge from 1993 to 2000. His books include *Breaking the Deadlock: The 2000 Election and the Courts* (2001) and *Public Intellectuals: A Study of Decline: A Critical Analysis* (2001). The following article on the limits of civil liberties was first published in the *Atlantic Monthly*.

——————————— ✦ ———————————

In the wake of the September 11 terrorist attacks have come many proposals for tightening security; some measures to that end have already been taken. Civil libertarians are troubled. They fear that concerns about national security will lead to an erosion of civil liberties. They offer historical examples of supposed overreactions to threats to national security. They treat our existing civil liberties—freedom of the press, protections of privacy and of the rights of criminal suspects, and the rest—as sacrosanct, insisting that the battle against international terrorism accommodate itself to them.

I consider this a profoundly mistaken approach to the question of balancing liberty and security. The basic mistake is the prioritizing of liberty. It is a mistake about law and a mistake about history. Let me begin with law. What we take to be our civil liberties—for example, immunity from arrest except upon probable cause to believe we've committed a crime and from prosecution for violating a criminal statute enacted after we committed the act that violates it—were made legal rights by the Constitution and other enactments. The other enactments can be changed relatively easily, by amendatory legislation. Amending the Constitution is much more difficult. In recognition of this the Framers left most of the constitutional provisions that confer rights pretty vague. The courts have made them definite.

Concretely, the scope of these rights has been determined, through an interaction of constitutional text and subsequent judicial interpretation, by a weighing of competing interests. I'll call them the public-safety interest and the liberty interest. Neither, in my view, has priority. They are both important, and their relative importance changes from time to time and from situation to situation. The safer the nation feels, the more weight judges will be willing to give to the liberty interest. The greater the threat that an activity poses to the nation's safety, the stronger will the grounds seem for seeking to repress that activity, even at some cost to liberty. This fluid approach is only common sense.

Supreme Court Justice Robert Jackson gave it vivid expression many years ago when he said, in dissenting from a free-speech decision he thought doctrinaire, that the Bill of Rights should not be made into a suicide pact. It was not intended to be such, and the present contours of the rights that it confers, having been shaped far more by judicial interpretation than by the literal text (which doesn't define such critical terms as "due process of law" and "unreasonable" arrests and searches), are alterable in response to changing threats to national security.

5 If it is true, therefore, as it appears to be at this writing, that the events of September 11 have revealed the United States to be in much greater jeopardy from international terrorism than had previously been believed—have revealed it to be threatened by a diffuse, shadowy enemy that must be fought with police meas-

ures as well as military force—it stands to reason that our civil liberties will be curtailed. They *should* be curtailed, to the extent that the benefits in greater security outweigh the costs in reduced liberty. All that can reasonably be asked of the responsible legislative and judicial officials is that they weigh the costs as carefully as the benefits.

It will be argued that the lesson of history is that officials habitually exaggerate dangers to the nation's security. But the lesson of history is the opposite. It is because officials have repeatedly and disastrously underestimated these dangers that our history is as violent as it is. Consider such underestimated dangers as that of secession, which led to the Civil War, of a Japanese attack on the United States, which led to the disaster at Pearl Harbor, of Soviet espionage in the 1940s, which accelerated the Soviet Union's acquisition of nuclear weapons and emboldened Stalin to encourage North Korea's invasion of South Korea; of the installation of Soviet missiles in Cuba, which precipitated the Cuban missile crisis; of political assassinations and outbreaks of urban violence in the 1960s; of the Tet Offensive of 1968; of the Iranian revolution of 1979 and the subsequent taking of American diplomats as hostages; and, for that matter, of the events of September 11.

It is true that when we are surprised and hurt, we tend to overreact—but only with the benefit of hindsight can a reaction be separated into its proper and excess layers. In hindsight we know that interning Japanese Americans did not shorten World War II. But was this known at the time? If not, shouldn't the Army have erred on the side of caution, as it did? Even today we cannot say with any assurance that Abraham Lincoln was wrong to suspend habeas corpus during the Civil War, as he did on several occasions, even though the Constitution is clear that only Congress can suspend this right. (Another of Lincoln's wartime measures, the Emancipation Proclamation, may also have been unconstitutional.) But Lincoln would have been wrong to cancel the 1864 presidential election, as some urged: by November of 1864 the North was close to victory, and canceling the election would have created a more dangerous precedent than the wartime suspension of habeas corpus. This last example shows that civil liberties remain part of the balance even in the most dangerous of times, and even though their relative weight must then be less.

Lincoln's unconstitutional acts during the Civil War show that even legality must sometimes be sacrificed for other values.

We are a nation under law, but first we are a nation. I want to emphasize something else, however: the malleability of law, its pragmatic rather than dogmatic character. The law is not absolute, and the slogan *"Fiat iustitia ruat caelum"* ("Let justice be done though the heavens fall") is dangerous nonsense. The law is a human creation rather than a divine gift, a tool of government rather than a mandarin mystery. It is an instrument for promoting social welfare, and as the conditions essential to that welfare change, so must it change.

Civil libertarians today are missing something else—the opportunity to challenge other public-safety concerns that impair civil liberties. I have particularly in mind the war on drugs. The sale of illegal drugs is a "victimless" crime in the special but important sense that it is a consensual activity. Usually there is no complaining witness, so in order to bring the criminals to justice the police have to rely heavily on paid informants (often highly paid and often highly unsavory), undercover agents, wiretaps and other forms of electronic surveillance, elaborate sting operations, the infiltration of suspect organizations, random searches, and monitoring of airports and highways, the "profiling" of likely suspects on the basis of ethnic or racial identity or national origin, compulsory drug tests, and other intrusive methods that put pressure on civil liberties. The war on drugs has been a big flop; moreover, in light of what September 11 has taught us about the gravity of the terrorist threat to the United States, it becomes hard to take entirely seriously the threat to the nation that drug use is said to pose. Perhaps it is time to redirect law-enforcement resources from the investigation and apprehension of drug dealers to the investigation and apprehension of international terrorists. By doing so we may be able to minimize the net decrease in our civil liberties that the events of September 11 have made inevitable.

Questions for Discussion

1. What approach to civil liberties does Posner propose? Explain why you agree or disagree with his point of view.
2. How does Posner use Supreme Court Justice Richard Jackson's decision on free speech to support his claim that civil liberties should be curtailed to protect the nation from the kind of terrorism evident in the events of September 11, 2001?
3. According to Posner, why do the lessons of history confirm his position that we need heightened security at the expense

of liberties in times when our nation is at grave risk? Explain why you agree or disagree with Posner's point of view.

4. How and why does Posner use the example of President Abraham Lincoln's unconstitutional acts during the Civil War that showed how "legality must sometimes be sacrificed for other values" to advance his own argument? Why does Posner also argue for a shift of emphasis on the detection of drug dealers to the detection of terrorists? Why do you think he ends his argument on this note? Is this an effective way to conclude?

Ideas for Writing

1. Write an argument in which you agree or disagree with Posner. Do you think that the government has gone too far in limiting civil liberties? What liberties should we be given back? If you think that the government has not gone far enough, what aspects of our communities need to be more closely regulated?

2. Research a specific aspect of increased security at the cost of civil liberties in your community. Write a paper with the intention of informing your audience on whether or not new regulations are essential for the protection of citizens.

Protecting Dr. King's Legacy: Justice and Liberty in the Wake of September 11th

NADINE STROSSEN

Nadine Strossen earned her J.D. from Harvard Law School in 1975. Since 1984, she has taught law at New York University and New York Law School, and beginning in 1991, has served as President of the American Civil Liberties Union. She has made public appearances at hundreds of college campuses and other forums. Her books include *Defending Pornography: Free Speech, Sex and the Fight for Women's Rights* (1995; 2000) and *The Government vs. Erotica: The Siege of Adam & Eve* (2001). The following selection, "Protecting Dr. King's Legacy: Justice and Liberty in the Wake of

September 11th," is taken from her testimony before Congressman John Conyers' Forum on National Security and the Constitution (2002).

———————— ✦ ————————

The American Civil Liberties Union is a non-partisan, non-profit organization consisting of nearly 300,000 members dedicated to protecting the principles of freedom and equality set forth in the Constitution and in our civil rights laws. We have been involved in responding to Congressional and Administrative actions in the wake of September 11th, some of which we find deeply troubling. Many of the policies are placebos—they are illusory "solutions" that do not make us safer but do threaten fundamental constitutional protections. We believe that it is possible to be both "Safe and Free." We can have effective law enforcement while also protecting individual rights.

As we start a new year and celebrate the birthday of Dr. Martin Luther King, Jr., we commend you, Mr. Chairman, for holding this forum. This is an appropriate time for the Congress to ensure that in our effort to remain secure, we do not sacrifice the very foundations of our democracy.

Dr. King's life is a testament to the power of the Constitution. Dr. King had the social insight and moral courage to challenge government and resist policies that undermined liberty, equality, and justice for all. He stood on the principles of the First Amendment to advocate equality under the Fourteenth Amendment.

Over the past several months, the Executive Branch has initiated an expansive array of new police powers and tactics that raise significant moral and constitutional questions—from secret tribunals and expanded wiretapping authority, to monitoring attorney-client conversations, riffling through confidential business and student records, rounding up and detaining immigrants in secret, and questioning certain young male lawful U.S. residents merely based on their national origin. It is up to the Congress to assert its oversight authority—and responsibility—to examine these dramatic actions.

5   As you consider the actions taken in response to terrorism, consider that threats to the constitutional rights of one group endanger the constitutional rights of everyone. As Dr. King said in a speech he gave in September 1967: "I have fought too hard and long to end segregated public accommodations to segre-

gate my own moral concerns. It is my deep conviction that justice is indivisible, that injustice anywhere is a threat to justice everywhere."

Justice means that each and every right and liberty in our Constitution must be as strong in a time of crisis as in a time of peace. We cannot sacrifice equality or privacy or basic checks and balances without eroding justice for all. We cannot allow discrimination against one group without threatening equality for all. We cannot allow the government to silence the voice of one dissenter without weakening the core of our democracy. These principles are the bedrock of American democracy.

SECRET DETENTION

The Department of Justice has launched what appears to be an extensive program of preventive detention. The Department admits that over 1,200 people have been detained in connection with the September 11 attacks. Some have been incarcerated for long periods of time, others held for only hours. Because of the secrecy surrounding the detentions, we do not have a full picture as to how many people are still incarcerated, where they are incarcerated, whether they have access to counsel and how they are being treated. Some of the stories being reported upon are disturbing. According to a *Washington Post* story, two Pakistani immigrants were held for 49 days before being charged with overstaying their visas; and an Israeli national was held for 66 days before being charged with entering the country illegally.

According to media accounts of the detentions, only a very small number of persons who have been arrested have any involvement with, or knowledge of, the attacks. Approximately 10 people are at what the *Washington Post* called the "hot center"— believed to have close ties to the Al-Qaeda network or some knowledge of the hijackers. An additional 18 people are believed to have more distant connections to the hijackers or connections to the people in the "hot center." The rest have been charged with unrelated technical immigration violations or minor criminal charges (usually under state law), or are being held as material witnesses under 18 U.S.C. sec. 3144.

It appears that the vast majority of the people being detained in connection with this investigation are being detained on pretexts: they are suspected of having committed minor offenses that give law enforcement or immigration authorities the power to detain them even though they would not normally be detained for such conduct. By all accounts, the overwhelmingly majority of detainees are Muslims or Arabs, come from Middle Eastern countries, and are non-citizens. However, as was previously mentioned, we know that there have been at least a few detainees from India and Pakistan. It seems that for the most part, similarly situated non-Muslims and non-Arabs who commit the same types of violations are not being detained.

10   We have the most urgent concern for the detainees who are being held on immigration charges because their access to legal counsel is limited. Although the Attorney General assures us that everyone being held has had access to counsel, many stories are coming to light that belie this assertion. For example, Dr. Al Bader Al-Hazmi, a San Antonio, Texas, Saudi national and a radiologist at the Texas Health Science Center was held incommunicado—denied access to either his lawyer or his family—for seven days. After nearly two weeks in detention, Dr. Al-Hazmi was finally released with no charges filed against him. Another troubling example is Tarek Mohamed Fayad, an Egyptian national and dentist residing in California. He was picked up by the FBI on September 13th and then transferred to the Brooklyn Detention Center in New York City, where we believe he remains to this day. According to the *Wall Street Journal,* it took his lawyer one month before she was able to locate and talk to him. If this is the treatment that prominent professionals are receiving, one can only imagine what is happening to people who are less fortunate.

The public has virtually no information about the whereabouts of persons held on immigration violations. Are they being held in custody or have they been released? Where are they being held? How long have they been held? Do they have attorneys? The fact that immigration detainees can be held in so many facilities, coupled with the secrecy surrounding the detention, makes it extremely difficult to determine whether the detainees have access to counsel, are allowed contact with their families, and are being properly treated. We know that at least one detainee—55-year-old Mohammed Rafiq Butt—died in custody. On October 23, Mr. Butt was found dead in his cell at the Hudson County jail in Kearny, New Jersey, the cause of death ruled heart failure. We know of others who have been held for weeks without any charges being lodged against them. This contradicts the Attorney General's assurances that all those who are being detained are being promptly charged within 48 hours. It also violates the recently enacted USA PATRIOT Act, which requires that, even for those individuals certified by the Attorney General as suspected terrorists, charges must be filed within 7 days or the individuals must be released.

It is not for lack of trying that we have been unable to get adequate information about the detainees. On October 17, 2001 the ACLU wrote to the Attorney General asking him for information about the detainees. He did not respond to that letter. We posed similar questions to the Director of the FBI, Robert Meuller, at two meetings on September 25 and October 25. When those requests for information failed, we filed, along with other organizations, a request under the Freedom of Information Act on October 29. Subsequent to filing the FOIA request, on October 30, we met with Commissioner Ziglar of the Immigration and Naturalization Service who also did not provide the information.

When our repeated attempts to obtain information failed, we filed suit in federal district court on December 5, 2001 along with other organizations including the American-Arab Anti-Discrimination Committee, the Arab American Institute, the Asian American Legal Defense and Education Fund, the Center for National Security Studies, the Council on American Islamic Relations, the Electronic Privacy Information Center, Human Rights Watch, and the Reporters Committee for Freedom of the Press.

Since filing suit, the government's response to our legal request for basic information on individuals arrested and detained after September 11th continues to be "incomplete and inaccurate." We are now seeking further information about the contradictory information contained in documents provided on January 11, 2002. Those documents revealed beyond any doubt that earlier assurances by government officials that rights were being respected were false. For example, while officials said that they were, in general, charging those who were arrested within the constitutionally required 48-hour period, the documents show instead that many individuals were not charged for several weeks, or even as long as two months.

We believe that a complete response to our FOIA request will 15 prove that the vast majority of people detained after September 11 had no connection to terrorism and may also show that the government placed severe obstacles in order to thwart access to counsel. Civil rights and human rights groups who had routinely been given access to detention facilities to offer legal assistance were not permitted to do so after September 11th. Individuals who retained lawyers were denied the right to have a lawyer present during questioning.

The documents that have been provided reveal that the government itself has determined that most of the detainees are not connected to terrorism and that the Attorney General no longer has any national security rationale for withholding information about these individuals. For instance, of the 725 detainees listed in documents, 344 are listed separately under the caption 'INACTIVE CASES,' which would seem to indicate that they have been cleared of any link to terrorism.

Our organization continues to press for basic information about the detainees and about any rights violations that have occurred. The ACLU of New Jersey announced on January 22 the filing of a lawsuit against Hudson and Passaic Counties, seeking disclosure of the names of all Immigration and Naturalization Service detainees held in those counties' jails. The filing was made under the state's strong public records law, which requires that jails make public the names and other information on all those being held.

ATTORNEY GENERAL PASSES EMERGENCY REGULATION TO MAKE IT EASIER TO DETAIN PEOPLE

Adding to the concern about unfair detention is a new regulation that makes it easier for the government to detain noncitizens. This regulation was issued by the Attorney General on October 26 and went into effect on October 29. Like many post-September 11 regulations, it was put into effect under the administration's "emergency rule-making authority" that exempts the Attorney General from complying with the normal notice and comment period. The new rule allows the Immigration and Naturalization Service to set aside any release order issued by an immigration judge, simply because it disagrees with the immigration judge's determination, in cases where the INS says it believes that the non-citizen poses a danger to the community or is a flight risk. Previously, the INS needed to request a stay from the Board of Immigration Appeals if it disagreed with an immigration judge's determination, except in limited circumstances where the individual had been convicted of certain crimes or accused of terrorism. Now, even for individuals who are merely accused of overstaying their visas, the hearing before the immigration judge has been rendered meaningless because the decision whether to detain or release rests exclusively with the INS.

THE QUESTIONING OF 5,000 MEN BASED ON THEIR COUNTRY OF ORIGIN

In addition to detaining people based on their ethnicity or country of origin, the Attorney General also is using these criteria as the primary reason for questioning people. In a November 9, 2001 directive, the Attorney General ordered the FBI and other law enforcement officials to conduct interviews of at least 5,000 men, 18 to 33 years old, who had entered the U.S. on non-immigrant visas in the past two years and come from countries where terrorist activities are known or believed to occur. The DOJ's list of the young men targeted for government questioning was compiled based on their national origin, age and gender, not on any individualized suspicion of criminal activity.

The DOJ acknowledged that it has no basis for believing that 20 any of the thousands of men on this list has any knowledge whatsoever that is relevant to the investigation, and it stresses that it has no basis for suspecting any of them of any involvement in any terrorist activities, or of any other criminal activity, or any violation of immigration laws.

The ACLU recognizes the right—indeed the responsibility—of federal law enforcement to gather relevant information in the course of its investigation into the September 11 terrorist attacks. But discriminatory, dragnet profiling is neither an effective investigative technique nor a permissible substitute for the constitutional requirement of individualized suspicion of wrongdoing.

The DOJ guidelines went far beyond any legitimate quest for factual information. Officials were instructed to inquire into the political beliefs of the targeted young men, and to ask them to report on the political beliefs of their families and friends. The Attorney General has reported that the interviews were "successful" and conducted professionally. However, the Attorney General has not claimed that the interviews succeeded in acquiring a significant amount of information relevant to the September 11th investigation. Besides raising constitutional concerns, this investigative technique seemed to be ineffective.

DEPORTING 6,000 PEOPLE BASED ON THEIR COUNTRY OF ORIGIN

The most recent discriminatory tactic is the administration's decision to deport 6,000 people who are in violation of their immigration status. The ACLU does not oppose deporting people who have broken immigration laws; we do, however, object strenuously to selective prosecution, a questionable law enforcement tactic that has never been proven effective. While there are over 300,000 outstanding deportation orders, the DOJ plans to focus on some 6,000 based solely on national or ethnic origin. There is no evidence that selectively deporting people with outstanding deportation orders would have prevented the events of September 11th. None of the highjackers had outstanding deportation orders. Many of the hijackers were in the country legally; in fact, the whole point of a "sleeper cell" is to remain innocuous until the last moment before springing into violent action.

A dragnet approach to removing individuals who overstay their visas based solely on national origin is counter-productive because Al-Qaeda is an organization that spans the globe. Focusing on men from the Middle East or North Africa won't prevent terrorism because the terrorists will simply come from a cell in a country far off the radar screen. The government should be encouraging those with information to come forward, rather than alienating individuals who might have information and discouraging them from coming forward because of the targeting and mistreatment of their communities.

25   Furthermore, a recent article in the *Washington Post* states that Asia and Africa are believed to be the next possible source of Al-Qaeda operatives. According to government officials, Al-Qaeda, by utilizing Asian and African terrorists, hopes to elude the racial profiles developed by law enforcement agencies.

RELAXING THE GUIDELINES ON POLITICAL SPYING

On December 1, 2001, the *New York Times* reported that Attorney General Ashcroft is considering a plan to relax restrictions on the FBI, giving them greater freedom to spy on religious and political organizations. Apparently, Mr. Ashcroft is not a student of history.

Many of us remember the horrific revelations made during the Church Hearings in the 1970s. The FBI "monitored political demonstrations, infiltrated civil rights groups, conducted illegal break-ins and warrant-less wiretaps of anti-war groups, sent anonymous poison-pen letters intended to break up marriages of political group leaders, and targeted, among others, Dr. Martin Luther King, Jr."

With regard to Dr. King, the FBI had no bona fide investigative purpose for its activities. The campaign against him was predicated on FBI Director J. Edgar Hoover's dislike of King. In 1962, Hoover wrote on a memorandum that Dr. King was "no good." A monograph compiled and published by the FBI and distributed to various officials was described by Burke Marshall, Assistant Attorney General for the Civil Rights Division under Robert Kennedy, as "a personal diatribe . . . a personal attack without evidentiary support on the moral character and person of Dr. Martin Luther King, and was only peripherally related to anything substantive . . ." Dr. King's real crime in the eyes of the FBI was that he "represented a clear threat to 'the established order' of the U.S."

The FBI's enmity toward Dr. King led it to bug his telephones and hotel rooms, obtaining highly person information that it then tried to use to break up his marriage and to encourage him to commit suicide. The FBI tried to discredit King in the eyes of the White House, Congress, the religious community, and even foreign governments—all done because Dr. King advocated social justice.

The documented excesses of the FBI in targeting individuals   30 or groups because of their beliefs led to Congressional hearings, and, eventually, guidelines adopted by the Attorney General. These guidelines regulate FBI activity in both foreign and domestic intelligence gathering, and make it clear that constitutionally protected advocacy of unpopular ideas or political dissent alone cannot serve as the basis for an investigation.

The primary safeguard is that the guidelines require a valid factual basis for opening an investigation, which largely precludes wholesale FBI fishing expeditions. The preamble to the Attorney General's Guidelines on General Crimes, Racketeering Enterprise and Domestic Security/Terrorism Investigations (hereinafter "Domestic Guidelines") notes investigation "must be performed with care to protect individual rights and to insure that investigations are confined to matters of legitimate law enforcement interest." A domestic terrorism investigation may only be initiated "when the facts or circumstances reasonably indicate that two or more persons are engaged in an enterprise for the purpose of furthering political or social goals wholly or in part through activities that involve force or violence and a violation of the criminal laws of the United States." One of the considerations when determining whether to open such an investigation is "the danger to privacy and free expression posed by an investigation."

The Attorney General Guidelines for FBI Foreign Intelligence Collection and Foreign Counterintelligence Investigations (hereinafter "Foreign Guidelines") state that investigations of groups or organizations "should focus on activities of foreign counterintelligence or international terrorism activities, not on unrelated First Amendment activities."

The threshold for opening a formal investigation is low, requiring only a "reasonable indication" that a crime is occurring or is about to occur. This standard is substantially lower than probable cause." The FBI is also authorized to open a preliminary inquiry based on even a lower evidentiary threshold, when it receives any information or allegation "whose responsible handling requires some further scrutiny." These preliminary inquiries are contemplated to be of short duration and more limited than a full investigation. A preliminary inquiry can turn into a full investigation upon the Bureau's receiving "reasonable indication" that a crime has been, or is about to be, committed.

Not only is there already a low standard for FBI investigations, but it is also clear the Bureau's hands are not tied. It need not wait for a crime to occur. The Guidelines recognize that "[i]n its efforts to anticipate or prevent crime, the FBI must at times initiate investigations in advance of criminal conduct."

35   The Guidelines also make it clear that the FBI may investigate based on advocacy of violence. While urging respect for the First Amendment, the Guidelines state: "When, however, statements advocate criminal activity or indicate an apparent intent to engage in crime, particularly crimes of violence, an investigation under these guidelines may be warranted."

We know from history what happens when the FBI is given too long a leash—it targets individuals and groups based on their advocacy and association rather than based on legitimate law enforcement concerns. The Guidelines were adopted to shorten that leash and to keep investigations properly focused. To relax the Guidelines and allow greater spying on groups based on their First Amendment activity is counter-productive and a waste of resources, as well as violating fundamental constitutional rights.

Political spying not only undermines our political freedom, chilling those who may disagree with the status quo, but it also diverts resources that could be better spent fighting real crime. Thousands of groups espouse views with which the government disagrees, but a relatively small number ever engage in criminal activity. Every FBI agent spending his or her days noting license plate numbers at a political rally or taping and transcribing political speeches is an agent not engaged in preventing or solving crime.

Political spying is also likely to exacerbate violence rather than stop it. Justice Louis Brandeis recognized long ago that the First Amendment acts as a safety valve. If those marginalized in our society are free to express their views and engage in political activity, they are less likely to resort to violence. Political spying plays into the hands of many anti-government extremist groups, driving them underground and encouraging the fanatics among them to respond with violence.

While the Attorney General drafts the Guidelines, Congress has the responsibility to oversee any proposed amendments and examine their effects on the constitutional right to dissent. Since the passage of the USA PATRIOT Act, Congress must be even more vigilant in overseeing the Justice Department because the USA PATRIOT Act permits law enforcement agencies to share sensitive information gathered in criminal investigations with intelligence agencies including the CIA and the NSA, and also with other federal agencies including the INS, Secret Service, and Department of Defense.

The PATRIOT Act also permits law enforcement officers to share with the CIA intercepts of telephone conversations and Internet communications. No court order would be necessary to authorize the sharing of this sensitive information and the law does not include any meaningful restrictions on subsequent use of the recorded conversations. For example, there is nothing in the Act that prevents this information from being used to screen candidates who apply for government jobs. Moreover, the Act does not prohibit the CIA from sharing with foreign governments surveillance information gleaned from a criminal investigation, even if sharing that information could put at risk members of a person's family who live abroad.

The PATRIOT Act also mandates disclosure to the CIA of "foreign intelligence information" obtained in connection with a criminal investigation, without defining "foreign intelligence information." These provisions represent extraordinary extensions

40

of the previous powers of the foreign intelligence agencies, including the CIA, to obtain information about Americans.

While some sharing of information may be appropriate in some limited circumstances, it should only be done with strict safeguards. The PATRIOT Act lacks essential safeguards, which may well lead to a recurrence of the very abuses that the Church Committee exposed—and sought to end—decades ago.

MONITORING PROTECTED ATTORNEY-CLIENT CONVERSATIONS

Not only are people being detained without access to counsel, but in addition, once they obtain counsel, there is no guarantee that their attorney-client communications will be kept confidential. The Attorney General promulgated regulations that permit the Department of Justice to monitor confidential attorney-client conversations in any case in which the Attorney General finds that there is "reasonable suspicion" to believe that a particular federal prisoner "may" use communications with attorneys or their agents "to further or facilitate acts of terrorism." The regulation requires that the Director of the Bureau of Prisons (BOP) "shall . . . provide appropriate procedures for the monitoring or review of communications between that inmate and attorneys or attorneys' agents who are traditionally covered by the attorney-client privilege.

In short, the Justice Department, unilaterally, without judicial oversight, and with no meaningful standards, is to decide when to monitor the confidential attorney-client conversations of a person whom the Justice Department itself may be seeking to prosecute. This regulation applies not only to convicted prisoners in the custody of the BOP, but also to all persons in the custody of the Department of Justice, including pretrial detainees who have not yet been convicted of any crime and are presumed innocent, as well as material witnesses and individuals who are being held on suspected immigration violations and who are not accused of any crime.

45   What makes the regulation even more disturbing is the fact that it is completely unnecessary. The Department of Justice already has legal authority to record attorney-client conversations by going before a judge and obtaining a warrant based on probable cause that the attorney is facilitating a crime. Indeed, the Supreme Court has even approved searches of an attorney's law

office, provided a warrant has first been obtained from a neutral and detached magistrate. Similarly, if prison officials have reason to believe that a particular prisoner is using the mail to violate the law or threaten security, they may obtain a search warrant to read and open the mail.

The Justice Department has not articulated a single reason why current law is insufficient to ensure that attorneys are not assisting their clients in committing crime. Indeed, during questioning before the Senate Judiciary Committee on November 27, 2001, Assistant Attorney General Michael Chertoff could not answer Senator Kennedy's question as to why the new regulation was necessary. Though it lacks any justification for doing so, the Department of Justice has made itself the arbiter of when conversations should be monitored, taking away the authority from a neutral judge. This regulation is an unprecedented frontal assault on the attorney-client privilege as well as on the right to counsel and the right of access to the courts guaranteed by the Constitution. . . .

CONCLUSION

Congress must resist any future "quick fix" "antiterrorism" or "security" measures that the administration proposes. Despite Attorney General Ashcroft's promises to uphold the Constitution and protect civil liberties, his actions belie his rhetoric. Our democracy is in real danger if any one branch of the government becomes too powerful. From establishing military tribunals without Congressional approval, to expanding wiretapping authority while limiting judicial oversight, this Administration is demonstrating its disregard for the other two branches of government. The precarious balance of powers is becoming dangerously tilted toward an excess of Executive Branch power. We urge the Congress to play an active role in guarding against continued excesses of the executive branch. We urge Congress to:

- Hold quarterly oversight hearings on the implementation of the USA PATRIOT Act to make sure that civil rights and liberties are protected.
- Ensure that the Department of Justice complies with section 1001 of the USA PATRIOT Act that requires the Inspector General of the Department of Justice to establish one position to review information and receive complaints alleging

abuses of civil rights and civil liberties by employees and officials of the DOJ and report to the Congress on those abuses.

- Establish an independent Civil Rights/Liberties Commission of prominent academics and national leaders to monitor and analyze the impact of the USA PATRIOT Act.
- Call upon the Department of Justice to give a full accounting of all persons held in detention since September 11, to ensure that all persons are being held on legitimate charges and have access to adequate legal counsel and to immediately release all people being held illegally.
- Urge the Attorney General to rescind immediately the regulations that permit the monitoring of attorney-client conversations and that permit the Attorney General to override release orders of immigration judges.

Lastly, I would like to point out that it is not only the ACLU that shares these concerns. Attached to this document is a "Call to Action" signed by 50 national organizations expressing similar concerns.

Thank you very much. I appreciate very much the opportunity to appear here today and look forward to continuing to work with you in the future.

Questions for Discussion

1. Strossen invokes the legacy of Martin Luther King, Jr. in her introductory remarks and elsewhere in her comments. What is the purpose of her references to King? Do you think it is relevant for her to bring up King in the aftermath of the September 11 terrorist attacks?
2. How have certain civil and legal rights been suspended in detention and questioning under the Patriot Act and related laws? How have the rights of a terrorist suspect to attorney-client privacy and an open trial been compromised? How well does Strossen establish the unjust nature of these disruptions and curtailments of rights? What counterarguments could be made in defense of these curtailments under the current crisis situation?
3. How have spying and sharing of data on suspects increased and become less controlled by law and civil rights under the Patriot Act? How does Strossen use the history of FBI harassment to emphasize the dangers of giving this agency too much power over our lives?

4. In the final section of her address, Strossen makes five proposals to help maintain a better balance of powers under the Patriot Act. Do her proposals seem reasonable and clearly stated?

Ideas for Writing

1. Do some research into the Patriot Act, its provisions, the controversy around it, and the circumstances that brought about its passage. Write an essay in which you either agree or disagree with Strossen's critical approach to this act and its curtailment of civil liberties. Give support from your reading on the subject and interviews with professionals and students (particularly foreign students) who have some knowledge of the law and its impact.

2. After doing some research into the Patriot Act, write an essay in which you evaluate Strossen's five proposals at the end of her address to the Forum. From your findings, do you think the proposals would be adequate to handle the negative effects of the Patriot Act on privacy and rights? Why or why not?

Extending the Theme

1. In "Rights as a Check on Democracy" Dershowitz explains how civil rights evolve through court decisions to protect individuals from the "tyranny of the majority," responding to new issues of civil rights that arise due to social change. Demonstrate how this concept of the evolution of civil rights in relationship to court decisions is demonstrated in the particular cases raised by Lawrence, Etzioni, and Posner.

2. Social activists Strossen and Lawrence present themselves as proponents of civil rights and liberties, particularly for minority or under-served groups. Contrast the different approaches of both of these authors; then examine the validity of each writer's position and explain which has more potential to affect social change.

3. Contrast the differing views on the right to privacy presented by Etzioni, Posner, and Strossen. Which of their approaches makes the most sense to you? Consider particularly the difference between an absolute versus a relative right to privacy.

4. In the essays written after September 11 by Strossen and Posner, both authors focus on whether issues of national security should take priority over

civil liberties in the climate of our current "war on terrorism." Contrast the positions that Posner and Strossen take in response to recent legislation (such as the Patriot Act) that limits our civil liberties. What is your position on the need to regulate civil liberties in an attempt to control the dangers of terrorism? Refer to specific events as you develop your argument.

5. Visit an organization or a protest event of an organization dedicated to the preservation of civil liberties such as the right to life, pro choice, freedom of speech, or religious freedom. Do some research on the organization; visit their Web site. You can also do library research and interview people at the organization. Then write a paper that discusses what you have learned and how your point of view on a civil liberties issue has developed and/or changed through studying the activist group.

The Media and
the Citizen

*"The communications media in America carry on an enterprise more
fundamental even than formal education to the well-being of an open
society."*   DOUGLASS CATER

*"The recurring conflict between media commercial interest and the public
interest distorts both the performance of the media and their capacity for
self-evaluation and self-criticism."*
                 R.K. BAKER AND S.J. BALL, *A REPORT TO THE NATIONAL
COMMISSION ON THE CAUSES AND PREVENTION OF VIOLENCE*

*"Television isolates people from the environment, from each other, and
from their own senses."*   JERRY MANDER

The quotation above by Douglass Cater indicates a common
conviction that effective and open media communications are
essential elements of a democracy. It is for this reason that the
First Amendment to the Constitution was designed—to assure
freedom of the press, the dominant communications medium of
the day. In the twentieth century, the face of mass media changed
dramatically, with the focus shifting from the press to radio, film,
television, and the Internet, as well as other forms of mass media.
Many critics have commented on how the mass media with their
centralized ownership and commercial power have developed an

unhealthy control over the minds of modern citizens. As Jerry Mander indicates above, mass media also can separate people from direct interaction with normal family and friendship interactions and have reduced the desire in many citizens to participate in the political process.

The essays in this chapter examine both the negative effects, as well as the potentially positive impact of media on the political beliefs and actions of citizens. Pratkanis and Aronson in "Pictures in Our Heads" from *The Age of Propaganda* demonstrate how citizens who are heavy television viewers and readers of sensational news stories are likely to display racial and gender prejudice and fear of violence in their communities. Furthermore, because of the limited range of story types reported by television and print journalists, elected political leaders find their positions and policies placed uppermost in the minds of citizens through extensive media coverage.

Next, the essays by Patricia Williams and Cathleen Cleaver focus on the anger and frustration that many citizens feel when confronted by offensive media content over which they have no control. Patricia Williams, an African-American lawyer and professor, writes in her essay "Hate Radio" of her feelings of outrage at talk radio programs which feature negative and abusive portrayals of blacks, women, and gays. Cathleen Cleaver in "The Internet: A Clear and Present Danger?" argues that the excessive amount of hard-core pornography on the Internet is easily available to children and must be controlled.

The next essay emphasizes the power of mainstream commercial media over the social views and actions of citizens. Jeffery Scheuer in "Media Literacy and Democratic Citizenship" offers a proposal to help citizens gain power over and understanding of the impact of media on their beliefs and daily lives by becoming more media literate and entering into a culture of critical thinking and viewing.

Feeling that mainstream media are inherently limited by commercial and corporate control, David Barsamian in his essay "Independent Media Alternatives" focuses on ways that alternative media, including public radio stations and the Internet, are changing the face of grassroots democracy by engaging citizens in active community participation. In our final essay, "Re-Thinking Virtual Communities: The Prospects for the Public Sphere," Howard Rheingold considers both the possibility that the Internet could have an important influence on grassroots democracy, as well as the dangers involved in the misuse of the medium for commercial and propaganda ends.

Pictures in Our Heads

ANTHONY PRATKANIS AND ELLIOT ARONSON

Anthony Pratkanis and Elliot Aronson are professors of psychology at the University of California, Santa Cruz. Pratkanis has taught courses in consumerism and advertising at Carnegie Mellon. He has written many articles for both popular and scholarly journals and is co-author with Aronson of *Social Psychology* (1993). Aronson is one of the world's most highly regarded social psychologists and the author of many books, including *The Jigsaw Classroom* (1978, 1997). The following article is from Pratkanis and Aronson's *The Age of Propaganda* (1992), which focuses on the ways people's views of the world are influenced and molded by the constant barrage of media propaganda.

--- ✦ ---

In *Public Opinion*, the distinguished political analyst Walter Lippmann tells the story of a young girl, brought up in a small mining town, who one day went from cheerfulness into a deep spasm of grief. A gust of wind had suddenly cracked a kitchen windowpane. The young girl was inconsolable and spoke incomprehensibly for hours. When she finally was able to speak intelligibly, she explained that a broken pane of glass meant that a close relative had died. She was therefore mourning her father, whom she felt certain had just passed away. The young girl remained disconsolate until, days later, a telegram arrived verifying that her father was still alive. It appears that the girl had constructed a complete fiction based on a simple external fact (a broken window), a superstition (broken window means death), fear, and love for her father.

The point of Lippmann's story was not to explore the inner workings of abnormal personality, but to ask a question about ourselves: To what extent do we, like the young girl, let our fictions guide our thoughts and actions? Lippmann believed that we are much more similar to that young girl than we might readily admit. He contended that the mass media paint an imagined world and that the "pictures in our heads" derived from the media influence what men and women will do and say at any particular moment. Lippmann made these observations in 1922. Seven decades later, we can ask: What is the evidence for his claim? To what extent do the pictures we see on television and in other mass media influence how we see the world and set the agenda for what we view as most important in our lives?

Let's look at the world we see on television. George Gerbner and his associates have conducted the most extensive analysis of television to date. Since the late 1960s, these researchers have been videotaping and carefully analyzing thousands of prime-time television programs and characters. Their findings, taken as a whole, indicate that the world portrayed on television is grossly misleading as a representation of reality. Their research further suggests that, to a surprising extent, we take what we see on television as a reflection of reality.

In prime-time programming, males outnumber females by 3 to 1, and the women portrayed are younger than the men they encounter. Nonwhites (especially Hispanics), young children, and the elderly are underrepresented; and members of minority groups are disproportionately cast in minor roles. Moreover, most prime-time characters are portrayed as professional and managerial workers: Although 67 percent of the work force in the United States are employed in blue-collar or service jobs, only 25 percent of TV characters hold such jobs. Finally, crime on television is ten times more prevalent than it is in real life. The average 15-year-old has viewed more than 13,000 TV killings. Over half of TV's characters are involved in a violent confrontation each week; in reality, fewer than 1 percent of people in the nation are victims of criminal violence in any given year, according to FBI statistics. David Rintels, a television writer and former president of the Writers' Guild of America, summed it up best when he said, "From 8 to 11 o'clock each night, television is one long lie."

5   To gain an understanding of the relationship between watching television and the pictures in our heads, Gerbner and his colleagues compared the attitudes and beliefs of heavy viewers (those who watch more than four hours a day) and light viewers (those who watch less than two hours a day). They found that heavy viewers (1) express more racially prejudiced attitudes; (2) overestimate the number of people employed as physicians, lawyers, and athletes; (3) perceive women as having more limited

abilities and interests than men; (4) hold exaggerated views of the prevalence of violence in society; and (5) believe old people are fewer in number and less healthy today than they were twenty years ago, even though the opposite is true. What is more, heavy viewers tend to see the world as a more sinister place than do light viewers; they are more likely to agree that most people are just looking out for themselves and would take advantage of you if they had a chance. Gerbner and his colleagues conclude that these attitudes and beliefs reflect the inaccurate portrayals of American life provided to us by television.

Let's look at the relationship between watching television and images of the world by looking more closely at how we picture criminal activity. In an analysis of "television criminology," Craig Haney and John Manzolati point out that crime shows dispense remarkably consistent images of both the police and criminals. For example, they found that television policemen are amazingly effective, solving almost every crime, and are absolutely infallible in one regard: The wrong person is never in jail at the end of a show. Television fosters an illusion of certainty in crime-fighting. Television criminals generally turn to crime because of psychopathology or insatiable (and unnecessary) greed. Television emphasizes criminals' personal responsibility for their actions and largely ignores situational pressures correlated with crime, such as poverty and unemployment.

Haney and Manzolati go on to suggest that this portrayal has important social consequences. People who watch a lot of television tend to share this belief system, which affects their expectations and can cause them to take a hard-line stance when serving on juries. Heavy viewers are likely to reverse the presumption of innocence, believing that defendants must be guilty of something, otherwise they wouldn't be brought to trial.

A similar tale can be told about other "pictures painted in our heads." For example, heavy readers of newspaper accounts of sensational and random crimes report higher levels of fear of crime. Repeated viewing of R-rated violent "slasher" films is associated with less sympathy and empathy for victims of rape. When television is introduced into an area, the incidence of theft increases, perhaps due partly to television's promotion of consumerism, which may frustrate and anger economically deprived viewers who compare their life-styles with those portrayed on television.

It should be noted, however, that the research just described—that done by Gerbner and colleagues and by others—is correlational; that is, it shows merely an association, not a causal relation, between television viewing and beliefs. It is therefore impossible to determine from this research whether heavy viewing actually causes prejudiced attitudes and inaccurate beliefs or whether people already holding such attitudes and beliefs simply tend to watch more television. In order to be certain that watching TV causes such attitudes and beliefs, it would be necessary to perform a controlled experiment in which people are randomly assigned to conditions. Fortunately, some recent experiments do allow us to be fairly certain that heavy viewing does indeed determine the pictures we form of the world.

10   In a set of ingenious experiments, the political psychologists Shanto Iyengar and Donald Kinder varied the contents of evening news shows watched by their research participants. In their studies, Iyengar and Kinder edited the evening news so that participants received a steady dose of news about a specific problem facing the United States. For example, in one of their experiments, some participants heard about the weaknesses of U.S. defense capabilities; a second group watched shows emphasizing pollution concerns; a third group heard about inflation and economic matters.

The results were clear. After a week of viewing the specially edited programs, participants emerged from the study more convinced than they were before viewing the shows that the target problem—the one receiving extensive coverage in the shows they had watched—was a more important one for the country to solve. What is more, the participants acted on their newfound perceptions, evaluating the current president's performance on the basis of how he handled the target issue and evaluating more positively than their competitors those candidates who took strong positions on those problems.

Iyengar and Kinder's findings are not a fluke. Communications researchers repeatedly find a link between what stories the mass media cover and what viewers consider to be the most important issues of the day. The content of the mass media sets the public's political and social agenda. As just one example, in a pioneering study of an election in North Carolina, researchers found that the issues that voters came to consider to be most important in the campaign coincided with the amount of coverage those issues received in the local media. Similarly, the problems of drug abuse, NASA incompetence, and nuclear energy were catapulted into the nation's consciousness by the coverage of dramatic events such as the drug-related death of basketball star Len Bias, the *Challenger* explosion, and the nuclear-reactor accidents at Three Mile Island and Chernobyl. Former Secretary of State Henry Kissinger clearly understood the power of the news media in setting agendas. He once noted that he never watched the content of the evening news but was only interested in "what they covered and for what length of time, to learn what the country was getting."

Of course, each of us has had extensive personal contact with many people in a myriad of social contexts; the media are just one source of our knowledge about political affairs and different ethnic, gender, and occupational groups. The information and impressions we receive through the media are relatively less influential when we can also rely on firsthand experience. Thus those of us who have been in close contact with several women who work outside the home are probably less susceptible to the stereotypes of women portrayed on television. On the other hand, regarding issues with which most of us have had limited or no personal experience, such as crime and violence, television and the other mass media are virtually the only vivid source of information for constructing our image of the world.

The propaganda value of the mass media in painting a picture of the world has not been overlooked by would-be leaders. Such social policy as a "get tough on crime" program, for example, can be easily sold by relating it to the prime-time picture of crime as acts committed by the psychopathic and the greedy, rather than dealing with situational determinants such as poverty and unemployment. In a similar vein, it is easier to sell a "war on drugs" after the drug-related death of a prominent basketball star or to promote an end to nuclear power after a fatal tragedy at a nuclear reactor.

It is even more important for a would-be leader to propagate 15 his or her own picture of the world. The political scientist Roderick Hart notes that since the early 1960s, U.S. presidents have averaged over twenty-five speeches per month—a large amount of public speaking. Indeed, during 1976, Gerald Ford spoke in public once every six hours, on average. By speaking frequently on certain issues (and gaining access to the nightly news), a president can create a political agenda—a picture of the world that is favorable to his or her social policies. Indeed, one of President Bush's key advisors is Robert Teeter, a pollster who informs the president on what Americans think and what issues should be the topic of his speeches. This can be of great importance in maintaining power. According to Jeffery Pfeffer, an expert on business organizations, one of the most important sources of power for a chief executive officer is the ability to set the organization's agenda by determining what issues will be discussed and when, what criteria will be used to resolve disputes, who will sit on what committees, and, perhaps most importantly, which information will be widely disseminated and which will be selectively ignored.

Why are the pictures of the world painted by the mass media so persuasive? For one thing, we rarely question the picture that is shown. We seldom ask ourselves, for example, "Why are they showing me this story on the evening news rather than some other one? Do the police really operate in this manner? Is the world really this violent and crime-ridden?" The pictures that television beams into our homes are almost always simply taken for granted as representing reality.

Once accepted, the pictures we form in our heads serve as fictions to guide our thoughts and actions. The images serve as primitive social theories—providing us with the "facts" of the matter, determining which issues are most pressing, and decreeing the terms in which we think about our social world. As the political scientist Bernard Cohen observed, the mass media

> may not be successful much of the time in telling people *what to think*, but it is stunningly successful in telling its readers *what to think about*. . . . The world will look different to different people, depending . . . on the map that is drawn for them by writers, editors, and publishers of the papers they read.

Questions for Discussion

1. What are the "pictures in our heads" that the authors comment on? How do these pictures both resemble and differ from dreams and fantasies? How do they influence our political behavior and beliefs?

2. What conclusions can be drawn from George Gerbner's television program analysis? How have the experiments of Iyengar and Kinder on evening news shows and their viewers helped to correct and support Gerbner's research?

3. How are criminals usually portrayed on television? What impact does this portrayal have on our attitudes and beliefs? How have politicians used stereotypical portrayals of criminals and crime to "sell" their programs to the public?

4. Explain Bernard Cohen's distinction between the media's telling us what to think as opposed to telling us "what to think about." What does Cohen consider the media's most stunning success? What examples does he provide?

Ideas for Writing

1. Do some research into recent intensive media coverage of a political event or a controversial issue such as the U.S.-Iraq war and its aftermath. Write an essay in which you discuss the media's impact on the public's perceptions of the reality of the situation. You might take a look at some public opinion polls that were taken during the period you are discussing and examine typical stories aired on television and in the newspapers. How do you think the media shaped citizens' political beliefs on this issue?

2. Write about your attitudes toward a political issue covered extensively by the mass media; explain to what degree the media, as opposed to direct experience and conversation influenced your political views and social outlook. Were the media an accurate source of information?

Hate Radio

PATRICIA J. WILLIAMS

Patricia Williams (b. 1951), an outspoken critic of racial inequality and gender discrimination, is a lawyer and Professor of American Law at Columbia University. Williams received her J.D. from Harvard Law School in 1975. She has been a contributor to many publications and writes a regular column for *The Nation*, "Diary of a Mad Law Professor." Her books include *The Rooster's Egg: On the Persistence of Prejudice* (1995) and *Seeing a Color-Blind Future: The Paradox of Race* (1997). In the following essay that first appeared in *Ms Magazine*, Williams argues that right-wing talk radio is a degrading and socially dangerous media phenomenon.

───────── ✦ ─────────

Three years ago I stood at my sink, washing the dishes and listening to the radio. I was tuned to rock and roll so I could avoid thinking about the big news from the day before—George Bush had just nominated Clarence Thomas to replace Thurgood Marshall on the Supreme Court. I was squeezing a dot of lemon Joy into each of the wineglasses when I realized that two smoothly radio-cultured voices, a man's and a woman's, had replaced the music.

"I think it's a stroke of genius on the president's part," said the female voice.

"Yeah," said the male voice. "Then those blacks, those African Americans, those Negroes—hey 'Negro' is good enough for Thurgood Marshall—whatever, they can't make up their minds [what] they want to be called. I'm gonna call them Blafricans. Black Africans. Yeah, I like it. Blafricans. Then they can get all upset because now the president appointed a Blafrican."

"Yeah, well, that's the way those liberals think. It's just crazy."

5   "And then after they turn down his nomination the president can say he tried to please 'em, and then he can appoint someone with some intelligence."

Back then, this conversation seemed so horrendously unusual, so singularly hateful, that I picked up a pencil and wrote it down. I was certain that a firestorm of protest was going to engulf the station and purge those foul radio mouths with the good clean soap of social outrage.

I am so naive. When I finally turned on the radio and rolled my dial to where everyone else had been tuned while I was busy watching Cosby reruns, it took me a while to understand that there's a firestorm all right, but not of protest. In the two and a half years since Thomas has assumed his post on the Supreme Court, the underlying assumptions of the conversation I heard as uniquely outrageous have become commonplace, popularly expressed, and louder in volume. I hear the style of that snide polemicism everywhere, among acquaintances, on the street, on television in toned-down versions. It is a crude demagoguery that makes me heartsick. I feel more and more surrounded by that point of view, the assumptions of being without intelligence, the coded epithets, the "Blafrican"-like stand-ins for "nigger," the mocking angry glee, the endless tirades filled with nonspecific, non-empirically based slurs against "these people" or "those minorities" or "feminazis" or "liberals" or "scumbags" or "pansies" or "jerks" or "sleazeballs" or "loonies" or "animals" or "foreigners."

At the same time I am not so naive as to suppose that this is something new. In clearheaded moments I realize I am not listening to the radio anymore, I am listening to a large segment of white America think aloud in even louder resurgent thoughts that have generations of historical precedent. It's as though the radio has split open like an egg, Morton Downey, Jr.'s clones and Joe McCarthy's ghost spilling out, broken yolks, a great collective of sometimes clever, sometimes small, but uniformly threatened brains—they have all come gushing out. Just as they were about to pass into oblivion, Jack Benny and his humble black sidekick Rochester get resurrected in the ungainly bodies of Howard Stern and his faithful black henchwoman, Robin Quivers. The culture of Amos and Andy has been revived and reassembled in Bob Grant's radio minstrelry and radio newcomer Daryl Gates's sanctimonious imprecations on behalf of decent white people. And in striking imitation of Jesse Helms's nearly forgotten days as a radio host, the far Right has found its undisputed king in the personage of Rush Limbaugh—a polished demagogue with a weekly radio audience of at least twenty million, a television show that vies for ratings with the likes of Jay Leno, a newsletter with a circulation of 380,000, and two best-selling books whose combined sales are closing in on six million copies.

From Churchill to Hitler to the old Soviet Union, it's clear that radio and television have the power to change the course of history, to proselytize, and to coalesce not merely the good and the noble, but the very worst in human nature as well. Likewise, when Orson Welles made his famous radio broadcast "witnessing" the landing of a spaceship full of hostile Martians, the United States ought to have learned a lesson about the power of radio to appeal to mass instincts and incite mass hysteria. Radio remains a peculiarly powerful medium even today, its visual emptiness in a world of six trillion flashing images allowing one of the few remaining playgrounds for the aural subconscious. Perhaps its power is attributable to our need for an oral tradition after all, some conveying of stories, feelings, myths of ancestors, epics of alienation, and the need to rejoin ancestral roots, even ignorant bigoted roots. Perhaps the visual quiescence of radio is related to the popularity of E-mail or electronic networking. Only the voice is made manifest, unmasking worlds that cannot—or dare not?—be seen. Just yet. Nostalgia crystallizing into a dangerous future. The preconscious voice erupting into the expressed, the prime time.

What comes out of the modern radio mouth could be the   10
Iliad, the *Rubaiyat*, the griot's song of our times. If indeed radio is a vessel for the American "Song of Songs," then what does it

mean that a manic, adolescent Howard Stern is so popular among radio listeners, that Rush Limbaugh's wittily smooth sadism has gone the way of prime-time television, and that both vie for the number one slot on all the best-selling book lists? What to make of the stories being told by our modern radio evangelists and their tragic unloved chorus of callers? Is it really just a collapsing economy that spawns this drama of grown people sitting around scaring themselves to death with fantasies of black feminist Mexican able-bodied gay soldiers earning $100,000 a year on welfare who are so criminally depraved that Hillary Clinton or the antichrist-of-the-moment had no choice but to invite them onto the government payroll so they can run the country? The panicky exaggeration reminds me of a child's fear. . . . *And then, and then, a huge lion jumped out of the shadows and was about to gobble me up, and I can't ever sleep again for a whole week.*

As I spin the dial on my radio, I can't help thinking that this stuff must be related to that most poignant of fiber-optic phenomena, phone sex. Aural Sex. Radio Racism with a touch of S & M. High-priest hosts with the power and run-amok ego to discipline listeners, to smack with the verbal back of the hand, to smash the button that shuts you up once and for all. "Idiot!" shouts New York City radio demagogue Bob Grant and then the sound of droning telephone emptiness, the voice of dissent dumped out some trap-door in aural space.

As I listened to a range of such programs what struck me as the most unifying theme was not merely the specific intolerance on such hot topics as race and gender, but a much more general contempt for the world, a verbal stoning of anything different. It is like some unusually violent game of "Simon Says," this mockery and shouting down of callers, this roar of incantations, the insistence on agreement.

But, ah, if you *will* but only agree, what sweet and safe reward, what soft enfolding by a stern and angry radio god. And as an added bonus, the invisible shield of an AM community, a family of fans who are Exactly Like You, to whom you can express, in anonymity, all the filthy stuff you imagine "them" doing to you. The comfort and relief of being able to ejaculate, to those who understand, about the dark imagined excess overtaking, robbing, needing to be held down and taught a good lesson, needing to put it in its place before the ravenous demon enervates all that is true and good and pure in this life.

The audience for this genre of radio flagellation is mostly young, white, and male. Two thirds of Rush Limbaugh's audience is male. According to *Time* magazine, 75 percent of Howard Stern's listeners are white men. Most of the callers have spent their lives walling themselves off from any real experience with blacks, feminists, lesbians, or gays. In this regard, it is probably true, as former Secretary of Education William Bennett says, that Rush Limbaugh "tells his audience that what you believe inside, you can talk about in the marketplace." Unfortunately, what's "inside" is then mistaken for what's outside, treated as empirical and political reality. The *National Review* extols Limbaugh's conservative leadership as no less than that of Ronald Reagan, and the Republican party provides Limbaugh with books to discuss, stories, angles, and public support. "People were afraid of censure by gay activists, feminists, environmentalists—now they are not because Rush takes them on," says Bennett.

U.S. history has been marked by cycles in which brands of this or that hatred come into fashion and go out, are unleashed and then restrained. If racism, homophobia, jingoism, and woman-hating have been features of national life in pretty much all of modern history, it rather begs the question to spend a lot of time wondering if right-wing radio is a symptom or a cause. For at least four hundred years, prevailing attitudes in the West have considered African Americans less intelligent. Recent statistics show that 53 percent of people in the U.S. agree that blacks and Latinos are less intelligent than whites, and a majority believe that blacks are lazy, violent, welfare-dependent, and unpatriotic.

I think that what has made life more or less tolerable for "out" groups have been those moments in history when those "inside" feelings were relatively restrained. In fact, if I could believe that right-wing radio were only about idiosyncratic, singular, rough-hewn individuals thinking those inside thoughts, I'd be much more inclined to agree with Columbia University media expert Everette Dennis, who says that Stern's and Limbaugh's popularity represents the "triumph of the individual" or with *Time* magazine's bottom line that "the fact that either is seriously considered a threat . . . is more worrisome than Stern or Limbaugh will ever be." If what I were hearing had even a tad more to do with real oppressions, with real white *and* black levels of joblessness and homelessness, or with the real problems of real white men, then I wouldn't have bothered to slog my way through hours of Howard Stern's miserable obsessions.

Yet at the heart of my anxiety is the worry that Stern, Limbaugh, Grant et al. represent the very antithesis of individualism's triumph. As the *National Review* said of Limbaugh's ascent, "It

15

was a feat not only of the loudest voice but also of a keen political brain to round up, as Rush did, the media herd and drive them into the conservative corral." When asked about his political aspirations, Bob Grant gloated to the *Washington Post*, "I think I would make rather a good dictator."

The polemics of right-wing radio are putting nothing less than hate onto the airwaves, into the marketplace, electing it to office, teaching it in schools, and exalting it as freedom. What worries me is the increasing-to-constant commerce of retribution, control, and lashing out, fed not by fact but fantasy. What worries me is the reemergence, more powerfully than at any time since the institution of Jim Crow, of a socio-centered self that excludes "the likes of," well, me for example, from the civic circle, and that would rob me of my worth and claim and identity as a citizen. As the *Economist* rightly observes, "Mr. Limbaugh takes a mass market—white, mainly male, middle-class, ordinary America—and talks to it as an endangered minority."

I worry about this identity whose external reference is a set of beliefs, ethics, and practices that excludes, restricts, and acts in the world on me, or mine, as the perceived if not real enemy. I am acutely aware of losing *my* mythic individualism to the surface shapes of my mythic group fearsomeness as black, as female, as left wing. "I" merge not fluidly but irretrievably into a category of "them." I become a suspect self, a moving target of loathsome properties, not merely different but dangerous. And that worries me a lot.

20   What happens in my life with all this translated license, this permission to be uncivil? What happens to the social space that was supposedly at the sweet mountaintop of the civil rights movement's trail? Can I get a seat on the bus without having to be reminded that I *should* be standing? Did the civil rights movement guarantee us nothing more than to use public accommodations while surrounded by raving lunatic bigots? "They didn't beat this idiot [Rodney King] enough," says Howard Stern.

Not long ago I had the misfortune to hail a taxicab in which the driver was listening to Howard Stern undress some woman. After some blocks, I had to get out. I was, frankly, afraid to ask the driver to turn it off—not because I was afraid of "censoring" him, which seems to be the only thing people will talk about anymore, but because the driver was stripping me too, as he leered through the rearview mirror. "Something the matter?" he demanded, as I asked him to pull over and let me out well short of my destination. (I'll spare you the full story of what happened from there—trying to get another cab, as the cabbies stopped for all the white businessmen who so much as scratched their heads near the curb; a nice young white man, seeing my plight, giving me his cab, having to thank him, he hero, me saved-but-humiliated, cabdriver pissed and surly. I fight my way to my destination, finally arriving in bad mood, militant black woman, cranky femi-nazi.) When Yeltsin blared rock music at his opponents holed up in the parliament building in Moscow, in imitation of the U.S. Marines trying to torture Manuel Noriega in Panama, all I could think of was that it must be like being trapped in a crowded subway car when all the portable stereos are tuned to Bob Grant or Howard Stern. With Howard Stern's voice a tinny, screeching backdrop, with all the faces growing dreamily mean as though some soporifically evil hallucinogen were gushing into their bloodstreams, I'd start begging to surrender.

Surrender to what? Surrender to the laissez-faire resegregation that is the metaphoric significance of the hundreds of "Rush rooms" that have cropped up in restaurants around the country; rooms broadcasting Limbaugh's words, rooms for your listening pleasure, rooms where bigots can capture the purity of a Rush-only lunch counter, rooms where all those unpleasant others just "choose" not to eat? Surrender to the naughty luxury of a room in which a Ku Klux Klan meeting could take place in orderly, First Amendment fashion? Everyone's "free" to come in (and a few of you outsiders do), but mostly the undesirable nonconformists are gently repulsed away. It's a high-tech world of enhanced choice. Whites choose mostly to sit in the Rush room. Feminists, blacks, lesbians, and gays "choose" to sit elsewhere. No need to buy black votes, you just pay them not to vote; no need to insist on white-only schools, you just sell the desirability of black-only schools. Just sit back and watch it work, like those invisible shock shields that keep dogs cowering in their own backyards.

How real is the driving perception behind all the Sturm and Drang of this genre of radio-harangue—the perception that white men are an oppressed minority, with no power and no opportunity in the land that they made great? While it is true that power and opportunity are shrinking for all but the very wealthy in this country (and would that Limbaugh would take that issue on), the fact remains that white men are still this country's most privileged citizens and market actors. To give just a small example, according to the *Wall Street Journal*, blacks were the only racial group to suffer a net job loss during the 1990–91 economic downturn at the companies reporting to the Equal Employment Opportunity Commission. Whites, Latinos, and Asians, meanwhile, gained thousands of jobs. While whites gained 71,144 jobs at these companies, Latinos gained 60,040, Asians gained 55,104, and blacks lost 59,479. If every black were hired in the United States tomorrow, the numbers would not be sufficient to account for white men's expanding balloon of fear that they have been specifically dispossessed by African Americans.

25   Given deep patterns of social segregation and general ignorance of history, particularly racial history, media remain the principal source of most Americans' knowledge of each other. Media can provoke violence or induce passivity. In San Francisco, for example, a radio show on KMEL called "Street Soldiers" has taken this power as a responsibility with great consequence: "Unquestionably," writes Ken Auletta in the *New Yorker*, "the show has helped avert violence. When a Samoan teenager was slain, apparently by Filipino gang members, in a drive-by shooting, the phones lit up with calls from Samoans wanting to tell [the hosts] they would not rest until they had exacted revenge. Threats filled the air for a couple of weeks. Then the dead Samoan's father called in, and, in a poignant exchange, the father said he couldn't tolerate the thought of more young men senselessly slaughtered. There would be no retaliation, he vowed. "And there was none." In contrast, we must wonder at the phenomenon of the very powerful leadership of the Republican party, from Ronald Reagan to Robert Dole to William Bennett, giving advice, counsel, and friendship to Rush Limbaugh's passionate divisiveness.

The outright denial of the material crisis at every level of U.S. society, most urgently in black inner-city neighborhoods but facing us all, is a kind of political circus, dissembling as it feeds the frustrations of the moment. We as a nation can no longer afford to deal with such crises by *imagining* an excess of bodies, of babies, of job-stealers, of welfare mothers, of overreaching immigrants, of too-powerful (Jewish, in whispers) liberal Hollywood, of lesbians and gays, of gang members ("gangsters" remain white, and no matter what the atrocity, less vilified than "gang members," who are black), of Arab terrorists, and uppity women. The reality of our social poverty far exceeds these scapegoats. This right-wing backlash resembles, in form if not substance, phenomena like anti-Semitism in Poland: there aren't but a handful of

Jews left in that whole country, but the giant balloon of heated anti-Semitism flourishes apace, Jews blamed for the world's evils.

The overwhelming response to right-wing excesses in the United States has been to seek an odd sort of comfort in the fact that the First Amendment is working so well that you can't suppress this sort of thing. Look what's happened in Eastern Europe. Granted. So let's not talk about censorship or the First Amendment for the next ten minutes. But in Western Europe, where fascism is rising at an appalling rate, suppression is hardly the problem. In Eastern and Western Europe as well as the United States, we must begin to think just a little bit about the fiercely coalescing power of media to spark mistrust, to fan it into forest fires of fear and revenge. We must begin to think about the levels of national and social complacence in the face of such resolute ignorance. We must ask ourselves what the expected result is, not of censorship or suppression, but of so much encouragement, so much support, so much investment in the fashionability of hate. What future is it that we are designing with the devotion of such tremendous resources to the disgraceful propaganda of bigotry?

Questions for Discussion

1. What does Williams mean by the simile "the radio has split open like an egg"? What is coming out of the egg?
2. According to Williams, what underlying fears do racist talk shows prey on? What kind of generalized contempt do such radio programs express? Do you agree with Williams on this point? Explain. Do these programs have any positive impact on listeners?
3. Despite the emphasis in the conservative belief system on individuality, how does right-wing talk radio represent "the very antithesis of individualism's triumph"?
4. What power, according to Williams, do right-wing talk radio programs have to change the public's beliefs? What examples does she give to support her arguments about the power and the dangers of the medium? Can talk radio undermine the democratic process? How?

Ideas for Writing

1. Although freedom of speech is protected by the First Amendment, some believe that censorship of extremist hate speech in the media such as the radio or the Internet should be an option

in our society. Write an essay in which you take a position on the issue of censorship of hate speech on radio or the Internet.

2. In paragraph 25, Williams introduces a positive note in her essay through her example of the San Francisco radio show *Street Soldiers*. Write an essay in which you examine other examples of radio shows whose purpose is to act as a positive social force for overcoming hatred and violence.

The Internet: A Clear and Present Danger?

CATHLEEN A. CLEAVER

Cathleen A. Cleaver often contributes op-ed articles on subjects related to the protection of children and families. Currently she serves as counsel to the U.S. House of Representatives subcommittee on the Constitution. Cleaver was working in Washington, D.C., at the Family Research Council (a research and advocacy organization) as director of legal education when she delivered the following speech on Internet pornography at Boston University in 1997.

— ✦ —

- Someone breaks through your firewall and steals proprietary information from your computer systems. You find out and contact a lawyer who says, "Man, you shouldn't have had your stuff online." The thief becomes a millionaire using your ideas, and you go broke, if laws against copyright violation don't protect material on the Internet.
- You visit the Antiques Anonymous Web site and decide to pay their hefty subscription fee for a year's worth of exclusive estate sale previews in their private online monthly magazine. They never deliver, and, in fact, never intended to—they don't even have a magazine. You have no recourse, if laws against fraud don't apply to online transactions.
- Bob Guccione decides to branch out into the lucrative child porn market, and creates a Teen Hustler Web site featuring nude adolescents and preteens. You find out and complain,

but nothing can be done, if child pornography distribution laws don't apply to computer transmissions.

- A major computer software vendor who dominates the market develops his popular office software so that it works only with his browser. You're a small browser manufacturer who is completely squeezed out of the market, but you have to find a new line of work, if antitrust laws don't apply online.
- Finally, a pedophile e-mails your son, misrepresenting himself as a 12 year old named Jenny. They develop an online relationship and one day arrange to meet after school, where he intends to rape your son. Thankfully, you learn in advance about the meeting and go there yourself, where you find a 40-year-old man instead of Jenny. You flee to the police, who'll tell you there's nothing they can do, if child-stalking laws don't apply to the Internet.

THE ISSUE

The awesome advances in interactive telecommunication that we've witnessed in just the last few years have changed the way in which many Americans communicate and interact. No one can doubt that the Internet is a technological revolution of enormous proportion, with outstanding possibilities for human advancement.

As lead speaker for the affirmative, I'm asked to argue that the Internet poses a "clear and present danger," but the Internet, as a whole, isn't dangerous. In fact, it continues to be a positive and highly beneficial tool, which will undoubtedly improve education, information exchange, and commerce in years to come. In other words, the Internet will enrich many aspects of our daily life. Thus, instead of defending this rather apocalyptic view of the Internet, I'll attempt to explain why some industry and government regulation of certain aspects of the Internet is necessary—or, stated another way, why people who use the Internet should not be exempt from many of the laws and regulations that govern their conduct elsewhere. My opening illustrations were meant to give examples of some illegal conduct which should not become legal simply because someone uses the Internet. In looking at whether Internet regulation is a good idea, I believe we should consider whether regulation is in the public interest. In order to do that, we have to ask the question: Who is the public? More specifically, does the "public" whose interests we care about tonight include children?

CHILDREN AND THE INTERNET

Dave Barry describes the Internet as a "worldwide network of university, government, business, and private computer systems, run by a thirteen-year-old named Jason." This description draws a smile precisely because we acknowledge the highly advanced computer literacy of our children. Most children demonstrate computer proficiency that far surpasses that of their parents, and many parents know only what their children have taught them about the Internet, which gives new relevance to Wordsworth's insight: "The child is father of the man." In fact, one could go so far as to say that the Internet is as accessible to many children as it is inaccessible to many adults. This technological evolution is new in many ways, not the least of which is its accessibility to children, wholly independent of their parents.

When considering what's in the public interest, we must consider the whole public, including children, as individual participants in this new medium.

PORNOGRAPHY AND THE INTERNET

5   This new medium is unique in another way. It provides, through a single avenue, the full spectrum of pornographic depictions, from the more familiar convenience store fare to pornography of such violence and depravity that it surpasses the worst excesses of the normal human imagination. Sites displaying this material are easily accessible, making pornography far more freely available via the Internet than from any other communications medium in the United States. Pornography is the third largest sector of sales on the Internet, generating $1 billion annually. There are an estimated seventy-two thousand pornographic sites on the World Wide Web alone, with approximately thirty-nine new explicit sex sites every day. Indeed, the *Washington Post* has called the Internet the largest pornography store in the history of mankind.

There is little restriction of pornography-related activity in cyberspace. While there are some porn-related laws, the specter of those laws does not loom large in cyberspace. There's an implicit license there that exists nowhere else with regard to pornography—an environment where people are free to exploit others for profit and be virtually untroubled by legal deterrent. Indeed, if we consider cyberspace to be a little world of its own, it's the type of world for which groups like the ACLU have long fought, but, so far, fought in vain.

I believe it will not remain this way, but until it changes, we should take the opportunity to see what this world looks like, if for no other reason than to reassure ourselves that our decades-old decisions to control pornography were good ones.

With a few clicks of the mouse, anyone, any child, can get graphic and often violent sexual images—the kind of stuff it used to be difficult to find without exceptional effort and some significant personal risk. Anyone with a computer and a modem can set up public sites featuring the perversion of their choice, whether it's mutilation of female genitals, eroticized urination and defecation, bestiality, or sites featuring depictions of incest. These pictures can be sold for profit, they can be sent to harass others, or posted to shock people. Anyone can describe the fantasy rape and murder of a specific person and display it for all to read. Anyone can meet children in chat rooms or via e-mail and send them pornography and find out where they live. An adult who signs onto an AOL chat room as a thirteen-year-old girl is hit on thirty times within the first half hour.

All this can be done from the seclusion of the home, with the feeling of near anonymity and with the comfort of knowing that there's little risk of legal sanction.

The phenomenon of this kind of pornography finding such a   10
welcome home in this new medium presents abundant opportunities for social commentary. What does Internet pornography tell us about human sexuality? Photographs, videos, and virtual games that depict rape and the dehumanization of women in sexual scenes send powerful messages about human dignity and equality. Much of the pornography freely available without restriction on the Internet celebrates unhealthy and antisocial kinds of sexual activity, such as sadomasochism, abuse, and degradation. Of course, by its very nature, pornography encourages voyeurism.

Beyond the troubling social aspects of unrestricted porn, we face the reality that children are accessing it and that predators are accessing children. We have got to start considering what kind of society we'll have when the next generation learns about human sexuality from what the Internet teaches. What does unrestricted Internet pornography teach children about relationships, about the equality of women? What does it teach little girls about themselves and their worth?

Opponents of restrictions are fond of saying that it's up to the parents to deal with the issue of children's exposure. Well, of course it is, but placing the burden solely on parents is illogical and ineffective. It's far easier for a distributor of pornography to control his material than it is for parents, who must, with the help of software, search for and find the pornographic sites, which change daily, and then attempt to block them. Any pornographer who wants to can easily subvert these efforts, and a recent Internet posting from a teenager wanting to know how to disable the filtering software on his computer received several effective answers. Moreover, it goes without saying that the most sophisticated software can only be effective where it's installed, and children will have access to many computers that don't have filtering software, such as those in libraries, schools, and at neighbors' houses.

INTERNET TRANSACTIONS SHOULD NOT BE EXEMPT

Opponents of legal restrictions often argue simply that the laws just cannot apply in this new medium, but the argument that old laws can't apply to changing technology just doesn't hold. We saw this argument last in the early '80s with the advent of the videotape. Then, certain groups tried to argue that, since you can't view videotapes without a VCR, you can't make the sale of child porn videos illegal, because, after all, they're just plastic boxes with magnetic tape inside. Technological change mandates legal change only insofar as it affects the justification for a law. It just doesn't make sense that the government may take steps to restrict illegal material in *every* medium—video, television, radio, the private telephone, *and* print—but that it may do *nothing* where people distribute the material by the Internet. While old laws might need redefinition, the old principles generally stand firm.

The question of enforcement usually is raised here, and it often comes in the form of: "How are you going to stop people from doing it?" Well, no law stops people from doing things—a red light at an intersection doesn't force you to stop but tells you that you should stop and that there could be legal consequences if you don't. Not everyone who runs a red light is caught, but that doesn't mean the law is futile. The same concept holds true for Internet laws. Government efforts to temper harmful conduct online will never be perfect, but that doesn't mean they shouldn't undertake the effort at all.

15   There's clearly a role for industry to play here. Search engines don't have to run ads for porn sites or prioritize search re-

sults to highlight porn. One new search engine even has *sex* as the default search term. Internet service providers can do something about unsolicited e-mail with hotlinks to porn, and they can and should carefully monitor any chat rooms designed for kids.

Some charge that industry standards or regulations that restrict explicit pornography will hinder the development of Internet technology. But that is to say that its advancement *depends upon* unrestricted exhibition of this material, and this cannot be true. The Internet does not belong to pornographers, and it's clearly in the public interest to see that they don't usurp this great new technology. We don't live in a perfect society, and the Internet is merely a reflection of the larger social community. Without some mitigating influences, the strong will exploit the weak, whether a Bill Gates or a child predator.

CONCLUSION: TECHNOLOGY MUST SERVE MAN

To argue that the strength of the Internet is chaos or that our liberty depends upon chaos is to misunderstand not only the Internet but also the fundamental nature of our liberty. It's an illusion to claim social or moral neutrality in the application of technology, even if its development may be neutral. It can be a valuable resource only when placed at the service of humanity and when it promotes our integral development for the benefit of all.

Guiding principles simply cannot be inferred from mere technical efficiency or from the usefulness accruing to some at the expense of others. Technology by its very nature requires unconditional respect for the fundamental interests of society.

Internet technology must be at the service of humanity and of our inalienable rights. It must respect the prerogatives of a civil society, among which is the protection of children.

Questions for Discussion

1. Do you believe that the examples Cleaver lists in the opening of her essay violate our civil liberties and that legislation should be passed to make the types of behavior she describes illegal? Does this list seem like an effective way to begin the essay?
2. What does Cleaver believe to be the positive potential of the Internet? Why does it need regulation?

3. Why is Cleaver especially concerned about the impact on children of Internet pornography? Why is pornography on the Internet more dangerous to children than other types of pornographic material?
4. What specific suggestions does Cleaver have for regulating Internet pornography? Do her ideas seem clear and feasible to you?

Ideas for Writing

1. Cleaver asks us to "start considering what kind of society we'll have when the next generation learns about human sexuality from what the Internet teaches." Write an essay in response to Cleaver's claim that the Internet today significantly affects children's ideas of sexuality and gender role.
2. An alternative to Cleaver's proposal for restricting Internet pornography through government control would be to have parents monitor more closely their children's Internet use and to discuss sexual issues more openly with them. Write an essay in which you discuss the strengths and weaknesses of each approach, indicating which would seem to be more effective.

Media, Literacy, and Democratic Citizenship

Jeffrey Scheuer

Jeffrey Scheuer graduated with honors from Swarthmore College (1975) and received a M.S. from the Columbia School of Journalism. He is on the board of directors of several social service agencies and has published articles in many national journals and newspapers. He is the author of *The Sound Bite Society: Television and the American Mind* (1999; 2001), from which the following selection is excerpted. News analyst Daniel Schorr has written that *The Sound Bite Society* is "the most searching book I have seen on television's assault on our psyches and society."

———————— ◆ ————————

In a sound bite society, we cannot be critical thinkers without also being critical viewers; the application of critical skills to mass media is therefore an essential counterpart of critical thinking. Media literacy has been defined as "the ability to access, analyze, evaluate, and create messages in various media."⁹ Neil Postman uses the term "media ecology" to describe "how the media control the form, distribution, and direction of information, and how such control affects people's cognitive habits, political beliefs, and social relations." Like verbal literacy and critical thinking, it has several important aims: to teach young viewers how to distinguish reality from fantasy and artifice; to examine the distinct codes and cues of visual images, words, music, etc.; to distinguish and decipher commercial, political, and other types of messages; to detect the cynical and the trivial; and in general, to understand how television and other media frame and package information and entertainment, and their influence on viewers, consumers, and citizens.

Students who spend more time watching television than in classrooms, and who have viewed an average of 18,000 TV murders by the time they graduate from high school, must learn to resist television's power to isolate, manipulate, deceive, simplify, palliate, and disguise. They must learn to detect submerged meanings, assess motives, and deconstruct narratives—the very skills we teach them to apply to literature and writing in general. As the boundary between factual messages and advertising is increasingly blurred by "infomercials," "advertorials," and commercialized news, and as corporate advertising creeps insidiously into the school environment, students need to know how to evaluate commercial and political advertising, how news is shaped for a mass audience, and how truth, accuracy, balance, and context are compromised by other interests and imperatives. Moreover, just as literacy involves writing as well as reading, media literacy should include experience in producing and critiquing audiovisual messages. All curriculum development should promote critical thinking; media literacy in particular should be mandatory in the American school curriculum, as it is in Great Britain, Canada, Australia, and elsewhere.

Media literacy cannot focus on television to the exclusion of film, video, radio, music, or the Internet. It must encompass study of the exploding media universe, and its increasingly tenuous relationship to genuine knowledge. (Instead of allocating scarce educational dollars to hardwire American classrooms to the Internet, on the simple assumption that knowledge equates with access to facts, we might better devote those resources to raising the pay and competency standards of teachers.) Nor does critical viewing imply that TV is an evil or all-powerful medium, that it does not gratify legitimate needs and desires, or that children do not bring to it critical faculties of their own. Media literacy should explore TV's positive as well as its negative potentials and the controversies surrounding them. The purpose of critical viewing is not to shield people from television, but to enable them to use and enjoy it intelligently, while recognizing the legitimacy of its sedative and entertaining functions.

Yet, like critical thinking generally, media literacy has an unavoidable ideological dimension. Critical viewing is subversive because, like critical thinking generally, it imparts mental skills which dispositionally favor a more complex view, not just of how television frames and filters reality, but of television itself as a social organism, and of society as a whole. It is subversive because it transfers some of the power over the message and its interpretation from the mediators (typically commercial enterprises) to the audience—democratic citizens. It is inherently skeptical, egalitarian, and anticommercial. It posits motives, causes, and contextual factors that interested parties would prefer to ignore. Thus, media literacy is bound to offend conservatives who would deny its relevance to informed citizenship. Like the Wizard of Oz, media corporations and advertisers will inevitably oppose (or in more sinister cases, co-opt and corrupt) efforts to look behind the curtain and reveal how they manipulate.

5   But there is also an important, if limited, political counterclaim to be made here. Media literacy is not simply "proliberal" or "anticonservative." In principle, it should appeal to dignified conservatives who value individual opportunity and citizenship over corporate hegemony. Open societies must tolerate many moral complexities and ostensible contradictions, including some things that warrant critical scrutiny, or even condemnation, but not wholesale proscription. On paramount issues such as the value of informed democratic citizenship, which at least partly transcend ideology, thoughtful conservatives will side with liber-

als. In this sense, the critical thinking and viewing agenda is not just a liberal one but a broader democratic one.

CRITICAL DIALOGUE AND DEMOCRATIC CITIZENSHIP

Certain progressive goals in the twenty-first century relate to more nebulous aspects of the American political-media culture. For example, that culture would survive if it tolerated more open discussion of class. Progressives have a particular stake in ending this taboo because their views on the subject of class are at greater variance with the status quo. Class mobility exists in America, up to a point, as does stratification, with intertwining racial, ethnic, educational, and economic barriers. The existence of such barriers in a market-driven society—and the acceptable range, and the costs of eliminating or reducing them—are not just valid but crucial matters of debate. In a more mobile and egalitarian society there would be less to differ about; then, we could all become conservatives. As it is, we dream two American Dreams: in the rosier conservative one, we are a society without obvious or eradicable barriers to class mobility; in the liberal one, it is not so simple.

More broadly, a culture of critical thinking and viewing would demand higher standards for media, government, and citizens alike. For instance, it would demand greater journalistic accountability both ethically and intellectually, on matters such as integrity and fairness, concealed bias, diligence, accuracy, and news judgement. News producers and consumers alike should understand how television drives, alters, and distorts events— and how covering them differently, or not at all, might serve or disserve a wider public interest. This cannot be done by the media alone, or on a judicial model of self-appointed news councils. An excellent place to begin, with strong public support, would be to make a clear distinction between the private and public lives of public figures. It isn't so difficult. Journalists can learn to just say no.

A more media-literate nation would not tolerate news media that accept evasive answers from politicians or shrink from offending them with a follow-up question, or buckle under corporate threats of litigation should inconvenient facts be exposed to consumers. It would not brook the barring of reporters from a battlefield where Americans are fighting, or countenance contempt for the press on the part of public officials, which is properly regarded as contempt for the people. When a president plays on public mistrust of the media by treating reporters like a pack of baying dogs, or deflecting their questions amid the whir of a waiting helicopter, we should have the critical sense to be affronted at this insult to democracy.

A media-literate audience would be more critical, not less, of individual news media—but not reflexively critical. Instead of carping about media negativism, it would insist on getting the bad news as well as the good: "My country right or wrong," said Carl Schurz, "when right to be kept right; when wrong to be put right."

10   As it is, Americans' mistrust of the media, as of politicians, is often uncritical: not based on performance, or on democratic criteria, but questioning the very legitimacy of those institutions. This is not just a failure to recognize the abundant examples of journalistic excellence, but indifference to the functions of news media in a democracy. Such broad based delegitimation of the media (and of Congress) is not just a vague threat to a democratic culture; it's a deep flaw in the fabric. Like government, the Media R Us; we elect them, from the choices available, every time we buy a periodical or tune into a broadcast. And we elect them for terms of our own choosing, lasting minutes or seconds.

In the human mind, neuroses arise as conflicts within the self that affect our perceptions and relationships. Likewise, in the public mind certain uncritical myths, perpetuated by the media and politicians, function as collective neuroses that distort our perceptions and behavior and the very climate of debate. While typically containing grains of truth that strike deep emotional chords in the national psyche, they also represent failures of critical thinking, and the failure to acknowledge our collective capacity and responsibility for political action or inaction.

Among the salient examples of such neuroses are indiscriminate hostility toward political incumbents and toward the media—institutions which are currently perceived more as alien forces than as imperfect mirrors of society. The anti-incumbent neurosis ignores the fact that we freely re-elect some 98 percent of officeholders, as well as the main reason for high incumbency rates: the system of political finance. Thus, Republican enthusiasm for term limits was cured by the reality therapy of electoral success in 1994.

Public mistrust of the news media reflects a similar pattern. Many news outlets (like many politicians) are shallow, sensational, dishonest, inaccurate, or scurrilous. We should be more critical of the media for specific failures and lapses, such as self-censorship or allowing corporate influence on news decisions; but less critical of the media for performing their function as surrogate messengers and watchdogs. A blind mistrust of either sector is a civic neurosis. Politics is sometimes futile, and politicians and the media are sometimes corrupt; but to hold these beliefs reflexively only reveals the low self-esteem of American democracy. In fact, it matters very much how the news is reported, whom we elect to represent us, and how those representatives conduct our business. It matters because lives, freedoms, and billions of dollars are at stake, including our own.

A more critical attitude here requires that we make a series of elementary, but routinely ignored; distinctions. The most important such distinction is between the paramount value of a free press and the quality of its performance. Thus, in addition to media-literacy curricula, greater democratic accountability demands more public criticism of, and self-criticism by, the press. Broadcasting, in particular, is devoid of such criticism; like print and cyberspace, it needs more independent critics and ombudsmen. At the same time, every democratic citizen should be educated for and capable of some level of informed media criticism. News media are not an afterthought of democratic life.

Another elementary distinction that we routinely obscure, when it suits our rhetorical purposes, is that between fair criticism and censorship. We degrade the First Amendment by impressing it into use as a shield against all criticism. Criticism does not threaten freedom of speech; it is not censorship. We need to distinguish between the rightness of an utterance and the right to say it; between the message and the messenger; and between a proper respect for quality and what philistines call "elitism." The American media have many shortcomings, based on commercialism and on ordinary human imperfection; but a mindless contempt for the media based on fear and ignorance is not the answer to the real and remediable problems of gathering and telling the news. It is rather a kind of bigotry toward informed citizenship.

15

THE ATTENTIVE SOCIETY: JOURNALISM
AND IDEOLOGICAL LITERACY

E.J. Dionne, Jr., has written that, "Lurking beneath the widespread criticism of the media is the sense that something is deeply defective in the public debate itself and that the press is not taking on a role that it ought to embrace: to make that debate more accessible, coherent and honest." For that to happen, media producers and consumers alike must become more ideologically literate. We must begin with agreement about indisputable facts; that is one of journalism's essential functions. But facts are only where we start from. Interesting and important debates are never about facts per se; they are about how we interpret them, and which facts are more relevant to some larger question or principle. Interesting arguments are not about facts, but about values: in effect, about the extent and complexity of our role as our brothers' and sisters' keepers.

Ideology is like weather: we may not like it, but it won't go away. To suggest that it is bad or unnecessary is a form of denial which, like blanket contempt for the media or government, can only impoverish debate. Awash in sound bites and electronic propaganda, both political and commercial, in clashing images, personalities, and parties, young Americans need to understand the ideas and values underlying different points on the spectrum, and the nature of the spectrum itself. Conservatives should embrace their simplicity; progressives should take equal pride in an agenda based on a more demanding and complicated social compact.

Greater ideological literacy is especially needed in the news media, which both lead and follow society at large. This does not mean that journalists should share any particular outlook, or should become philosophers; rather, they need greater understanding of, and respect for, the range of democratic ideological debate. This applies equally, of course, to politicians and their spokesmen, pundits, academicians, and their audiences. In an ideologically literate society, politicians would identify with their visions, not blur them; citizens and journalists would respect both the legitimacy and the proper boundaries of partisanship. They would distinguish between the political strength of arguments and their moral force; between the political status of the left or the right at a given moment, and the validity of their claims or broader goals; between issues amenable to neutral problem solving and those on which there can never be complete political consensus. Such distinctions are frequently obscured in a sound bite society, and most often at the expense of the left.

We should distinguish, further, between fiscal prudence—government not spending more than it takes in—and fiscal priorities: how much, and for what purposes, the government should take in and spend. We should distinguish between government regulation in the public interest and authoritarian government; between our individual notions of the good life, and the collective value of our common freedom to pursue those individual goods. Making such distinctions is a quintessential liberal project, and one that dignified conservatives and radicals can share.

What E.J. Dionne, Jr. and Glenn Tinder have called an "attentive society" is not a grand mutual pursuit of truth; truth is crucial, but only as a premise for the conduct of dignified argument. Neither is it the pursuit of universal consensus on all important issues, which the complexity spectrum precludes. It is rather about a higher level of understanding and respect. As Christopher Lasch has written, "what democracy requires is vigorous public debate, not [just] information." In a society where journalists often wield more influence than public officials, the quality of political representation, public discourse, journalism, and mass education are closely intertwined. Like our schools, television has the potential to contribute to a more, and not less, attentive society. It is erroneous to suppose that what we teach our children, and what television teaches them, about tolerance, democratic conversation, or ideology, are not similarly intertwined. The objective of journalism, writes Dionne, should be

> to salvage [Walter] Lippmann's devotion to accuracy and fairness by putting these virtues to the service of the democratic debate that [John] Dewey so valued. This means, in turn, that journalism needs to be concerned with far more than its professional rules and imperatives.

Whatever their particular failings, the media as a whole constitute the only portion of the private sector that is protected by the Constitution and essential to the democratic process. That is why quality, and not just quantity or profits, is important. Among other things, we have lost sight of the purpose of journalistic competition; the public would be better served if journalists worried less about getting it first, and more about getting it best. Certain elements of the media inevitably will—and should—focus on

the impregnation of celebrities by alien visitors. But if the need
for bread and circuses cannot be dismissed, neither can the need
for quality in the flow of information relevant to democratic life,
and for education that builds the demand for it.

American journalism is founded on a glorious contradiction.
Virtually all of it is commercially based or market dependent,
even in the nonprofit sector. It is sometimes compromised, and
always limited, by that dependence and its attendant pressures.
In this sense, the media can't help being conservative. Yet while
the media must sell, they also have a democratic mission to inform, and to provide a forum for debate; and for these reasons the
journalistic enterprise has inherently liberal and democratic tendencies: tendencies which, contrary to their commercial foundations, challenge power, question authority, and empower ordinary
citizens by diffusing information more widely than corporate or
private interests would like. Thus, however ensconced in the private sector, serious journalism—like public libraries and public
education—also has an intrinsically egalitarian public purpose.

There are several important ways in which this dilemma can
be mitigated. One is a diverse and competitive environment of
media pluralism—which the present media oligopoly is not. Another is for the mainstream media to follow the polestar of being
fierce advocates—for democratic argument. The civic journalism
movement has got it half right: we need journalism that promotes
active and informed citizenship. What we don't need is journalism driven by surveys, opinion polls, or focus groups, which is
market research masquerading as democracy.

To service democratic debate, the media must understand
and respect all shades of opinion, and the dignity of ideological
argument. Television's harsh, impatient gaze—oriented toward
means and gamesmanship rather than ends, issues, or values;
quick to expose scandal and flaws of character, slow to consider
deeper motives or broader intentions or ideas—is part of the
problem. In its institutional cynicism it inhibits and ignores serious ideological debate; hence the persistence of the naive suppo-
sition that bipartisan "solutions" can be found to important problems, and that partisanship is merely a fog obscuring the real
political terrain, and not, in fact, the terrain itself. And when ideology is scanted, complex ideology is taxed disproportionately.

25   If facts are only a point of departure for democratic discourse, then journalism schools, an awkward anomaly within the
American university with no clear public purpose or intellectual

focus, ought to provide more than vocational training for the harvesting of facts (or worse, the unseemly commingling of truth and propaganda, in misalliance with advertising and public relations). To suggest that journalists are not merely brokers of information but educators, who should themselves be students of human values and society, is to realize both the vital role of the journalism profession and the deep impatience with real knowledge—about ideas, theories, and values—in American culture.

Instead of just teaching people how to produce journalism—a misuse of our national educational resources—we should teach them to be better critics and consumers of journalism. In effect, we need to relocate journalism education to the elementary and secondary levels, to educate younger Americans about the technical, economic, and moral imperatives of the media. In short, America needs less journalism education, and more media education. While the two are not mutually exclusive, it is far more important for kids to learn what goes into doing and using journalism, than for young adults to learn how to meet a deadline. And instead of just training and credentializing reporters, producers, and Webmasters, universities should prepare them for their wider role as educators.

Information—to return to our introductory theme—is indeed power. That is no mere sound bite. But there is also a deep and naive faith in American culture: that all information is equally useful, and we can never have too much of it; that a rising information tide lifts all boats; that information is somehow tantamount to wisdom, mastery, or sensitivity. We need more critical thinking and robust debate—not just the classic American quick fix of more technology. The Internet may be bountiful, but so is the local public library or the inspiring teacher. The Web won't save us, or make our children smarter, and neither will the simplistic policy of putting more computers in classrooms.

Real education—whether the medium be TV, video, computer, radio, a classroom, or a park bench—admits no such technological shortcuts. It is not about the glutting of minds with facts, but the culture of critical thinking and respectful debate. It is not, said Yeats, the filling of a pail, but the lighting of a fire. Commercial television, more than anything else in our society, under-cuts those values by inuring us, and our political and media surrogates, to solutions that are easy, visible, quick, cheap, short-term, and simple.

As Roderick Hart and others have urged, a new critical ethic of the moving image is needed for the twenty-first century. More than that, the sheer scope and complexity of the fusion between politics and the media warrant a new avenue of scholarly inquiry, combining the tools and techniques of media studies, moral and political discourse, and the social and information sciences, to explore the cognitive, psychological, political, and behavioral impact of all visual and interactive media, especially on children.

30   One option for the left, in the face of the corporate media oligopoly, lies in alternative sources of media production and distribution, in areas such as public access TV, microradio, and the Internet. The good news is that the cost of media production is declining; and here video, cable, and the Internet offer real possibilities. But so long as commercial television retains its dominance, and public television remains underfunded and subservient to political and private interests, market economics remains a powerful barrier to alternative voices. Ultimately, quality journalism, alternative or otherwise, will remain a ghetto until some information media are decommercialized, and until America invests more heavily in its schools.

Even with additional resources and channels, the structural barriers remain. These barriers at least partly explain why alternative programming efforts, in Graham Knight's words, "often turn out to be, in comparison with mainstream television, dull, long-winded, and sanctimonious. . . ." What is important, Knight concludes, "is not [the appropriation of existing] techniques per se (*as if they had some naturalized ideological essence*), [my italics] but rather how they are combined and used." This book has argued that there is precisely such a 'naturalized ideological essence' in the media, against the grain of which progressives must labor.

Questions for Discussion

1. What strategies for critical viewing and media literacy does Scheuer discuss? Why does he believe that it is important for these to become part of the mandatory school curriculum? Why is such media literacy "subversive" and likely to "offend conservatives"? What would a "media-literate nation" refuse to tolerate?

2. According to Scheuer, what is so dangerous about our current attitude of generalized hostility towards both politicians and the media? How would developing media literacy help us to reevaluate some of our blanket rejection of the media and politicians? Do you agree?

3. Why does Scheuer believe that ideological literacy within and in response to the news media is so greatly needed? Why are mere facts inadequate? What examples does he provide of important value distinctions that can be drawn through ideological literacy?
4. What are some of the reforms and strategies through which Scheuer believes the news media can achieve an "egalitarian public purpose"? Why is a college education in journalism inadequate as it is presently taught?

Ideas for Writing

1. Drawing on Scheuer's ideas and your own observations, write an essay in which you discuss and analyze both the causes for and ways to help people get beyond the blanket rejection of media information and politicians that leads many young people to feel alienated from public life and unwilling to exercise their fundamental citizenship right of voting.
2. Argue whether you believe that media-literate people would necessarily be any more engaged in citizenship and the nation's political decision-making than our current citizenry.

Independent Media Alternatives
DAVID BARSAMIAN

David Barsamian is the producer of the award-winning syndicated audio program *Alternative Radio*, which he founded in 1986. Barsamian is also the national producer of another weekly radio program, *Making Contact*, and is a regular contributor to *The Progressive* and *Z* magazines. His books include *Propaganda and the Public Mind* (1998) and *Conversations with Noam Chomsky* (1999). The selection that follows is excerpted from Barsamian's *The Decline and Fall of Public Broadcasting* (2001).

———————— ✦ ————————

More and more young people are taking to heart Jello Biafra's call to "Become the Media." They aren't just criticizing and complaining about the mainstream media; they're producing their own. This is very important not just for political reasons but also psychologically. While it is crucial to have an ongoing critique and understanding of corporate media, we have to produce alternatives.

Independent Media Centers (IMCs) are springing up all over the United States and around the world. They been instrumental, if not in reversing the tide of globalization, certainly in putting some roadblocks in its path. IMCs played a prominent role not only in organizing but in disseminating information about major demonstrations that took place during the past few years in Prague, Seattle, Washington, D.C., at the Republican convention in Philadelphia, and the Democratic convention in Los Angeles. They provided a demonstrator's-eye-view of these historic events with live and archival coverage that you couldn't see on television or read about in your local paper.

Independent media organizing has a long history. During the 1960s, underground newspapers, film collectives, and radio newswires were instrumental in bringing about political change and reached millions of people. Organizations like the Detroit-based Dodge Revolutionary Union Movement not only put out their own paper, they helped make an independent documentary film about their struggle. But indy media has experienced a renaissance since mass demonstrations shut down the World Trade Organization's ministerial meetings in Seattle, Washington, in November 1999.

In Seattle, more than 400 Internet, print, photo, radio, and television journalists converged to create an ad hoc newsroom and called it the Independent Media Center. Its goal was to make sure that protesters would not be silenced by corporate-owned media outlets and that the corporate media's version of events, "all the news that's fit to print," would not be the only one. The IMC produced up-to-the-minute coverage throughout the week of the protests.

5   When CNN, citing official police sources, reported that no rubber bullets were fired in Seattle, the IMC posted photos and video of the actual rubber bullets fired into crowds of clearly nonviolent demonstrators. The IMC web site was flooded with hits that day, and CNN had to change its story.

Since Seattle, IMCs have multiplied around the globe. Currently, around 60 IMCs are in operation across five continents.

"Of course, IMC prospects aren't all sunny," notes Eric Galatas, of Free Speech TV, a progressive television network based in Boulder, Colorado, who has worked closely with the IMCs.

Nearly two years into a non-hierarchical and consensus-based experiment, a formal decision making policy has yet to be adopted. More importantly, IMCs face the challenge of balancing the ratio of privileged and mostly white indy media contributors with youth, women, and people of color. A real commitment is essential to create IMCs that more accurately reflect the diversity of the communities most impacted by neoliberalism. And fundraising prospects are grim, in part due to a recent MacArthur Foundation decision to cut support for media centers. Who to turn to, when the only public funds available for media are reserved for corporate-friendly operations like PBS and NPR?

In spite of these hurdles, the IMC print team is now publishing a regular distillation of reports from international affiliates. This weekly two-page document is available in five languages. It's published as a PDF file, which means that anyone with access to the Internet can become their own printing press.

These are exciting intiatives taking place outside of corporate control. Independent presses like Odonian, Seven Stories, South End, and others are publishing radical books that are selling in large numbers. That's very encouraging. This is all the more remarkable as these books have virtually no publicity, and receive few reviews, even in the left press. A whole series of CDs with Angela Davis, Howard Zinn, and Noam Chomsky has also sold in the thousands. A lot of these digital recordings are circulating like *samizdat* in the old Soviet Union. MP3 technology is allowing for distribution in informal networks. New technologies are helping countercultural ideas reach a young audience that's completely turned off to NPR and PBS.

And while it is difficult to get on public radio and public television, you can do it, particularly outside the iron corridor that runs from Boston to Miami. In the rest of the country, it's somewhat easier to break through. So it's possible to get on the air in states such as Colorado and New Mexico. My program, Alternative Radio (AR), is aired on Montana Public Radio. One would think AR would be on in "liberal" Boston and have no chance at all in Montana, but it's just the opposite.

While there are several hundred NPR-type stations airing predictable fare, the U.S. has a fairly sophisticated community radio network. These stations range from big cities like Tampa to small towns like Astoria, Oregon. Many of these stations are also reaching out beyond their broadcast range through streaming audio

10

over the Internet. There are some excellent stations you can listen to now through this medium. The station that I'm rooted in, KGNU in Boulder, one of the best in the country, has a great mix of music, information, and news. You can now listen to it online. You can also hear WMNF in Tampa, Florida, and KUNM in Albuquerque, New Mexico, on the web.

If you want to hear "Democracy Now!" or "Making Contact," you can find out what time they're broadcasting on a particular station and tune into the live feed. Or you can often go to the show's web site and listen to archived broadcasts.

Another encouraging development in community broadcasting is grassroots radio. The Grassroots Radio Coalition (GRC) mission statement speaks about building the "cornerstones of participatory democracy." As the statement explains, "More than audio outlets, volunteer-based community radio stations are cultural institutions in their communities, reflecting the unique concerns and passions of the people who live there."

The grassroots radio movement in the United States grew organically within community radio as it became evident that community radio was falling prey to the negative forces of commercialization, corporatization, and homogenization which have infiltrated so much of the media, says Marty Durlin, station manager at KGNU in Boulder, "including public broadcasting."

The CPB has cut back support for such community broadcasting efforts, notably ending a provision that credited stations for volunteer hours worked at the station. "By rewarding the creation of new funding sources, including 'enhancing' and increasing underwriting and creating profit-making ventures," Durlin explains, "CPB shifted the burden of financial support away from listeners and federal funds and toward the commercial sector."

15   In response to these pressures, grassroots activists have tried to organize themselves to effectively counter the homogenization of the public airwaves. A network of community radio stations hosted the first Grassroots Radio Conference in Boulder, Colorado, in 1996, and have organized a series of successful gatherings since. The first conference had 85 participants, the second had more than 100, and the third had 130. Some 160 people participated in the 2000 gathering.

Such positive developments are also being extended into public television. Since May 2000, Free Speech TV (FSTV), the first full-time, progressive television channel in the United States, has broadcast 24 hours a day, seven days a week on Echostar's Dish Network. FSTV's roots are in the 90s Channel, started by John Schwartz, which broadcast into selected markets as a paid access station on the TCI cable system (now a part of AT&T). TCI's John Malone eventually forced the channel off the air through huge rate increases. After a failed legal battle, Mallone and others regrouped and launched FSTV in 1995, providing four hours a week of social documentaries to a network of 50 public access cable channels. Today, through a combination of its public access and dish outlets, FSTV estimates it reaches at least 10 million homes in the United States.

"The work of progressive producers and film-makers that is censored or screened out from PBS and corporate television is seen on Free Speech TV," explains Brian Drolet, Internet director for FSTV in Boulder. "Most significantly, FSTV provides a new national venue for grassroots organizations and activists." Like the IMCs, FSTV has played an important role in broadcasting news from protests around the globe, including live coverage of the protests at the Republican and Democratic conventions in Philadelphia and Los Angeles in 2000. FSTV plans to go on the road with a mobile studio in 2002, bringing stories that might otherwise be largely unheard to a national television audience.

Questions for Discussion

1. What are IMCs and what have they accomplished? What hurdles do they need to overcome?
2. What are some of the recent developments independent publishing and CD/MP3 distribution? How do these new outlets help spread countercultural ideas?
3. Distinguish "grassroots" radio from NPR stations. List several of the most interesting and effective developments in the grassroots community radio broadcasting that Barsamian discusses. How do these stations network to support one another and resist commercialization?
4. How is public television beginning to follow the lead of grassroots radio? What is Free Speech TV (FSTV)?

Ideas for Writing

1. Do some research into independent radio stations and write a paper that examines a number of the significant ways that this grassroots type of radio is broadening and deepening the coverage of crucial events in the United States and around the world.

2. Listen to Barsamian's *Alternative Radio* show on the Internet and do some research on the broadcasts by visiting its Web site; then write an informative and evaluative review of the program. In your final paragraph, discuss what important insights you have had through researching and writing this paper.

Rethinking Virtual Communities: The Prospects for the Public Sphere

HOWARD RHEINGOLD

Howard Rheingold has been writing about computer technology and its social implications since the early 1980s. He is also a science fiction writer and artist. He has been an editor of online magazines and was the founder of the online community Electronic Minds. His books on computer technology and its impact include *The Cognitive Connection: Thought and Language in Man and Machine* (1987), *Virtual Reality* (1991), and *Smart Mobs: The Next Social Revolution* (2002). The selection that follows is excerpted from Rheingold's *The Virtual Community: Homesteading on the Electronic Frontier* (1993; 2000).

———————— ✦ ————————

Will citizens use the Internet to influence the nations of the world to become more democratic? Or will our efforts be ineffectual or even work to amplify the power of state or corporate autocracies? All other social questions about the impact of life online are secondary to this one. . . .

In the first edition of *The Virtual Community*, I coined the neologism *disinfotainment* to describe that sphere in which special effects, television laugh tracks, manufactured "news" programming, and cross-media promotion of cultural products serve to distract and misinform a pacified population of unprotesting consumers, as well as to return profits to the owners of the cultural producers. I also dabbled in the work of Jürgen Habermas, because his notion of the "public sphere" intuitively seemed to me the best way to frame the political import of social cyberspace. If I can be allowed to temporarily jack up the theoretical infrastructure for a social theory of cyberspace I started building into the clear blue sky of 1993, I need to insert Adorno and Horkheimer's ideas.

Adorno and Horkheimer were concerned with the fusion between the culture industry and mindless entertainment. Amusement is specific to the twentieth century mass cultural industry and is simply another part of the cycle of routinization. Their attack on the culture industry, first published in 1944, claimed that mass art was based on "a medicinal bath" of amusement and laughter, rather than on transcendence or happiness (Adorno and Horkheimer, 1972). People were amused and liberated from the need to think and their laughter affirmed existing society.

Are virtual communities part of a last hold out from the commodification of media culture, a place of resistance and autonomy and self-empowerment? A place where we have a chance of seeing reality for what it is, so that we can refuse to accept the present and try to change the future. Or are they disinfotainment in the guise of antidisinfotainment? Is it another way to amuse ourselves to death? These are the key questions Adorno and Horkheimer would most likely raise about the new phenomena of social cyberspaces. . . .

The most serious critique of this book and the most serious   5
concern about the social impact of the Internet is the challenge to my claim that many-to-many discussions could contribute to the health of democracy by making possible better communications among citizens. It seems that a great deal of the critique, although not all, is directed at one specific paragraph. I wrote this in 1993:

> We temporarily have access to a tool that could bring conviviality and understanding into our lives and might help revitalize the public sphere. The same tool, improperly controlled and wielded, could become an instrument of tyranny. The vision of a citizen-designed, citizen-controlled worldwide communications network is a version of technological utopianism that could be called the vision of "the electronic agora." In the original democracy, Athens, the agora was the marketplace, and more—it was where citizens met to talk, gossip, argue, size each other up, find the

weak spots in political ideas by debating about them. But another kind of vision could apply to the use of the Net in the wrong ways, a shadow vision of a less utopian kind of place—the Panopticon.

Two of the criticisms directed at this paragraph have caused me to reconsider my original statement. The phrase "tool that could bring" has an implication of technological determinism that I simply let slip through because I wasn't paying sufficient attention. Now, I pay more attention when discussing the way people, tools, and institutions affect each other. It's not healthy to assume we don't have a choice. Tools aren't always neutral. But neither do they determine our destinies, immune to human efforts. The rest of the book isn't overly deterministic, but that paragraph is probably cited and challenged by dozens of scholarly essays over the years for reasons I have humbly come to understand.

Another flaw in my original draft is that I failed to make it clear that I was identifying, not advocating, the utopian version of an "electronic agora." I also should have mentioned that the affluent zeitgeist of Athenian democracy rested on the backs of slaves. As David Silver, one of the most thoughtful critical commentators, told me: "I'd make it clear in your new edition: neither Athens nor America nor cyberspace is a utopia."

I agree, now that critics have helped educate me. I would argue that we can still learn something from both experiments about the social nature of democracy, and about the influence of public communications on political action. . . .

In an age in which most of the journalism seen by most of the world is produced by a subsidiary of one of a few multinational entertainment companies, the question of what will remain truly "public" about communications is central today. It might not make sense tomorrow. If a theme park is all you know, you aren't going to be asking where all the real parks are. In America, the idea of "public property" has grown increasingly unfashionable in the physical world of freeways, malls, and skyscrapers. Is there still space in cyberspace for public property, public discourse, public opinion that emerges from informed deliberation among citizens?

10   Which brings us to the most serious challenge to the original draft of this book, that virtual communities might be bogus substitutes for true civic engagement or outright directly harmful to the public sphere. In 1995, two scholars, Jan Fernback and Brad

Thompson, presented a talk, "Computer-Mediated Communication and the American Collectivity," at the annual convention of the American Communication Association. With the permission of the authors, I've hosted it on my web site since then <http://www.Well.com/user/hlr/texts/VCcivil.html>. . . .

Perhaps the most useful point Fernback and Thompson raise is: "Ultimately, we believe, the hope placed in CMC is misplaced because change will occur not by altering the technology but by reforming the political and social environment from which that technology flows." If any population is to succeed in this alteration, are we to do it without tools? And assuming the success of such a reformation of the political and social environment, aren't we still faced with the challenge of learning how to use technology? Or are we to abandon the factories and office buildings and return to hunting and gathering? I agree, and must emphasize, that hopes placed in CMC or any technology are false hopes. Hopes must be placed in humans. I believe that knowing how to use tools is part of any successful human enterprise.

Fernback and Thompson's serious challenges must also be weighed in the light of reports such as Christopher Mele, who documents the story of how a group of low-income residents of public housing, all African-American women, used online communications to transform and empower the residents association in a two-year battle with the housing authority: "Once wired, it is difficult to predict the effects of online communication for collective action conducted by disempowered groups. For the women activists at Jervay, their connection to the Internet peeled away some of the historic and systematic layers that blanketed access to essential information. Whether it translates to long-term success is perhaps less important than the positive effect upon the activist role of the women themselves" (Mele, 1999).

The power to publish and communicate has no magical ability to make democracy happen. Only people can do that. No tool can make democracy happen without the actions of millions of people—but those millions of people won't succeed without the right tools. Most of what needs to be done has to be done face to face, person to person—civic engagement means dealing with your neighbors in the world where your body lives. But an important part of the work to be done will be mediated by new communication technologies. We need to relearn and continue to teach the communication skills necessary for maintaining healthy democracies.

Information sources and communication media that were until recently the province of the wealthy and powerful are used daily by millions. Discourse among informed citizens can be improved, revived, restored to some degree of influence—but only if a sufficient number of people learn how to use communication tools properly, and apply them to real-world political problem-solving. Surely, this opportunity is worthy of serious consideration. Surely, we owe it to ourselves to make an effort to discover whether the charges of Fernback and Thompson and other critics are true in practice as well as theory.

15 The global corporations that have consolidated control of distribution of news and entertainment will continue to command attention, reap profits, and exert influence. But they are no longer the only game in town. If there is one question that lies at the foundation of the uncertainty about the Internet's future it is whether the technical democratization of publishing will prove to be a credible challenge to existing publishing interests.

I believe the publicness of democracy has been eroded, for the reasons Neil Postman cited in *Amusing Ourselves to Death* (Postman, 1985): The immense power of television as a broadcaster of emotion-laden images, combined with the ownership of more and more news media by fewer and fewer global entertainment conglomerates, has reduced much public discourse, including discussions of vital issues, to soundbites and barrages of images.

In theory and a few practical examples, centralized opinion-shaping mechanisms are challenged by the decentralization afforded by many-to-many media. But that is far from saying that the future will be less manipulated and more freely chosen by informed citizens. Much remains to be done for that rosy scenario to become a reality.

Theories and opinions about the Internet are plentiful. A good question to ask is how many real online tools exist for citizens to use today? Are there examples of successful experiments in online civic involvement that ought to be widely replicated? As a definition of "civic involvement," I suggest the one offered in Robert Wuthnow's *Loose Connections: Joining Together in America's Fragmented Communities*: "Broadly conceived, civic involvement consists in participation in social activities that either mediate between citizens and government or provide ways for citizens to pursue common objectives with or without the help of government."

The public sphere is where Kim Alexander operates when her organization, the California Voter's Foundation <http://www.-

calvoter.org/aboutcvf.html>, uses email to organize a campaign to require political candidates to put their financial disclosures on the Internet. Civic involvement is what Paul Resnick and his students are trying to foster when they go door to door in their neighborhoods in Ann Arbor, Michigan, creating web pages and email lists intended to help people who live on the same block get to know one another <http://www.whothat.org>. The public sphere is what Steven Clift and colleagues at the Minnesota E-Democracy project <http://www.e-democracy.org> seek to extend when they bring candidates for state office online to publish position statements and field questions from citizens. A little investigation reveals that dozens, probably hundreds, of profit-making and nonprofit enterprises are experimenting with different tools for civic involvement. Among the most notable are:

- CapAdvantage <http://www.capitoladvantage.com/> for communication with officials, and other citizens. Their page, titled "Tools for Online Grassroots Advocacy and Mobilization," offers a comprehensive guide to Congressional publications, directories to identify state and national congressional representatives, spot news and issues tracking.
- E-The People <http://www.ethepeople.com/> for petitions. "Welcome to America's Interactive Town Hall: Where Active Citizens Connect with Their Government and Each Other"

  If your car is swallowed up by a pothole the size of Poughkeepsie, E-The People can help you find the person you need to tell about it. Simply come to our site, click on "roads and transportation," type in your address and we'll forward your note to the right officials in your city. And if your public works commissioner doesn't have Internet access, we'll convert your concern to a fax! Are you an organizer? With E-The People, you can start a petition about the same pothole and contact 10 neighbors to sign it—all on one site.

- Freedom Forum <http://www.freedomforum.org/> is a good example of vibrant discussion of political issues via message boards, along with Internet radio and news on rights. "The Freedom Forum is a nonpartisan, international foundation dedicated to free press, free speech and free spirit for all people."
- Civic Practices Network <http://www.cpn.org/> describes itself thus: "Born of the movement for a "new citizenship" and "civic revitalization," CPN is a collaborative and nonpartisan project

dedicated to bringing practical tools for public problem solving into community and institutional settings across America."
- The title of the Freespeech.org page <http://www.freespeech .org/>. is "Free Speech Internet Television."
- VolunteerMatch <http://www.volunteermatch.org> matches volunteers with opportunities, enables nonprofit organizations and potential volunteers to get together. Since 1987, CompuMentor <http://www.compumentor.org/> has provided volunteer-based technology assistance to nonprofits.
- National Strategy for Nonprofit Technology <http://www.nten .org/nsnt.htm> is "a leadership network of nonprofit staff members, funders, and technology assistance providers working together to analyze the technology needs of the nonprofit sector, and to develop a blueprint for how it can use technology more effectively and creatively."
- Guidestar <http://www.guidestar.org> is a clearinghouse for financial information: "Find information on the activities and finances of more than 650,000 nonprofit organizations, the latest news on philanthropy, and resources for donors and nonprofits."
- While many big organizations are incorporating donation activities into their web sites, smaller sites are going with a donation service like i-charity <http://www.i-charity.net/>: "Free Internet fundraising service and online donations portal."
- Cause-related marketing type services like GreaterGood <http://www.greatergood.com/> provide online consumers the ability to send a portion of product purchase prices to designated organizations: "Shop where it matters."
- VoxCap <http://www.voxcap.com> aggregates tools and resources for online civic engagement as well as for "building a community of engaged citizens, where social capital can be accumulated and brought to bear," according to Jeff Fisher, VoxCap's Director of Community Development.
- Two enterprising political satirists quit their jobs in the winter of 2000 and hit the road in a van, following the early stages of the presidential campaign from the road, updating their web site daily from their own zany and well-informed angle. The site <http://www.y2kwhistlestop.com/> is well designed and informative as well as funny. Perhaps political journalism might follow their lead and loosen up.
- The Association for Community Networking <http://www.bcn.boulder.co.us/afcn/> is a community of in-

terest and support for the hundreds of people working to use Internet communications to improve social capital in face to face communities.

• The Living Constitution Society <http://www.wethepeople.org> is dedicated to creating a continuous flow of interrelationship between government, industry, academia, citizens, and nonprofit organizations.

If the public sphere is where people act as citizens by discussing   20
the issues that concern them, and civil society is the general name for the associations that citizens organize for social, charitable, and political purposes, the name for the common wealth that they gain from acting cooperatively, in concert, rather than competitively as individuals seeking to maximize individual gain, is "social capital." Civic Practices Network defines social capital this way (http://www.cpn.org/sections/tools/models/social_capital.html):

> Social capital refers to those stocks of social trust, norms and networks that people can draw upon to solve common problems. Networks of civic engagement, such as neighborhood associations, sports clubs, and cooperatives, are an essential form of social capital, and the denser these networks, the more likely that members of a community will cooperate for mutual benefit. This is so, even in the face of persistent problems of collective action (tragedy of the commons, prisoner's dilemma, etc.), because networks of civic engagement:
>
> • foster sturdy norms of generalized reciprocity by creating expectations that favors given now will be returned later;
> • facilitate coordination and communication, and thus create channels through which information about the trustworthiness of other individuals and groups can flow, and be tested and verified;
> • embody past success at collaboration, which can serve as a cultural template for future collaboration on other kinds of problems;
> • increase the potential risks to those who act opportunistically that they will not share in the benefits of current and future transactions.
>
> Social capital is productive, since two farmers exchanging tools can get more work done with less physical capital; rotating credit

associations can generate pools of financial capital for increased entrepreneurial activity; and job searches can be more efficient if information is embedded in social networks. Social capital also tends to cumulate when it is used, and be depleted when not, thus creating the possibility of both virtuous and vicious cycles that manifest themselves in highly civic and uncivic communities.

The question of how to measure social capital is central to understanding the health of the public sphere. Indeed, as I will show later, there are those who question the idea that the social should be considered to be a form of capital. In an influential article, "Bowling Alone: America's Declining Social Capital" (*Journal of Democracy* 6:1, January 1995, 65–78), Robert Putnam documented a broad decline in civic engagement and social participation in the United States over the past 35 years. Citizens vote less, go to church less, discuss government with their neighbors less, are members of fewer voluntary organizations, have fewer dinner parties, and generally get together less for civic and social purposes. Putnam argues that this social disengagement is having major consequences for the social fabric and for individual lives. At the societal level, social disengagement is associated with more corrupt, less efficient government and more crime. When citizens are involved in civic life, their schools run better, their politicians are more responsive, and their streets are safer. At the individual level, social disengagement is associated with poor quality of life and diminished physical and psychological health. When people have more social contact, they are happier and healthier, physically and mentally.

Putnam concluded his article prescriptively:

> In the established democracies, ironically, growing numbers of citizens are questioning the effectiveness of their public institutions at the very moment when liberal democracy has swept the battlefield, both ideologically and geopolitically. In America, at least, there is reason to suspect that this democratic disarray may be linked to a broad and continuing erosion of civic engagement that began a quarter-century ago. High on our scholarly agenda should be the question of whether a comparable erosion of social capital may be under way in other advanced democracies, perhaps in different institutional and behavioral guises. High on America's agenda should be the question of how to reverse these

adverse trends in social connectedness, thus restoring civic engagement and civic trust.

The questions raised in Putnam's articles are about as serious as questions get: Is the social "glue" that holds together democratic societies going to dissolve as we retreat from civic participation into more private pursuits? If, as Putnam proposed in a follow-up article, "The Strange Disappearance of Civic America," (PS, American Political Science Association, winter 1996), the diffusion of television through the population over the past forty years was strongly correlated with the disintegration of civic participation during that time, it is indeed important to ask now which way the Internet might push us in the future—toward or away from authentic community and deep personal ties. Or are we using the wrong assumptions and terminology when addressing the way civic practices are changing, the way Wellman and Cerulo believe we are misframing social science research in cyberspace?

Another contemporary student of community, also a Harvard professor, Robert Wuthnow, recently wrote a book, *Loose Connections: Joining Together in America's Fragmented Communities* (Cambridge: Harvard University Press, 1998), that addresses the way social affiliations seem to be changing. These paragraphs describing the book <http://hupress.harvard.edu/Fall98/catalog/loose_connect .html> summarize Wuthnow's thesis, offering an alternative to Putnam's view of the changes that seem to be taking place:

> It has become common to lament Americans' tendency to pursue individual interests apart from any institutional association. But to those who charge that Americans are at home watching television rather than getting involved in their communities, Robert Wuthnow answers that while certain kinds of civic engagement may be declining, innovative new forms are taking their place.
>
> Acknowledging that there has been a significant change in group affiliations—away from traditional civic organizations— Wuthnow shows that there has been a corresponding movement toward affiliations that respond to individual needs and collective concerns. Many Americans are finding new and original ways to help one another through short-term task-oriented networks. Some are combining occupational skills with community interests in nonprofit and voluntary associations. Others use communication technologies, such as the World Wide Web, to connect with like-minded people in distant locations. And people

are joining less formal associations, such as support groups and lobbying efforts, within their home communities.

People are still connected, but because of the realities of daily life, they form "loose connections." These more fluid groups are better suited to dealing with today's needs than the fraternal orders and ladies' auxiliaries of the past. Wuthnow looks at the challenges that must be faced if these innovative forms of civic involvement are to flourish, and calls for resources to be made available to strengthen the more constructive and civic dimensions of these organizations. . . .

Outlining a program for measuring the health of civil society and defining social capital in a way that doesn't transform human relationships into commodities is beyond the scope of this book. However, it is at the very heart of the kinds of discussions that must take place on a broad basis, online and offline, among millions of people. It is in the service of this broad, citizen-driven, democratic discourse that online tools for publishing and communicating hold out a hope. If online community is NOT a commodity, it is only because people work to make it so. The hope I hold out for myself and suggest to others is that people will accomplish a task using a tool. Hope should not be vested in the tool itself. One important way of using tools wisely is informed government regulation. A tax break for corporations that donate to the public sphere, for example, might do more good than all the rhetoric and all the books decrying the deterioration of civic engagement. Consider the following scenario, not as a recipe for utopia, but a thought-experiment.

A tiny proportion of the gargantuan profits reaped by telecommunications service providers could be contributed to a well-managed fund (with its own budget and expenditures open for public inspection) that insures that every citizen has access to publicly available terminals, a free email account, and free access to introductory classes on citizen use of the Net. In a world where everyone has affordable access and citizens become actively engaged in informing themselves and communicating with one another, will it be possible to make government more responsive to citizen needs—and perhaps more responsible to the public trust? All proceedings and filings at the city, state, and national level could be made available to all citizens in dynamically updated databases, with easy-to-use web interfaces. GIS systems could enable citizens to visualize the impacts of proposed development on regional cultural and ecosystems. We could know when our legislators trade stock in companies their legislation affects.

The scenario offered in the previous paragraph is offered as an example of what I believe we should work to build, not as an unattainably ideal society expected to emerge magically from technology. There is no guarantee that the potential power of many-to-many communications will make a difference in political battles about the shape of our future. Indeed, the odds are against a media-literate population seizing the opportunities the Internet offers. But I believe the opportunity for leverage is there, waiting to be seized, ignored, or mishandled. The hegemony of culture, power, and capital that critics from Marx to Fernback and Thompson describe is a potent force to be reckoned with. But if we don't try to make a difference in the way tools are used and people are treated, we definitely *won't* make a difference.

The first step in acting effectively is to know what you are acting on. Collectively, we know only a small amount about human behavior in social cyberspaces. We need to know a lot more. I hope that this chapter helps inspire and orient those who pursue that knowledge, debate its meaning, and put it into action in meaningful ways.

Questions for Discussion

1. What is meant by the term "disinfotainment"? How do Adorno and Horkheimer's ideas reflect on this phenomenon? How does disinfotainment challenge the validity of virtual communities?

2. How does Rheingold counter the criticism that "virtual communities might be bogus substitutes for true civic engagement"? How do Christopher Mele's reports support the efficacy and real-life contributions of online communities?

3. How is the measuring of social capital "central to understanding the health of the public sphere"? Using the social capital measurement, how healthy is American society today? In contrast, how does Wuthnow's idea of "loose connections" suggest that we might be doing better in terms of civic interaction than traditional social critics believe?

4. What hope does Rheingold hold out in his conclusion? What does he believe we need to do and to learn in order to establish strong online communities that will make a difference in reviving democracy?

Ideas for Writing

1. Do some research into community building and activism using computers and the Internet over the last decade; then write an essay in which you consider whether computer-mediated communities have shown potential for reviving democracy in the public sphere.

2. Pick one of the criticisms of electronic technology that Rheingold develops in his essay and do some further research into it. How serious a threat is the misuse of electronic technology such as the Internet to our personal freedom and privacy, sense of reality, and/or sense of ourselves as citizens in a democracy?

Extending the Theme

1. Pratkanis and Aronson, Williams, and Cleaver all discuss the ways that media influence our impressions of the realities of being a citizen in the United States. Contrast the causal relationships that each of the authors perceives between the media and our beliefs about the realities of politics, sexuality, and criminals. Whose point of view do you find most accurate? How did these writers help you to more fully understand the impact of the media on our identities as citizens?

2. Scheuer, Barsamian, and Rheingold present different perspectives on the relationships between the media and democratic citizenship. Contrast the writers' views and discuss how their arguments help you better understand how the media help define democracy in the United States. Include your own point of view on the impact that the media have had, using examples from your own experiences when relevant.

3. Compare the views of Barsamian and Rheingold on the importance of independent media as vehicles for social change. Do further research into the subject and write an essay that reflects your point of view.

4. Observe the functioning of an alternative medium such as alternative public radio or television, independent journals, newspapers, or Web sites devoted to social change. If possible, interview those in charge of an organization and do research into the organization's impact and success. Draw some conclusions about the efficacy of alternative media in helping shape citizens' political and social beliefs and behavior.

The Public
Citizen

"No man can enjoy the privileges of education and thereafter with a clear conscience break his contract with society. To respect that contract is to be mature, to strengthen it is to be a good citizen, to do more than your share under it is noble."

ISAIAH BOWMAN, PRESIDENT OF JOHN HOPKINS UNIVERSITY, 1935–1948

"The fundamental law of human beings is interdependence. A person is a person through other persons."

BISHOP DESMOND TUTU

"We are supposed to preach without preaching not by words, but by our example, by our actions. All works of love are works of peace."

MOTHER TERESA

In this chapter, we move from considerations of individual rights, entertainment, and the world of the private citizen to the role of the citizen in the public realm. In recent years, voting in national and state elections has reached an all-time low in the United States; on the other hand, we have seen a remarkable rise in the level of citizen commitment to various forms of public service and social activism. Many secondary schools and colleges make service learning a requirement—both students and adults are working for non-profit organizations caring for the impover-ished and the environment, joining the Teacher Corps, or working for groups dedicated to ending discrimination and war. Why do so many people today choose to serve as volunteers or for minimal financial rewards in a society that seems to value material success and consumerism? The quotations above and the essays that follow in this chapter give us some insights into the changing devotion to activism and service in today's communities. Many citizens believe, as Isaiah Bowman did, that a good citizen has a contract with society which is realized and strengthened through service and engagement with the struggle to improve the quality of life for all citizens. As Bishop Desmond Tutu says in the quotation above, "The fundamental law of human beings is interdependence." We become fully human through helping others.

In the first essay in this chapter, "The Moral Obligations of Living in a Democratic Society," Cornel West argues that America needs a renewed democratic sensibility that acknowledges and works actively in the public interest to help the most disadvantaged in our society. We need to go beyond the current market culture that focuses on the individual and work together with hope and empathy for a better future for all Americans. Next, Charles Derber, in his essay "Civic Responsibility," proposes an idea of social citizenship that extends the rights defined and protected in our Constitution to include affirmative rights and obligations on both the government and citizens. Derber believes claims that all citizens of the United States should have the right to food, health care, shelter, and a healthy environment.

The next two essays move from a focus on theories of social action to examples of individuals who have devoted their lives to serving others and improving society. Anti-AIDS activist Cleve Jones tells how his vision of the AIDS quilt gave birth to one of the best-known national and international statements about the losses suffered because of the AIDS epidemic. In her speech "The Artist as Citizen," actress and singer Barbra Streisand argues for the continuation of federal funding for the arts and for a recognition of the value of the contributions that artists make as good citizens when they perform in fund-raising benefits and create works that draw attention to important social issues.

Our next selection, "A Match Made in Heaven," social rights activist Suzanne Pharr illuminates an important aspect of social activism that is often overlooked. Through her dialogue with a member of the Christian men's group the Promise Keepers, Pharr demonstrates how important it is for activists to be able to listen to and communicate their ideas to people and organizations that have different values and political agendas. Our final article by Lani Guinier, "The Tyranny of the Majority," examines a fundamental and yet often-neglected aspect of the citizen's engagement with the political process, the act of voting. Guinier explains various alternatives to winner-take-all solutions in voting. She believes that such voting and leadership methods will lead to better dialogue and intergroup communication that is necessary to create a meaningful consensus form of decision making in public affairs and government.

Becoming a public citizen has more responsibilities than many Americans have considered. Now is the time to think about what obligations you want to fulfill as a citizen and how the action of serving others can enrich your own life as a public citizen and a human being.

The Moral Obligations of Living in a Democratic Society

CORNEL WEST

Cornel West (b. 1953) earned his M.A. at Princeton University in 1975 and his Ph.D. at Union Theological Seminary in 1980. West has taught at Yale, Princeton, and Harvard universities. The ideas and traditions of the Baptist Church, European Liberal Philosophy, American Transcendentalism, Democratic Populism, and the Black Panther Party have influenced his work. West, the author of many books, is best known for *Beyond Eurocentrism and Multiculturalism* (1992) and *Race Matters* (1993). The piece that follows is included in the anthology *The Good Citizen*.

---------------- ✦ ----------------

One of the fundamental questions of our day is whether the tradition of struggle can be preserved and expanded. I refer to the struggle for decency and dignity, the struggle for freedom and democracy.

In *Tradition and Individual Talent* (1919) T. S. Eliot claims that tradition is not something you inherit—if you want it, you must sacrifice for it. In other words, tradition must be fought for. . . .

In any discussion about race matters it is vital to situate your-self in a tradition, in a larger narrative that links the past to the present. When we think of Sojourner Truth, Harriet Tubman, Ida Buelle, Wells Barnett. A. Philip Randolph, Marcus Garvey, Ella Baker, James Baldwin, and so many nameless and anonymous ones, we cannot but be moved by their standards of vision and courage. They are wind at one's back.

The recovery of a tradition always begins at the existential level, with the experience of what it is to be human under a specific set of circumstances and conditions. It is very difficult to engage in a candid and frank critical discussion about race by assuming it is going to be a rational exchange. Race must be addressed in a form that can deal with its complexity and irrationality.

5   Perhaps no one understood the existential dimension of be-ing human and African in America better than W. E. B. Du Bois. He recognized the absurd in American society and realized that being Black in America is to be a problem. Du Bois asserted that race in this country is the fetishization of a problem, black bodies in white space. He understood what it meant to be cast as part of a problem people rather than people with problems. Once the hu-manity of a people is problematized, they are called into question perennially. Their beauty is attacked: wrong hips, lips, noses, skin texture, skin pigmentation, and hair texture. Black intelligence is always guilty before proven innocent in the court of the life of the mind: *The Bell Curve* is just a manifestation of the cycle. Perhaps the gravest injustice is the image of the welfare queen. Looking at the history of black women in America, on the plantation taking care of white children in white households, how is it possible that they could become the symbol of laziness? All of the foregoing are signs of a humanity that has been problematized.

Du Bois also underscored that to be part of a problem people is to be viewed as part of an undifferentiated blob, a monolithic block. Problem people become indistinguishable and inter-changeable, which means that only one of them has to be asked to find out what all the rest of them think.

It is rare in human history, of course, that the notion of indi-viduality and the civic are coupled so that a democratic project is generated. For most of history ordinary people have been viewed as "weeds and rain drops," as part of a mob, a rabble, all of which are ways of constituting them as an undifferentiated mob. Even the Greeks, despite their glorious yet truncated democratic exper-iment, would only apply the tragic to the elite. Ordinary people were limited to the idyllic and the comic, the assumption being that their lives were less complex and one-dimensional.

A democratic sensibility undeniably cuts against the grain of history. Most of human history is the history of elites, of kings, queens, princes, prelates, magistrates, potentates, knights, earls, and squires, all of whom subordinated and exploited everyday people.

This is why it becomes vital to talk about prevailing forms of oligarchy and plutocracy, and to some degree "pigmentocracy," in America. One percent of the population owns 48 percent of the total net financial wealth. The top 10 percent owns 86 percent of the wealth, while the top 20 percent owns 94 percent of the wealth. Meanwhile, 80 percent of the population is experiencing stagnating and declining wages.

Corporations speak glibly about downsizing—bureaucratic   10 language that simply means you do not have a job even though we have the highest profits we have had since 1948. And yet 25 percent of all of America's children live in poverty, and 42 percent of young brown brothers and sisters live in poverty, and 51 percent of young black brothers and sisters live in poverty in the richest nation in the history of the world. These sets of conditions are immoral.

When I examine the present state of American democracy, I believe we are living in one of the most terrifying moments in the history of this nation. We are experiencing a lethal and unprecedented linkage of relative economic decline (i.e., working class wage stagnation), cultural decay, and political lethargy. No democracy can survive with a middle class so insecure that it is willing to accept any authoritarian option in order to provide some sense of normalcy and security in their lives. It also opens the door for significant segments of that middle class to scapegoat those who are most vulnerable.

It is past time that we consider in our public discourse the civic responsibilities of corporations. There must be prescribed forms of public accountability for institutions that have a disproportionate amount of wealth, power, and influence. This is not a matter of demonizing corporations, but an issue of democratic survival.

We are all in the same boat, on the same turbulent sea. The boat has a huge leak in it and in the end, we go up and down together. A corporate executive recently said to me, "We are not in the same boat. We're global." His response suggests why it is vital to inquire when corporate commercial interests must be subordinate to the public interest.

Democracy always raises the fundamental question: What is the role of the most disadvantaged in relation to the public interest? It is similar in some ways to the biblical question: What are you to do with the least of these? If we do not want to live in a democracy, we are not obliged to raise that question. In fact, the aristocracy does not address that question at all. Chekhov wrote in a play. "The Czar's police, they don't give a damn about raising that question. That's not the kind of society they are." But within a democratic society that question must be continually raised and pushed.

15   The conversation matters because the preservation of democracy is threatened by real economic decline. While it is not identical to moral and cultural decay, it is inseparable from it. Even though the pocketbook is important, many Americans are concerned more about the low quality of their lives, the constant fear of violent assault and cruel insult, the mean spiritedness and cold heartedness of social life, and the inability to experience deep levels of intimacy. These are the signs of a culturally decadent civilization.

By "decadent" I mean the relative erosion of systems of nurturing and caring, which affects each of us, but which has an especially devastating impact on young people. Any civilization that is unable to sustain its networks of caring and nurturing will generate enough anger and aggression to make communication near impossible. The result is a society in which we do not even respect each other enough to listen to each other. Dialogue is the lifeblood of democracy and is predicated on certain bonds of trust and respect. At this moment of cultural decay, it is difficult to find places where those ties of sympathy may be nurtured.

The roots of democracy are fundamentally grounded in mutual respect, personal responsibility, and social accountability. Yet democracy is also about giving each person a dignified voice in the decision-making processes in those institutions that guide and regulate their lives. These deeply moral suppositions have a certain spiritual dimension. John Dewey and Josiah Royce, among others, identified a spirituality of genuine questioning and dialogical exchange that allows us to transcend our egocentric predicaments. Spirituality requires an experience of something bigger than our individual selves that binds us to a community. It could be in an authoritarian bind, of course, which is why the kind of spiritual and moral awakening that is necessary for a democracy to function is based on a sense of the public—a sense of what it is to be a citizen among citizens.

Nurturing spirituality is so difficult today because we are bombarded by a market culture that evolves around buying and selling, promoting and advertising. The market tries to convince us that we are really alive only when we are addicted to stimulation and titillation. Given the fact that so much of American culture revolves around sexual foreplay and orgiastic intensity, for many people the good life might mean being hooked up to an orgasm machine and being perennially titillated.

The ultimate logic of a market culture is the gangsterization of culture: I want power now. I want pleasure now. I want property now. Your property. Give it to me.

Young black people call their block a "hood" now. I grew up   20
in a neighborhood; it is a big difference. A neighborhood was a place not only for the nuclear family, but also included aunts and uncles, friends and neighbors, rabbis and priests, deacons and pastors, Little League coaches and dance teachers—all of whom served as a backdrop for socializing young people. This backdrop provided children with a sense of what it is to be human, with all its decency, integrity, and compassion. When those values are practiced, a neighborhood emerges.

Unfortunately, neighborhoods often took shape in my boyhood under patriarchal and homophobic conditions, and that history must be called into question. Still, we must recover its flow of nonmarket values and nonmarket activity.

These days we cannot even talk about love the way James Baldwin and Martin Luther King Jr. did. Nobody wants to hear that syrupy, mushy stuff. James Baldwin, however, said love is the most dangerous discourse in the world. It is daring and difficult because it makes you vulnerable, but if you experience it, it is the peak of human existence.

In our own time it is becoming extremely difficult for nonmarket values to gain a foothold. Parenting is a nonmarket activity; so much sacrifice and service goes into it without any assurance that the providers will get anything back. Mercy, justice; they are nonmarket. Care, service; nonmarket. Solidarity, fidelity; nonmarket. Sweetness and kindness and gentleness. All nonmarket.

Tragically, nonmarket values are relatively scarce, which is one of the reasons why it is so tough to mobilize and organize people in our society around just about any cause. It is hard to convince people that there are alternative options for which they ought to sacrifice. Ultimately, there can be no democratic tradition without nonmarket values.

In the last decade we have witnessed within popular culture   25
wonderful innovation in forms of hip hop and rap. Compare that phenomenon to the 1960s when the Black Panther Party emerged

and note the big difference between the two movements. One has to do with sacrifice, paying the price, dealing with the consequences as you bring power and pressure to bear on the prevailing status quo. The other has to do with marketing black rage. One movement had forty-seven local branches across the nation, the other sells millions of albums and CDs. The comparison is not a matter of patronizing this generation. Frankly, it is a critique of each us who has to deal with this market culture and through market mechanisms try to preserve some nonmarket values.

What then are we to do? There is no overnight solution or panacea, of course. We need to begin with something profoundly un-American, namely, recalling a sense of history, a very deep, tragic, and comic sense of history, a historical sensibility linked to empathy. Empathy is not simply a matter of trying to imagine what others are going through, but having the will to muster enough courage to do something about it. In a way, empathy is predicated upon hope.

Hope has nothing to do with optimism. I am in no way optimistic about America, nor am I optimistic about the plight of the human species on this globe. There is simply not enough evidence that allows me to infer that things are going to get better. That has been the perennial state and condition of not simply black people in America, but all self-conscious human beings who are sensitive to the forms of evil around them. We can be prisoners of hope even as we call optimism into question.

To be part of the democratic tradition is to be a prisoner of hope. And you cannot be a prisoner of hope without engaging in a form of struggle in the present moment that keeps the best of the past alive. To engage in that struggle means that one is always willing to acknowledge that there is no triumph around the corner, but that you persist because you believe it is right and just and moral. As T. S. Eliot said, "Ours is in the trying. The rest is not our business."

We are not going to save each other, ourselves, America, or the world. But we certainly can leave it a little bit better. As my grandmother used to say. "If the Kingdom of God is within you, then everywhere you go, you ought to leave a little Heaven behind."

Questions for Discussion

1. How does West define the "tradition of struggle"? Why is it so important that we recover this struggle? Do you agree with him?

2. What is the significance of the casting of African Americans as a "problem people" as opposed to being "people with problems"? What happens once the humanity of a people is problematized?

3. West says, "Democracy always raises the fundamental question: What is the role of the most disadvantaged in relation to the public interest?" What examples does he give to demonstrate that America is a "culturally decadent civilization"? Why does West believe that our country's market values make democracy impossible?

4. What is West's solution to revitalizing democracy and escaping the domination of market values? Why does he place more emphasis on hope than on optimism?

Ideas for Writing

1. Write an essay in which you explain why you agree or disagree with West's analysis of the failure of democracy in the United States today. Present examples of the actions of institutions and events to support your point of view.

2. Write a profile of a socially active organization that works to help realize the ideals of a democratic society. Discuss the principles of this organization and how it manages its workers and implements its programs. Report on the positive outcomes that the program has achieved.

Civic Responsibility
Charles Derber

Born in 1944, Charles Derber, who earned a Ph.D. from the University of Chicago, is a professor of sociology at Boston College, as well as an activist and an author who often writes about globalization, corporate power, and communitarianism. He has worked with community groups around the country in hopes of engendering a new politics based on "democratizing our corporate system." His books include *The Wilding of America: How Greed and Violence Are Eroding Our Nation's Character* (1996;

2001) and *Corporate Nation: How Corporations are Taking Over Our Lives and What We Can Do About It* (2000). The following essay on the rights and responsibilities of a civic society is taken from Derber's book, *Money, Murder, and the American Dream: Wilding from Wall Street to Main Street* (1992).

———————— ✦ ————————

America's romance with individualism and the free market has its virtues, but it has clouded Americans' understanding of what makes society tick. Civil society arises only when people develop strong obligations to the larger "us" that can override the perennial, very human preoccupation with "me, me, me." Such larger commitments bloom only under special conditions, when the community shows that it cares so deeply for each of its members that each, in turn, fully understands his debt to society and seeks to pay it back in full.

The Japanese and Europeans, in their very different ways, seem to appreciate this "deal" or contract that preserves civil society. The Japanese corporation smothers the Japanese worker in a cocoon of secure employment, health benefits, housing, and other social necessities that make it almost impossible for workers to imagine life outside of the group. Through their expansive welfare states, the Europeans deliver their own bushel of benefits and entitlements that the citizen recognizes as indispensable to personal survival and happiness. Both systems bring their own serious problems, but succeed in creating the allegiance to the larger community that breeds immunity to the wilding epidemic.

Each civil society has to find its own way of inspiring its members' devotion, but all must deliver those rock bottom necessities essential to the pursuit of life, liberty, and happiness. These include a minimal level of personal safety, food, shelter, and a livelihood. "Social orphans" deprived of these essentials are unable to fulfill any larger obligation to society, for their existence is entirely consumed by the brutish struggle for personal survival.

This leads to the idea of "social citizenship," an extension of the familiar but narrower concept of political citizenship. The rights to health care, housing, and a job can be seen as social rights, parallel to our political rights to vote and to free speech enshrined in our constitution. Political rights apply to all citizens automatically, because they are the precondition of democracy as a system. Analogously, social rights should be extended automatically to everyone, for they are the precondition of civil society's survival.

The Japanese deliver such social rights through a paternalistic 5
corporate extended family, largely private, while the Europeans do
it through the welfare state. America will have to find its own way.
Ideally, the emerging institutions of the social market would, in the
long run, provide a local, democratic, and nonstatist solution. One
possibility is an American version of the success achieved by Mondragon, a remarkable complex of over one hundred industrial cooperatives in the Basque region of Spain. Mondragon has succeeded
during the past forty years in guaranteeing job security, housing,
health care, and education to its members with scarcely any help
from the state. Workers in the cooperatives have created cooperative schools, hospitals, insurance companies, and banks that offer
robust social security from birth to death. The Mondragon complex, which is the largest manufacturer of durable goods in Spain
and employs thousands of "worker-owners," has never permanently
laid off a worker, reproducing the equivalent of the Japanese system
of lifetime employment, while also entrepreneuring new cooperatives in one of the most impressive rates of job creation in the world.

Whether an American social market could evolve in such a direction is purely speculative, but clearly there are ways to provide
social rights that are realistic, democratic, and do not require big
government. America is the only major industrialized country not
to offer health care as a social right to all its citizens. The problem
could be easily rectified through a national health care system
that is neither burcaucratic nor necessarily public. The 1990s has
already seen the proliferation of a variety of proposals for privately financed national health care, relying on the existing network of health deliverers and insurers and largely financed by
employers. More comprehensive publicly financed plans, including the Health USA Act of 1991 proposed by Nebraska senator
Bob Kerrey, could simultaneously solve problems of cost and access without creating a huge government bureaucracy. Similarly,
proposals abound for providing affordable housing in ways that
integrate private and public financing mechanisms and do not
make Uncle Sam everybody's landlord.

While government is not the preferred agent, it is the guaran-
tor of last resort. When people are homeless, starving, or jobless,
civil society has failed, and a wilding virus is activated. It is not
silly idealism or bleeding heart liberalism, but a conservative and
prudent defense of the social order that requires public action.

For this reason, legal scholars like Columbia University law
professor Louis Henkin are pointing to "genetic defects" in our

Bill of Rights that constitutionally guarantee political but not social citizenship rights. Chief Justice William Rehnquist, in a 1989 court opinion, argued that the Constitution confers "no affirmative right to governmental aid, even when such aid may be necessary to secure life." This leads constitutional attorney Paul Savoy, former dean of John F. Kennedy University School of Law, to point out that "Our civil rights and civil liberties are rights in the negative sense" and "do not include affirmative obligations on government. We do not have a constitutional right," Savoy observes, "to have the state provide us with health care, or give us shelter if we are homeless, or prevent a child from being beaten or from starving to death." A coalition of unions, environmentalists, and community groups has responded by calling for a second Bill of Rights that would entitle all citizens to the elementary social rights of shelter, food, and health care.

Social rights are not a free ride for the population, for with them come demanding social obligations. Citizenship is an intimate dance of rights and obligations, and "social citizens" need to embrace enthusiastically the moral obligations that come with their new entitlements. This means not only willingly paying the taxes required to keep civil society healthy, but also devoting time and effort, as we detail below, to "community-building" at work, in the neighborhood and in the country at large.

10   The problem with the Left is that it demands rights without spelling out the obligations that have to accompany them; the problem with the Right is that it expects obligations to be fulfilled without ceding social rights in return. Both positions are absurd, since rights and obligations are flip sides of civil society's coin of the realm. We need a new politics that marries the Left's moral passion for rights with the Right's sober recognition of duty.

DEFENDING OUR LIVES: GETTING FROM HERE TO THERE

But what do we do now? Americans are a pragmatic people and want down-to-earth answers. While there is no recipe or magic formula, we can act now to stop the wilding epidemic. If we want to survive with our humanity intact, we really have no alternative.

Since the wilding epidemic is a cancer that can destroy society, we are all patients fighting to stay alive. Obviously, if we each felt we had a desperate illness, we would mobilize ourselves to act immediately, to save ourselves. But since wilding is a societal disease and not a biological illness, individuals can feel a deceptive immunity. It is possible to feel healthy, have fun, and enjoy life as society begins to come undone.

But as the epidemic spreads, everyone will increasingly feel at risk. The personal meaning of the wilding epidemic is that we each have to spend more and more time simply defending our lives. Defending our property, defending our livelihood, defending our health, defending our physical safety, defending our ego. This imposes a terrible burden on the individual, and it can easily fuel the "me" mentality at the heart of the problem, but it also unlocks the riddle of what to do. Not only will the illusion of immunity diminish, but the wisdom of dealing with the underlying disease and not just the symptoms will become more apparent.

One can start defending one's life, as Albert Brook's film comedy of that title suggests, either wisely or foolishly. The short-sighted approach involves trying to save oneself by abandoning everyone else, exemplified by the suburbanites who cocoon within homes wired with the latest security technology and refuse to pay taxes to support the center city. Robert Reich suggests that such a "politics of secession" is sweeping upper middle-class America. If so, it is a blind and morally unsustainable choice, for it creates short-term symptomatic relief while worsening the disease.

Since the disease is social, so too must be the cure. As the social infrastructure begins to ulcerate and bleed, the rational long-term way to defend one's life is to help repair the damaged societal tissue, whether it be potholes in the road, hungry people sleeping on grates, or sociopathic competitiveness in the office. "Doing the right thing," then, is defending one's life by cooperating to build up community strength and bolster personal and collective resistance. This requires no saintly sacrifice for the common good, but tough-minded and clear-eyed assessment of where the threat lies. When facing a wilding threat, the first question to ask is, "What in myself or my social environment is creating this threat?" Once that question is answered, the next is, "What can I do about it?" Some cases will require purely personal change, falling back on all one's psychological and moral strength, as well as love and support from family, friends or mentors, to counter wilding impulses within oneself or susceptibility to wilding influence in the environment. Most cases will also require acting for some form of social change to extirpate the external poison, whether at work, in the neighborhood, or in the White House, typically achievable only with the help of others.

Fortunately, the wisdom of social action is obvious in a huge variety of circumstances, and Americans are already responding, especially where their own health is involved. When kids in Woburn, Massachussets, were getting sick because of toxic chemicals, parents got together to clean up the toxic dump and hold the wilding factory accountable. In the 1990s, Americans are recognizing that staying healthy has become a political-action project requiring a massive environmental clean-up, and they are not waiting for lackadaisical governments to take the lead. "People are recognizing they can in fact control their environment," Hal Hiemstra, a Washington environmental activist notes. "They're starting to say, 'we've had it.' " The *Boston Globe* reports that "an environmental wake-up call" is "being sounded nationwide by communities alarmed by the federal government's inertia and inspired by their own sense of power to reshape the landscape." The activists are not only defending their life but, the *Globe* observes, are "local heroes on planetary matters."

Heroes of a different sort are the suburban communities around Minneapolis, who swam against the tide and rejected the "politics of secession," the suburban wilding that has helped push Bridgeport, Connecticut, into Chapter Eleven bankruptcy and left New York City and hundreds of other cities tottering on the brink. The Minnesota suburbs joined with Minneapolis in the mid-1980s and formed a regional pact "whereby any community enjoying 40 percent more than the average growth of the region in any given year would have to share with the other signers of the pact." Such apparent sacrifice for the larger good is just plain common sense, since if the city center failed, it would bring the surrounding communities down with it. The great irony, as John Shannon of the Urban Institute notes, "is that Minneapolis is now enjoying boom times and must pay *out* to the suburbs." A modern Aesop's fable, it shows how cooperation for the common good is, indeed, a form of enlightened self-interest.

We can begin to cure the wilding sickness by doing more of what we have always done well and doing it better: taking responsibility for our lives through civic participation. Tocqueville was amazed at the richness of America's democracy; its dense web of voluntary associations and democratic town meetings made it unique. "The free institutions which the inhabitants of the United States possess, and the political rights of which they make so much use," Tocqueville explains, "remind every citizen, and in a thousand ways, that he lives in society."

In other words, democracy, and more democracy, is the best antidote for wilding and the most nourishing food for the social infrastructure.

Americans have become apathetic and indifferent to national politics, but we still retain our propensity to join together in what Tocqueville called "an immense assemblage of associations." One researcher suggests that there are now over 500,000 self-help groups in the United States with over 15 million members; many, whether alcoholics, abused children, battered spouses, or "codependents," are casualties of the wilding epidemic who by joining with others are taking enlightened first steps toward not only recovering personally but rebuilding civil society. The same can be said of the millions of others involved in volunteer efforts or political activism at local or higher levels.

In a recent study, the Kettering Institute of Dayton, Ohio, 20 concluded that Americans' indifference to national politics reflected less pure selfishness or apathy than despair about leaders and the absence of real choices. America desperately needs a new generation of political leaders who will tell the truth about the wilding crisis and articulate a new moral vision. But since no such leaders are now in view, the burden falls on the rest of us, where it ultimately belongs. It remains to be seen whether Americans will find in themselves the emotional and moral strength to forge a new collective dream.

Questions for Discussion

1. How does Derber define the concept of civil society in his introduction, and how does his contrast between American versus Japanese and European societies contribute to his definition? What can the U.S. learn from these societies?

2. According to Louis Henkin of Columbia Law School, what defects exist in the Bill of Rights? What additional "social citizenship" rights are needed? Do you agree with Henkin?

3. What social and moral obligations does Derber believe should be linked with social citizenship rights? What is the "problem with the Left"? According to Derber, how does his position on social obligation bring both the Left and Right together?

4. What are the "wilding sickness" and the "politics of secession"? What examples does Derber give of positive, community-based solutions to these social diseases?

Ideas for Writing

1. Write an essay in which you evaluate the idea of "social citizenship rights" that would supplement the other rights guaranteed in the Constitution. How would you respond to the view that this would just create an immense "welfare state"?

2. Derber provides examples of community projects and regulations involving cooperation for the common good. Do some research and then write an essay in which you describe a similar community project that you think would provide a positive alternative to the feelings of powerlessness and apathy that have infiltrated many cities and suburban areas today.

A Vision of the Quilt

CLEVE JONES AND JEFF DAWSON

Cleve Jones has been a gay activist since the early 1970s, when he lived in San Francisco and worked as a fundraiser for Senator Art Agnos. "A Vision of the Quilt" is excerpted from Jones and Jeff Dawson's book, *Stitching a Revolution* (2000), which tells the story of his role in creating the AIDS Memorial Quilt, a powerful visual reminder of the AIDS epidemic. The Quilt now contains more than 44,000 individual three-by-six-foot memorial panels, each one commemorating the life of someone who has died of complications related to AIDS. In 1996, the entire Quilt was displayed for the last time in Washington, D.C., at the National Mall, where the Quilt covered it completely. The Quilt was nominated for a Nobel Peace Prize in 1989 and is the largest community art project in the world today.

━━━━━━━━━━ ✦ ━━━━━━━━━━

After eight months on Maui I was back in the Castro. I had no job, no money, and was sleeping on a friend's couch (Jim Foster had taken me in). But I had a plan. I'd written a speech that I hoped would reignite the will to fight. I would give my speech at the candlelight march commemorating the day Harvey Milk and George Moscone had been shot. After that, who knows? I never really worried about career and fortune in those days. I was surviving, and that seemed quite a lot.

It's hard to communicate how awful it was in the fall of 1985. I'd left town out of my own fear and frustration. And somehow that sabbatical had been recuperative. Physically I felt fine. The shingles had left with only lingering tingles. And I'd gotten myself out of the coke and drinking routine thanks in part to Randy Shilts, an old friend from the Haight-Ashbury days. He, alone among my friends, had encouraged me to go to an AA meeting. It was hard as hell to attend those first meetings. Then, slowly, I broke the pattern and eventually learned to sleep without numbing myself with drink.

But there was something different in the San Francisco I returned to. Everyone seemed exhausted, almost fatalistic about AIDS. I understood that, certainly; but I also detected signs of hope within the despair. For one, the media had caught on to what was happening. Randy, who'd been a staff writer for the *Advocate*, was hired full-time by the *Chronicle* to write weekly AIDS columns, and he was extremely dogged in his attempts to puncture all the myths. There was a piece on the fallacy of AIDS being transmitted by mosquito bites, by tainted water, by waiters handling dinner plates. He went into AIDS wards and interviewed the nursing staff and doctors, and the truth was coming out.

Other newspapers followed his lead, and the public began to learn, if not always to accept, that this disease was not divine retribution. And other "points of light" flared up. Bobbi Campbell and his lover sat smiling on the cover of *Newsweek* in an article on the new disease—appearing shockingly alive and productive. There were respected physicians speaking out and against the panic. These were all important achievements, but still it was just so much whistling in the dark. We desperately needed an immediate fix, and it wasn't even on the horizon.

Seven years before, on the night of Harvey Milk's murder, I swore to myself that he would not be forgotten and began organizing a candlelight march to mark the day of his and Mayor Moscone's deaths. It had become a ritual, with thousands attending every year. A few days prior to the 1985 march, my friend Joseph Durant and I were working the Castro handing out leaflets reminding people of the candlelight memorial. We stopped to get a slice at Marcello's Pizza and I picked up a *Chronicle*. The front-page heading was chilling: "1,000 San Franciscans Dead of AIDS." I'd known most of them from my work with the KS Foundation. Virtually every single one of them had lived within a ten-block radius of where we were standing at Castro and Market.

5

When I walked up Eighteenth Street from Church to Eureka, I knew the ugly stories behind so many windows. Gregory died behind those blue curtains. Jimmy was diagnosed up that staircase in that office behind the venetian blinds. There was the house Alex got kicked out of when the landlord found an empty bottle of AZT in his trash can: "I'm sorry, we just can't take any chances." I wasn't losing just friends, but also all the familiar faces of the neighborhood—the bus drivers, clerks and mailmen, all the people we know in casual yet familiar ways. The entire Castro was populated by ghosts.

And yet, as I looked around the Castro with its charming hodge-podge of candy-colored Victorians, there were guys walking hand in hand, girls kissing each other hello, being successfully, freely, openly who they were. So much had been accomplished since the closeted days when the community met furtively in a black-alley culture. The Castro was a city within the city, an oasis and harbor for thousands who lived there and millions of gay men and lesbian women around the world for whom it symbolized freedom. And now, in what should have been its prime, it was withering.

Angrily, I turned to Joseph: "I wish we had a bulldozer, and if we could just level these buildings, raze Castro. . . . If this was just a graveyard with a thousand corpses lying in the sun, then people would look at it and they would understand and if they were human beings they'd have to respond." And Joseph, always the acid realist, told me I was the last optimist left standing: "Nobody cares, Cleve. This thing doesn't touch them at all."

November 27, 1985, the night of the memorial march, was cold and gray. As we waited for people to gather, Joseph and I handed out stacks of poster board and Magic Markers, and through the bullhorn I asked everyone to write down the name of a friend who'd been killed by AIDS. People were a little reluctant at first, but by the time the march began we had a few hundred placards. Most of the marchers just wrote first names, Tom or Bill or George; some of the signs said "My brother" or "My lover," and a few had the complete names—first, middle, and last—in bold block letters.

That Thanksgiving night we marched as we had for six years down Market Street to city hall, a sea of candles lighting up the night. One of the marchers asked me who else would be speaking this year and I said, "No one else. Just me. People are tired of long programs anyway." I was an angry, arrogant son of a bitch. The candles we'd been carrying were stumps by the time we'd gathered at Harvey Milk Memorial Plaza at city hall.

"... We are here tonight to commemorate the deaths of Supervisor Harvey Milk and Mayor George Moscone, victims of an assassin's bullets seven years ago this very day . . ." I talked of Harvey and how even back then he was not really our first martyr, that we'd lost many people to murder and suicide and alcohol and AIDS. "Yes, Harvey was our first collective martyr, but now we have many more martyrs and now our numbers are diminished and many of us have been condemned to an early and painful death. But we are the lesbian women and gay men of San Francisco, and although we are again surrounded by uncertainty and despair, we are survivors and we shall survive again and the dream that was shared by Harvey Milk and George Moscone will go forward. . . ."

Then we moved down Market to the old federal building. At that time it housed the offices of Health and Human Services—not such an effective rallying point as city hall, but perfect for our next demonstration, one that turned out to have more impact than I ever imagined. Earlier in the day, Bill Paul, a professor at San Francisco State University, and I had hidden extension ladders and rolls of tape in the shrubbery around the building's base. As the federal building came into view, I ended the chanting ("Stop AIDS now! Stop AIDS now!") and explained through the bullhorn that we were going to plaster the facade with posters inscribed with our dead. And that's what happened. The crowd surged forward, the ladders were set in place, and we crawled up three stories, covering the entire wall with a poster-board memorial.

It was a strange image. Just this uneven patchwork of white squares, each with handwritten names, some in script and some in block letters, all individual. We stared and read the names, recognizing too many. Staring upward, people remarked: "I went to school with him" . . . "I didn't know he was dead" . . . "I used to dance with him every Sunday at the I-Beam" . . . "We're from the same hometown" . . . "Is that our Bob?"

There was a deep yearning not only to find a way to grieve individually and together but also to find a voice that could be heard beyond our community, beyond our town. Standing in the drizzle, watching as the posters absorbed the rain and fluttered down to the pavement, I said to myself, *It looks like a quilt.* As I said the word *quilt*, I was flooded with memories of home and family and the warmth of a quilt when it was cold on a winter night.

10

And as I scanned the patchwork, I saw it—as if a Technicolor slide had fallen into place. Where before there had been a flaking gray wall, now there was a vivid picture and I could see quite clearly the National Mall, and the dome of Congress and a quilt spread out before it—a vision of incredible clarity.

15   I was gripped by the same terror and excitement that I'd felt standing before other large works commemorating other large issues. Not long ago I'd seen Christo's running fence in Sonoma County. It was a beautiful and moving sight, and I was struck by the grandeur of those vast expanses of shimmering opalescent fabric zigzagging up and down the golden hills. How it billowed in the breeze with the light playing off it, like a string of azure tall ships sailing on a golden sea. And there was the memory of Judy Chicago's *The Dinner Party*. This was a long table, maybe one hundred feet in length, with each place setting designed by a different artist. Both Christo and Judy Chicago had taken commonplace items, sheets drying on a line in his case, plates and utensils in hers, and by enlarging them had made the homely a dramatic, powerfully moving statement. It seemed an apt synthesis: individual quilts, collected together, could have the same immense impact.

When I told my friends what I'd seen, they were silent at first, and as I tried to explain it, they were dubious: "Cleve, don't you realize the logistics of doing something like that? Think of the difficulty of organizing thousands of queers!" But I knew there were plenty of angry queens with sewing machines. I wouldn't be working alone, I told my friends. Everyone understands the idea of a quilt. "But it's gruesome," they said.

That stopped me. Was a memorial morbid? Perhaps it was. And yet there is also a healing element to memorials. I thought of the Vietnam Veterans Memorial wall. I did not expect to be moved by it. I was influenced by the Quakers, who are suspicious of war memorials, which they believe tend to glorify war rather than speak to the horror of it. But I was overwhelmed by the simplicity of it, of that black mirrorlike wall and the power it had to draw people from all across America to find a beloved's name and touch it and see their face reflected in the polished marble and leave mementos.

So I thought about all these things and also about how quilting is viewed as a particularly American folk art. There was the quilting bee with its picture of generations working together, and the idea that quilts recapture history in bits of worn clothing, curtains, jackets—protective cloth. That it was women who did the sewing was an important element. At the time, HIV was seen as the product of aggressive gay male sexuality, and it seemed that the homey image and familial associations of a warm quilt would counter that.

The idea made so much sense on so many different levels. It was clear to me that the only way we could beat this was by acting together as a nation. Though gays and lesbians were winning political recognition in urban centers, without legitimate ties to the larger culture we'd always be marginalized. If we could somehow bridge that gap of age-old prejudice, there was hope that we could beat the disease by using a quilt as a symbol of solidarity, of family and community; there was hope that we could make a movement that would welcome people men and women, gay or straight, of every age, race, faith, and background.

To this day, critics ignore one of the most powerful aspects of the Quilt. Any Quilt display, no matter how small or large, is filled with evidence of love—the love between gay men and the love we share with our lesbian sisters as well as love of family, father for son, mother for son, among siblings. Alongside this love, the individual quilts are filled with stories of homophobia and how we have triumphed over it. There's deep and abiding pain in letters attached to the quilts from parents bemoaning the fact that they didn't accept their dead son. And there's implacable anger in the blood-splashed quilts blaming President Reagan for ignoring the killing plague. All these messages are part of a memorial that knows no boundaries. We go to elementary schools, high schools, the Bible Belt of the Deep South, rural America, Catholic churches, synagogues, and wherever we unfold this fabric we tell the story of people who've died of AIDS.

That night, standing with those few men and women in the damp and dark, I saw a way out for all of us, a method surmounting our fears and coming together in a collective memorial of our experience: all the sadness, rage, and anger; all the hope, all the dreams, the ambitions, the tragedy.

Eleven years later, this picture in my mind's eye became reality. But that night in November 1985 it was just an idea, and on the 8 Market bus up to the Castro, my friend Joseph Durant and Gilbert Baker and Joseph Canalli were unimpressed. Reagan will never let you do it, they said. Straight families won't join any cause with a bunch of San Francisco queers. It was late, they were tired. An AIDS quilt was a sweet idea, but it was morbid, corny, impossibly complicated. Give it up. But I was on fire with the vision. The idea made so much sense, in so many ways—the irony and truth of it. I couldn't get it out of my head.

Questions for Discussion

1. Why was November 27, 1985, chosen for the AIDS memorial march? What strategic planning did Jones make for the launching of the quilt? In what ways was he acting as a public citizen as he launched this project?
2. Why was the situation in the Castro District bleak and depressing in 1985? What forms of support did Jones have as he launched the project? What kinds of progress have been made to stop the spread of AIDS along with the success of the Names Quilt?
3. What was the impact of plastering the façade of the old federal building on Market Street with a patchwork of white squares, each memorializing the loss of a loved one to AIDS?
4. Why is a quilt an appropriate symbol for the struggle against AIDS? How does the success of the AIDS Quilt suggest that private citizens can act as public citizens by leading or participating in a community-based activist project?

Ideas for Writing

1. Do some research into the AIDS Quilt and the NAMES Project; then, write a paper that highlights the history of the project's impact and successes.
2. Write an essay in which you argue either for or against the efficacy of symbolic statements such as the AIDS Quilt in drawing public attention and funding to social and health issues.

The Artist as Citizen

Barbra Streisand

Barbra Streisand, best known for her career as a singer and an actress, has also played an important role as a political activist, donating and raising millions of dollars through benefits and personal appearances. She also produces films related to causes such as civil liberties, AIDS research, help for abused women, and the struggle against racism. In the following speech, delivered at the John F. Kennedy School of Government at Harvard University, Streisand argues for public money to support the arts, and defends moviemakers and other artists as socially responsible citizens. Her speech was published in *New Perspectives Quarterly* in the spring of 1995.

———————— ✦ ————————

A year ago, I was much more optimistic than I am today. We had seven women in the Senate, bringing the hope of full representation for more than half the population. And we had a President who judged our ethnic, cultural and artistic diversity as a source of strength rather than weakness.

Then came the election of 1994, and suddenly the progress of the recent past seemed threatened by those who hunger for the "good old days" when women and minorities knew their place. In this resurgent reactionary mood, artists derided as the "cultural elite" are convenient objects of scorn; and those institutions that have given Americans access to artistic works—such as the National Endowment for the Arts (NEA) and the Corporation for Public Broadcasting (PBS)—are in danger of being abolished.

Part of the profound conflict is between those who would widen freedom and those who would narrow it; those who defend tolerance and those who view it as a threat.

All great civilizations have supported the arts. However, the new Speaker of the House, citing the need to balance the budget, insists that the arts programs should be the first to go. But the government's contribution to the NEA and PBS is actually quite meager. To put it in perspective, the entire budget of the NEA is equal to one F-22 fighter jet—a plane that some experts say may not even be necessary—yet the Pentagon is planning to buy 442 of them. One less plane could fund the whole arts budget! Seventy-two billion dollars for fighterjets—that is real money. On the other hand, PBS costs each taxpayer less than one dollar a year and National Public Radio, 29 cents annually.

Perhaps, then, balancing the budget is not at issue; maybe it's about shutting the minds and mouths of artists who might have something thought-provoking to say.

5

William Bennett, the former United States education secretary who called recently for the elimination of the arts agencies, charged that they were corrupt for supporting artists whose work undermines "mainstream American values." Art does not exist only to entertain—but also to challenge one to think, to provoke, even to disturb, in a constant search for the truth. To deny artists, or any of us, free expression and free thought—or worse, to force us to conform to some rigid notion of "mainstream American values"—is to weaken the very foundation of our democracy.

The far right is waging a war for the soul of America by making art a partisan issue; by trying to cut these arts programs, which bring culture, education and joy into the lives of ordinary Americans, they are hurting the very people they claim to represent.

I find it ironic that Newt Gingrich claims that "the NEA and PBS are protected by a bunch of rich upper-class people." Isn't it hypocritical to lobby for tax cuts for these same rich upper-class people, but resent them when they try to protect the arts?

The persistent drumbeat of cynicism on the talk shows and in the new Congress reeks of disrespect for the arts and artists. But what else is new? Even Plato said that artists were nothing but troublemakers and wanted to ban poets from his perfect republic. In Victorian times there were signs requiring actors and dogs to eat in the kitchen. As recently as last year, artists who have spoken out politically have been derided as airheads, bubble-heads and nitwits—and this is not just by someone like Rush Limbaugh, who has called people in my industry the "spaced-out Hollywood left"—it is also the rhetoric of respectable publications.

10   The editor of *The New Republic* wrote of actors: "In general, they are an excruciating bunch of egomaniacs. They have little to say for themselves . . . and their politics are uniformly idiotic." To me, this is about jealousy. He specifically singled out Paul Newman, Whoopi Goldberg and Tom Hanks as subjects for his wrath after last year's Academy Awards.

What is the sin? Is it caring about your country? Why should the actor give up his role as citizen just because he's in show business? For his role in the movie *Philadelphia*, Tom Hanks had to learn quite a bit about being a gay man with AIDS. Should he have remained silent on this issue? For 30 years, Paul Newman has been an outspoken defender of civil liberties and a major philanthropist. Would it be better if he just made money and played golf? Should Whoopi Goldberg retreat into her home and not do anything for the homeless? Or is Robert Redford a bubblehead because he knows more about the environment than most members of Congress?

Imagine talking about the leaders of any other group in our society this way—say, leaders of the steelworkers union, agribusiness, or chief executives of the automobile industry. Imagine having this kind of contempt for an industry that is second only to aerospace in export earnings abroad. According to *Business Week*, Americans spent $340 billion on entertainment in 1993. Maybe policy makers could learn something from an industry that makes billions while the government owes trillions.

The presumption is that people in my profession are too insulated, too free-thinking, too subversive. One can almost hear the question—are you now or have you ever been a member of the Screen Actors Guild? Never mind that the former president of our guild did become President of the United States. The Hollywood smear seems to apply only to liberals.

Ironically, contempt for the artist as citizen is often expressed by those most eager to exploit the celebrity of the entertainer. Both journalists and politicians feed off the celebrity status of the successful artist. We can attract a crowd and raise astounding amounts of money for the politicians—and make good copy for the journalists. Which is precisely why we are courted and resented by both. I recall various leading newspapers and magazines trying to entice Hollywood celebrities to join their tables at the White House correspondents' dinner, only to trash them afterward. One can almost hear them thinking—you make money, you're famous, you have to have political opinions, too?

But we, as people, are more than what we do as performers, professors or plumbers; we also are—and we also should be—participants in the larger life of society.

In the past, in the days of the dominant movie studios, an artist wasn't allowed to express political opinions. But with the breakup of the studio system, creative people gained independence. And with the rise of the women's, environmental and gay rights movements, there has been an increase in artists who support liberal causes.

Most artists are on the humanist, compassionate side of public debate because it is consistent with the work we do. The basic task of the artist is to explore the human condition. In order to do what we do well, the writer, the director, the actor has to inhabit other people's psyches, understand other people's problems. We have to walk in other people's shoes and live in other people's skins. This does tend to make us more sympathetic to politics that are more tolerant. In our work, in our preparation and in our research, we are continuously trying to educate ourselves. And with learning comes compassion. Education is the enemy of bigotry and hate. It's hard to hate someone you truly understand.

15

Our participation in politics is a natural outgrowth of what we do, and it can and should be a responsible use of celebrity. Since we do have the ability to raise issues, reach people and influence opinion, as with Charlton Heston lobbying against gun control and, thank God, for the NEA, we do have a greater responsibility to be informed.

I will not defend everything that comes out of the entertainment industry. A lot of junk is produced; gratuitously violent, sexist, exploitive and debasing of the human spirit. I don't like it and I won't defend it. This is a profit-driven industry that produces the best and the worst in its attempt to find a market.

20   Further, the far right rarely attacks the violent movies—in fact, their candidates campaign alongside some of the major practitioners of this so-called art form. What disturbs them is often the best work of the mass media. They have attacked programming, beginning with *All in the Family* because it dealt with the controversial issues of racism and sexism. They attacked *Murphy Brown* which is a thoughtful attempt to deal with American lives that, for better or for worse, are very different from the lives of Ozzie and Harriet.

Art is the signature of a generation; artists have a way of defining the times. Marian Anderson, singing on the steps of the Lincoln Memorial because, as a black woman, she was forbidden to sing at Constitution Hall, forced Americans to confront the outrageousness of segregation. Art can illuminate, enlighten, inspire. Art finds a way to be constructive. It becomes heat in cold places; it becomes light in dark places.

When there was chaos in the 1960s, Bob Dylan said it was like "Blowin' in the Wind." During the riots of the 1960s, when people tried to explain the inexplicable, Aretha Franklin sang simply what was being asked for, "R-E-S-P-E-C-T."

Then there are the movies that spoke for their times. The movie version of John Steinbeck's *The Grapes of Wrath* brought the sad reality of the Depression home to those who wanted to ignore it. In the 1940s, a movie called *Gentleman's Agreement* raised the issue of anti-semitism in America. *In the Heat of the Night* was named Best Picture of 1967 and is remembered for its unsparing look at the issue of race. *Mr. Smith Goes to Washington* focused on buying votes and favors—a problem we still haven't solved. A generation ago, *Inherit the Wind* took on the Scopes trial and the subordination of science to one narrow religious view—and the movie is powerfully relevant today in light of the Christian Coalition's efforts to reintroduce creationism into the public school curriculum.

Just last year, we saw a motion picture called *Schindler's List* bring the subject of the Holocaust to millions of people around the world. Steven Spielberg rescued it from fading newsreels and recast it in black and white that made it vivid, real and undeniable.

Moviemakers can be late to a subject, or afraid, but often they are brave and ahead of their time. Artists were criticized for their involvement in the civil rights struggle and their early opposition to the Vietnam War. In those cases at least, I would suggest that the painters and performers were wiser than most pundits and politicians.

I am not suggesting that actors run the country; we have already tried that. I am suggesting, for example, that on the issue of AIDS, I would rather have America listen to Elizabeth Taylor, who had the courage to sponsor the first major fund-raiser against this dreaded disease, than to Jesse Helms, who has consistently fought legislation that would fund AIDS research.

Our role as artist is more controversial now because there are those, claiming the absolute authority of religion, who detest much of our work as much as they detest most of our politics. Instead of rationally debating subjects such as abortion or gay rights, they condemn as immoral those who favor choice and tolerance. They disown their own dark side and magnify everyone else's until, at the extreme, doctors are murdered in the name of protecting life. Who is this God they invoke, who is so petty and mean? Is God really against gun control and food stamps for poor children?

All people need spiritual values in their lives. But we can't reduce the quest for eternal meaning to a right-wing political agenda. What is dangerous about the far right is not that it takes religion seriously—most of us do—but rather that it condemns all other spiritual choices—the Buddhist, the Jew, the Muslim and many others who consider themselves to be good Christians. The wall of separation between church and state is needed precisely because religion, like art, is too important a part of the human experience to be choked by the hands of censors.

Artists have long felt the stranglehold of censorship by officially established religions. A 16th-century Pope ordered loincloths painted on the figures in Michelangelo's "Last Judgement"; 19th-century clerics damned Walt Whitman. Tolstoy was viewed as a heretic; and today, Islamic extremists, sanctioned by governments, are still hunting down Salman Rushdie.

25

30   It is interesting that Americans applaud artists in other parts of the world for speaking out, in China, for example. It is very often the artist who gives a voice to the voiceless by speaking up when no one else will. The playwright Vaclav Havel went to jail because of that. Now he is the president of his country.

Fortunately, there are reasonable Republicans. But I am worried about the direction in which the new Congress now seeks to take the country. I am worried about the name calling, the stereotypical labeling. I want to believe that these people have good intentions, but I think it was dangerous when Newt Gingrich developed a strategy in the last campaign of pitting President Clinton against so-called "normal Americans." The Speaker attacked again more recently when he said, "I fully expect Hollywood to have almost no concept of either normal American behavior, in terms of healthy families, healthy structures, religious institutions, conservative politics or the free enterprise system." This from a politician who held up a Hollywood movie, *Boy's Town*, as his answer to welfare reform. And, how can he say that Hollywood doesn't know anything about free enterprise?

Most of all, I deeply resent the notion that one politician or political party owns the franchise on family values, personal responsibility, traditional values and religion.

We are all normal Americans, even with our problems and complexities, including people in my community. We were not born in movie studios. We come from every part of this country and most of us are self-made. We have worked hard to get where we are and we do not forget where we came from, whether it's Iowa, Cincinnati or Brooklyn.

The notion of "normal Americans" has a horrible historical echo. It presupposes that there are "abnormal" Americans who are responsible for all that is wrong. The new scape-goats are members of what Gingrich calls the "counterculture McGoverniks."

35   I did a concert for George McGovern in 1972, and I still think that he would have made a better President than Richard Nixon. I am disappointed that I have read so little in defense of McGovern. Was McGovern countercultural? This son of a Republican Methodist minister has been married to the same woman for 51 years and flew 35 combat missions in World War II. Isn't it odd that his patriotism be disputed by a person who never served in the military and whose own family can hardly be called exemplary? But then again no one should have to conform to some mythical concept of the ideal family—not even Mr. Gingrich.

I am also very proud to be a liberal. Why is that so terrible these days? The liberals were liberators—they fought slavery, fought for women to have the right to vote, fought against Hitler, Stalin, fought to end segregation, fought to end apartheid. Thanks to liberals we have Social Security, public education, consumer and environmental protection, Medicare and Medicaid, the minimum wage law, unemployment compensation. Liberals put an end to child labor and they even gave us the five-day workweek! Such a record should be worn as a badge of honor!

Liberals have also always believed in public support for the arts. At the height of the Depression, Franklin Delano Roosevelt created the Works Progress Administration, which helped struggling artists. Willem de Kooning, Jackson Pollock and John Cage were among those who benefited from the support of the WPA.

Art was a way out for me. I represent a generation of kids who happened to benefit from government support of the arts in public schools. I was a member of the choral club at Erasmus Hall High School in Brooklyn. Sadly, the current generation of young people does not have the same opportunities.

How can we accept a situation in which there are no longer orchestras, choruses, libraries or art classes to nourish our children? We need more support for the arts, not less—particularly to make this rich world available to young people whose vision is choked by a stark reality. How many children, who have no other outlet in their lives for their grief, have found solace in an instrument to play or a canvas to paint on? When you take into consideration the development of the human heart, soul and imagination, the arts take on just as much importance as math or science.

As the difference between the elections of 1992 and 1994 shows, the outcome is not pre-ordained; progress, whatever one's definition of it, is not inevitable. I thought the current administration was doing a good job: reducing the deficit by $700 billion, creating six million jobs, downsizing government and passing a significant amount of important legislation.

We also need to keep in mind some words spoken by President John F. Kennedy who said he valued what artists could give because they "knew the midnight as well as the high noon (and) understood the ordeal as well as the triumph of the human spirit." He also said, "In serving his vision of the truth, the artist best serves his nation." President Kennedy was also the first to suggest the creation of the National Endowment for the Arts.

Well aware that art can be controversial, he concluded, "[the artist] must often sail against the currents of his time. This is not a popular role."

In 1995 I continue to believe it is an indispensable role. Artists, especially those who have had success, and have won popularity in their work, not only have the right, but the responsibility, to risk the unpopularity of being committed and active. And until women are treated equally with men, until gays and minorities are not discriminated against and until children have their full rights, artists must continue to speak out. I will be one of them. Sorry, Rush, Newt and Jesse, but the artist as citizen is here to stay.

Questions for Discussion

1. What does Streisand believe is the real reason for cutting money for programs such as the National Endowment for the Arts (NEA) and the Corporation for Public Broadcasting (PBS)?

2. Why does Streisand claim that to censor the arts "is to weaken the foundation of our democracy"? What evidence does she present? Do you agree or disagree with her?

3. Why does Streisand believe that there is often contempt for the artist as citizen? What are the reasons for this contempt, and how does she refute its efficacy?

4. Streisand claims that "Art is the signature of a generation." In what sense is this true or false? What work of art—a song, a film, television show, painting, or play—was the signature of your generation? In what ways did this work of art affect political and social values?

Ideas for Writing

1. Streisand claims, "The wall of separation between church and state is needed precisely because religion, like art, is too important a part of the human experience to be choked by the hands of censors." Write an essay that supports or refutes her analogy between art and religion. Use strong examples and evidence to support your point of view.

2. Streisand quotes President Kennedy's statement that, "In serving his vision of the truth, the artist best serves the nation." Write an argument that supports or refutes Kennedy's point of view. Do some research at your college library and on

the Internet to learn more about current visionary art and its impact on American values and the American spirit. Consider other ways that artists have served the nation.

A Match Made in Heaven

SUZANNE PHARR

An author and longtime social activist based in Arkansas, Suzanne Pharr endorses a progressive view of politics, social oppression, and economic inequality and has worked to combat racism, sexism, and homophobia. Pharr is the founder of Women's Project, an activist group that has done political education in Arkansas and nationally. She is the author of *Homophobia: A Weapon of Sexism* (rev. ed., 1997) and *In the Time of the Right: Reflections of Liberation* (1996).

———————— ✦ ————————

LESBIAN LEFTIE CHATS WITH A PROMISE KEEPER

In February, as I boarded a plane to Portland, Oregon, I overheard a man say to a woman, "We're almost all Promise Keepers on this flight. We are returning from an Atlanta meeting of 43,000 pastors."

"Forty-three thousand pastors," I thought. "That's like 43,000 organizers because they have influence over their congregations." I entered the plane thinking, "We're sunk."

For the last couple of years I have been watching the growth of the Promise Keepers with fascination and fear. As a Southern lesbian-feminist and anti-racist worker, I am keenly interested in any group of white men organizing around issues related to women and people of color.

As a long-time community organizer, I have to admire the brilliance of the Promise Keepers' organizing strategy. How smart it is to recognize not only the anger and confusion that men have about this changing society, but also their desire for connection and purpose. How smart to bring them into sports stadiums around the country to sing, touch, do the wave, and bond through physical and emotional contact they rarely allow themselves.

5   I believe the Promise Keepers are the ground troops in an authoritarian movement that seeks to merge church and state. It does not matter that a right wing agenda is not overt in the formative stages of this movement; when the leaders are ready to move their men in response to their agenda, they will have thousands disciplined to obey and command.

The plane was full of men dressed in casual clothes, many sporting new Promise Keepers shirts. During the flight, they stood in the aisles, talking excitedly. The scene reminded me of the 1987 March on Washington, which I attended along with thousands of lesbians and gay men. For the first time in our lives, we were the majority in airplanes, subways, buses, restaurants, and the streets. The experience was exhilarating. The Promise Keepers on the plane seemed to be having a similar experience, as though they had found each other for the first time.

After trying to escape through reading, I finally gave up and began chatting with the man next to me, dressed in a blue work shirt and jeans and reading a Tom Clancy novel. He reminded me very much of my brothers from rural Georgia. I asked if he was returning from Atlanta. "Yes," he replied. "I've just been to the Promise Keepers meeting, and I'm returning to my small town in Oregon."

I told him that I was a feminist, a civil-rights worker, and a lesbian, that I have very mixed feelings about the Promise Keepers, and that I wanted him to tell me about them.

He told me that he was pastor at a Baptist church, married, father of a teenage son, and that he would enjoy talking about his experience with the Promise Keepers. "You are the second homosexual I've ever met," he said, adding with a grin, "I think." With that introduction, we launched into an hour-and-a-half-long conversation.

10   The pastor told me that the first thing the Promise Keepers make clear is that men are responsible for all that's wrong with the family; they are not victims.

I told him that was going a little too far for this feminist—I think women might have some responsibility for the negative side of the ledger, too.

He said the Promise Keepers were not to dominate their wives but to lead them. When I asked what this meant, he said, "Man's role is laid out in the Bible—'As God is to man, man is to the family'—and it is to take charge of his family. This means listening to their needs and wishes, then deciding what is best for them."

I said, "As a feminist, I am deeply concerned about shared decision-making, about equality."

"We share the conversations, but I make the decisions," he said. "My job is to lead."

This talk about leadership made me feel that I was in a time 15 warp in which the women's movement had never occurred. I thought about the current status of women struggling with families, jobs, and intimate relationships. I thought about stories I have read that mention how pleased some Promise Keepers' wives are to have their husbands taking a dominant role in the family. With some sadness I considered how damning this is of many male-female relationships: that men are often so absent emotionally that women would be willing to give up autonomy in order to gain their husbands' presence.

I suggested the Promise Keepers could make an enormous contribution to women if they added an additional promise to their credo: that they would not lift their hand against women, and that they would stop other men from committing violence against women and children.

The Promise Keepers are against harming women, he said. They want to protect them. But adding an eighth promise would have to be up to the leadership.

Of everything that happened to this pastor at the meeting, the most life-changing, he said, was racial reconciliation. He said he had never thought about himself as someone prejudiced or discriminatory, and he came to recognize it in himself: "I'm not an emotional man, but I cried along with the audience when the men of color were called to the stage and they could not get there because they were intercepted by white pastors hugging them, shaking their hands, pounding them on the back."

The pastors were sent home, he said, to work to bring about racial reconciliation in their churches.

Since my conversation with the pastor on the airplane, Ralph 20 Reed has been calling for racial reconciliation in the wake of the recent rash of black church burnings in the South. At a meeting with black pastors, Reed admitted that the Christian Coalition has a history of being on the "wrong side" when it comes to race. Now it wants to be on the right side, he says. But why? Calls from the Christian Coalition and the Promise Keepers for racial reconciliation do not include any effort to end institutional racism, or to stop coded attacks on "welfare mothers" or immigrants or affirmative action. Rather, moving into black churches gives the religious right a foothold in the black community. In this way, the call for racial reconciliation is one of the most insidious aspects of the Promise Keepers and their allies on the Christian right. Just as the right is hungry for people of color who are willing to denounce affirmative action and the civil-rights struggles that have traditionally benefited their communities, the Promise Keepers' recruitment of black church leaders looks like a way to persuade the black community to act against its own best interests.

I asked the pastor about the Promise Keepers' attitudes toward lesbians and gays.

The pastor said it was not for a Promise Keeper to judge homosexuals ("That is God's job") but that they believe homosexuality is immoral because the Bible says it is.

"This is not judging?" I thought.

He said that he was sure there were many of us who were fine people but that we suffered from being identified with our "fringe" people who marched in those San Francisco parades.

25   I asked him if Jesus today would not be thought of as gay—an unmarried thirty-three-year-old who spent almost all of his time with twelve close male friends, one of whom in particular was "beloved."

He said, "No doubt if Jesus returned today, he might not be accepted in many churches."

We then talked about how few were the references in the Bible to same-sex relationships and how many were the references to sharing wealth, caring for those who have less, and opening one's home and heart to others. Why, then, did fundamentalists not have a strong economic agenda for the redistribution of wealth?

It's true, he said. This is a contradiction.

In the end, I thought we had communicated honestly with each other and that on some points, we had moved toward one another in understanding. It seemed to me that a great difference between us was his belief in the literal truth of the Bible, and my belief that it is a historical document with great spiritual content. I told him I thought that almost all of Christendom falls somewhere between those two positions. He agreed.

30   I wondered, can people who have very different beliefs and cultural practices live in peace with one another?

My final question to him was: Can you and I live in homes side by side, borrow sugar from one another, and encourage our children to play together? He said yes.

This conversation led me to think more deeply about the difference between the right's leaders (those engaged in an organizing strategy that threatens democracy) and its followers (those searching for solutions to social and economic instability, whose heartfelt beliefs make them easy targets for manipulation). Many progressives write off the latter, discarding them as ignorant or mean.

Our conversation stayed on my mind for weeks afterwards, and I thought of this one Promise Keeper with respect and continued interest. Then one day he phoned me long distance from his small town, saying he was just calling to keep in touch and to say what a profound effect our conversation had had on him.

"It eliminated whole areas of ignorance for me," he said.

"Me too," I replied.   35

My conversations with this Promise Keeper made me understand that progressive people must rethink their relation to the American right.

How do we point out the differences between the generals of this army and their recruits?

How do we talk to people who are different from ourselves?

How do we hold different beliefs and still live in harmony?

Is there any hope for preventing the merger of church and   40
state if we do not hold authentic conversations with those who believe fervently in the inerrancy of the Bible?

How do we get closer to people's real needs and their values in our organizing for change?

Finally, how do we carry on this conversation and organize as progressives committed to equal rights for everyone—nothing more, nothing less?

Questions for Discussion

1. Who are the Promise Keepers and what is their organizational strategy? Why does Pharr both admire and fear them?
2. How does the Promise Keeper movement interpret and apply the Bible to their philosophy of relationships between men and women and family structure? What are their attitudes toward racial reconciliation and homosexuality?
3. How effectively does Pharr express her areas of disagreement with the pastor? Do they come to a better understanding of one another's positions through their discussion? What are the areas on which they fail to agree?
4. What life-changing realization did the pastor have at the Promise Keepers' meeting in Atlanta? What realization did Pharr have after the discussion she had with him, and what advice does she have to present to her fellow activists?

Ideas for Writing

1. Pharr asks a final question to the pastor: "Can you and I live in homes side by side, borrow sugar from one another and encourage our children to play together?" While the pastor's answer was "Yes," from what you have learned reading this essay and life experiences, do you agree that right-wing fundamentalists and progressives could live happily together in the same neighborhoods? Argue in favor of the pastor's position or in opposition to it.

2. Write an essay that presents a debate on an issue related to public citizenship between two speakers who come from opposite points of view. Guide the debate and decide upon how much, if any, reconciliation will occur.

The Tyranny of the Majority
LANI GUINIER

Lani Guinier (b. 1950) is a professor of law at Harvard University with strong interests in public law, civil rights, and electoral reform. She is the founder of Commonplace, a national nonprofit organization dedicated to connecting people around the country to facilitate collective decision-making and problem-solving. In addition to her extensive publishing in law reviews, Guinier has written several books, including *The Tyranny of the Majority* (1994), *Lift Every Voice: Turning Civil Rights Setback into a New Vision of Social Justice* (1998), and *The Miners' Canary: Rethinking Race and Power* (2002). In the following essay, Guinier defends her controversial ideas on electoral reform, which were attacked by congressional questioners during her confirmation hearings for head of the Civil Rights Division for the Department of Justice in 1993.

───────────── ✦ ─────────────

I have always wanted to be a civil rights lawyer. This lifelong ambition is based on a deep-seated commitment to democratic fair play—to playing by the rules as long as the rules are fair. When the rules seem unfair, I have worked to change them, not subvert them. When I was eight years old, I was a Brownie. I was especially proud of my uniform, which represented a commitment to good citizenship and good deeds. But one day, when my Brownie group staged a hatmaking contest, I realized that uniforms are only as honorable as the people who wear them. The contest was rigged. The winner was assisted by her milliner mother, who actually made the winning entry in full view of all the participants. At the time, I was too young to be able to change the rules, but I was old enough to resign, which I promptly did.

To me, fair play means that the rules encourage everyone to play. They should reward those who win, but they must be acceptable to those who lose. The central theme of my academic writing is that not all rules lead to elemental fair play. Some even commonplace rules work against it.

The professional milliner competing with amateur Brownies stands as an example of rules that are patently rigged or patently subverted. Yet, sometimes, even when rules are perfectly fair in form, they serve in practice to exclude particular groups from meaningful participation. When they do not encourage everyone to play, or when, over the long haul, they do not make the losers feel as good about the outcomes as the winners, they can seem as unfair as the milliner who makes the winning hat for her daughter.

Sometimes, too, we construct rules that force us to be divided into winners and losers when we might have otherwise joined together. This idea was cogently expressed by my son, Nikolas, when he was four years old, far exceeding the thoughtfulness of his mother when she was an eight-year-old Brownie. While I was writing one of my law journal articles, Nikolas and I had a conversation about voting prompted by a *Sesame Street Magazine* exercise. The magazine pictured six children: four children had raised their hands because they wanted to play tag; two had their hands down because they wanted to play hide-and-seek. The magazine asked its readers to count the number of children whose hands were raised and then decide what game the children would play.

Nikolas quite realistically replied, "They will play both. First they will play tag. Then they will play hide-and-seek." Despite the magazine's "rules," he was right. To children, it is natural to take turns. The winner may get to play first or more often, but even the "loser" gets something. His was a positive-sum solution that many adult rule-makers ignore.

The traditional answer to the magazine's problem would have been a zero-sum solution: "The children—all the children—will

5

play tag, and only tag." As a zero-sum solution, everything is seen in terms of "I win; you lose." The conventional answer relies on winner-take-all majority rule, in which the tag players, as the majority, win the right to decide for all the children what game to play. The hide-and-seek preference becomes irrelevant. The numerically more powerful majority choice simply subsumes minority preferences.

In the conventional case, the majority that rules gains all the power and the minority that loses gets none. For example, two years ago Brother Rice High School in Chicago held two senior proms. It was not planned that way. The prom committee at Brother Rice, a boys' Catholic high school, expected just one prom when it hired a disc jockey, picked a rock band, and selected music for the prom by consulting student preferences. Each senior was asked to list his three favorite songs, and the band would play the songs that appeared most frequently on the lists.

Seems attractively democratic. But Brother Rice is predominantly white, and the prom committee was all white. That's how they got two proms. The black seniors at Brother Rice felt so shut out by the "democratic process" that they organized their own prom. As one black student put it "For every vote we had, there were eight votes for what they wanted. . . . [W]ith us being in the minority we're always outvoted. It's as if we don't count."

Some embittered white seniors saw things differently. They complained that the black students should have gone along with the majority: "The majority makes a decision. That's the way it works."

10   In a way, both groups were right. From the white students' perspective, this was ordinary decisionmaking. To the black students, majority rule sent the message: "we don't count" is the "way it works" for minorities. In a racially divided society, majority rule may be perceived as majority tyranny.

That is a large claim, and I do not rest my case for it solely on the actions of the prom committee in one Chicago high school. To expand the range of the argument, I first consider the ideal of majority rule itself, particularly as reflected in the writings of James Madison and other founding members of our Republic. These early democrats explored the relationship between majority rule and democracy. James Madison warned, "If a majority be united by a common interest, the rights of the minority will be insecure." The tyranny of the majority, according to Madison, requires safeguards to protect "one part of the society against the injustice of the other part."

For Madison, majority tyranny represented the great danger to our early constitutional democracy. Although the American revolution was fought against the tyranny of the British monarch, it soon became clear that there was another tyranny to be avoided. The accumulations of all powers in the same hands, Madison warned, "whether of one, a few, or many, and whether hereditary, self-appointed, or elective, may justly be pronounced the very definition of tyranny."

As another colonist suggested in papers published in Philadelphia, "We have been so long habituated to a jealousy of tyranny from monarchy and aristocracy, that we have yet to learn the dangers of it from democracy." Despotism had to be opposed "whether it came from Kings, Lords or the people."

The debate about majority tyranny reflected Madison's concern that the majority may not represent the whole. In a homogeneous society, the interest of the majority would likely be that of the minority also. But in a heterogeneous community, the majority may not represent all competing interests. The majority is likely to be self-interested and ignorant or indifferent to the concerns of the minority. In such case, Madison observed, the assumption that the majority represents the minority is "altogether fictitious."

Yet even a self-interested majority can govern fairly if it cooperates with the minority. One reason for such cooperation is that the self-interested majority values the principle of reciprocity. The self-interested majority worries that the minority may attract defectors from the majority and become the next governing majority. The Golden Rule principle of reciprocity functions to check the tendency of a self-interested majority to act tyrannically.

So the argument for the majority principle connects it with the value of reciprocity: You cooperate when you lose in part because members of the current majority will cooperate when they lose. The conventional case for the fairness of majority rule is that it is not really the rule of a fixed group—The Majority—on all issues; instead it is the rule of shifting majorities, as the losers at one time or on one issue join with others and become part of the governing coalition at another time or on another issue. The result will be a fair system of mutually beneficial cooperation. I call a majority that rules but does not dominate a Madisonian Majority.

The problem of majority tyranny arises, however, when the self-interested majority does not need to worry about defectors. When the majority is fixed and permanent, there are no checks

15

on its ability to be overbearing. A majority that does not worry about defectors is a majority with total power.

In such a case, Madison's concern about majority tyranny arises. In a heterogeneous community, any faction with total power might subject "the minority to the caprice and arbitrary decisions of the majority, who instead of consulting the interest of the whole community collectively, attend sometimes to partial and local advantages."

"What remedy can be found in a republican Government, where the majority must ultimately decide," argued Madison, but to ensure "that no one common interest or passion will be likely to unite a majority of the whole number in an unjust pursuit." The answer was to disaggregate the majority to ensure checks and balances or fluid, rotating interests. The minority needed protection against an overbearing majority, so that "a common sentiment is less likely to be felt, and the requisite concert less likely to be formed, by a majority of the whole."

20   Political struggles would not be simply a contest between rulers and people; the political struggles would be among the people themselves. The work of government was not to transcend different interests but to reconcile them. In an ideal democracy, the people would rule, but the minorities would also be protected against the power of majorities. Again, where the rules of decisionmaking protect the minority, the Madisonian Majority rules without dominating.

But if a group is unfairly treated, for example, when it forms a racial minority, *and* if the problems of unfairness are not cured by conventional assumptions about majority rule, then what is to be done? The answer is that we may need an *alternative* to winner-take-all majoritarianism. With Nikolas's help, I now call the alternative the "principle of taking turns." In a racially divided society, this principle does better than simple majority rule if it accommodates the values of self-government, fairness, deliberation, compromise, and consensus that lie at the heart of the democratic ideal.

In my legal writing, I follow the caveat of James Madison and other early American democrats. I explore decisionmaking rules that might work in a multi-racial society to ensure that majority rule does not become majority tyranny. I pursue voting systems that might disaggregate The Majority so that it does not exercise power unfairly or tyrannically. I aspire to a more cooperative political style of decisionmaking to enable all of the students at

Brother Rice to feel comfortable attending the same prom. In looking to create Madisonian Majorities, I pursue a positive-sum, taking-turns solution.

Structuring decisionmaking to allow the minority "a turn" may be necessary to restore the reciprocity ideal when a fixed majority refuses to cooperate with the minority. If the fixed majority loses its incentive to follow the Golden Rule principle of shifting majorities, the minority never gets to take a turn. Giving the minority a turn does not mean the minority gets to rule; what it does mean is that the minority gets to influence decisionmaking and the majority rules more legitimately.

Instead of automatically rewarding the preferences of the monolithic majority, a taking-turns approach anticipates that the majority rules, but is not overbearing. Because those with 51 percent of the votes are not assured 100 percent of the power, the majority cooperates with, or at least does not tyrannize, the minority.

The sports analogy of "I win; you lose" competition within a political hierarchy makes sense when only one team can win; Nikolas's intuition that it is often possible to take turns suggests an alternative approach. Take family decisionmaking, for example. It utilizes a taking-turns approach. When parents sit around the kitchen table deciding on a vacation destination or activities for a rainy day, often they do not simply rely on a show of hands, especially if that means that the older children always prevail or if affinity groups among the children (those who prefer movies to video games, or those who prefer baseball to playing cards) never get to play their activity of choice. Instead of allowing the majority simply to rule, the parents may propose that everyone take turns, going to the movies one night and playing video games the next. Or as Nikolas proposes, they might do both on a given night.

Taking turns attempts to build consensus while recognizing political or social differences, and it encourages everyone to play. The taking-turns approach gives those with the most support more turns, but it also legitimates the outcome from each individual's perspective, including those whose views are shared only by a minority.

In the end, I do not believe that democracy should encourage rule by the powerful—even a powerful majority. Instead, the ideal of democracy promises a fair discussion among self-defined equals about how to achieve our common aspirations. To redeem that promise, we need to put the idea of taking turns and disaggregating the majority at the center of our conception of representation. Particularly as we move into the twenty-first century as

25

a more highly diversified citizenry, it is essential that we consider the ways in which voting and representational systems succeed or fail at encouraging Madisonian Majorities.

To use Nikolas's terminology, "it is no fair" if a fixed, tyrannical majority excludes or alienates the minority. It is no fair if a fixed, tyrannical majority monopolizes all the power all the time. It is no fair if we engage in the periodic ritual of elections, but only the permanent majority gets to choose who is elected. Where we have tyranny by The Majority, we do not have genuine democracy.

My life's work, with the essential assistance of people like Nikolas, has been to try to find the rules that can best bring us together as a democratic society. Some of my ideas about democratic fair play were grossly mischaracterized in the controversy over my nomination to be Assistant Attorney General for Civil Rights. Trying to find rules to encourage fundamental fairness inevitably raises the question posed by Harvard Professor Randall Kennedy in a summary of this controversy: "What is required to create political institutions that address the needs and aspirations of all Americans, not simply whites, who have long enjoyed racial privilege, but people of color who have long suffered racial exclusion from policymaking forums?" My answer, as Professor Kennedy suggests, varies by situation. But I have a predisposition, reflected in my son's yearning for a positive-sum solution, to seek an integrated body politic in which all perspectives are represented and in which all people work together to find common ground. I advocate empowering voters and their representatives in ways that give even minority voters a chance to influence legislative outcomes.

30 But those in the majority do not lose; they simply learn to take turns. This is a positive-sum solution that allows all voters to feel that they participate meaningfully in the decisionmaking process. This is a positive-sum solution that makes legislative outcomes more legitimate.

I have been roundly, and falsely, criticized for focusing on outcomes. Outcomes are indeed relevant, but *not* because I seek to advance particular ends, such as whether the children play tag or hide-and-seek, or whether the band at Brother Rice plays rock music or rap. Rather, I look to outcomes as *evidence* of whether all the children—or all the high school seniors—feel that their choice is represented and considered. The purpose is not to guarantee "equal legislative outcomes"; equal opportunity to *influence* legislative outcomes regardless of race is more like it.

For these reasons, I sometimes explore alternatives to simple, winner-take-all majority rule. I do not advocate any one procedural rule as a universal panacea for unfairness. Nor do I propose these remedies primarily as judicial solutions. They can be adopted only in the context of litigation after the court first finds a legal violation.

Outside of litigation, I propose these approaches as political solutions if, depending on the local context, they better approximate the goals of democratic fair play. One such decisionmaking alternative is called cumulative voting, which could give all the students at Brother Rice multiple votes and allow them to distribute their votes in any combination of their choice. If each student could vote for ten songs, the students could plump or aggregate their votes to reflect the intensity of their preferences. They could put ten votes on one song; they could put five votes on two songs. If a tenth of the students opted to "cumulate" or plump all their votes for one song, they would be able to select one of every ten or so songs played at the prom. The black seniors could have done this if they chose to, but so could any other cohesive group of sufficient size. In this way, the songs preferred by a majority would be played most often, but the songs the minority enjoyed would also show up on the play list.

Under cumulative voting, voters get the same number of votes as there are seats or options to vote for, and they can then distribute their votes in any combination to reflect their preferences. Like-minded voters can vote as a solid bloc or, instead, form strategic, cross-racial coalitions to gain mutual benefits. This system is emphatically not racially based; it allows voters to organize themselves on whatever basis they wish.

Corporations use this system to ensure representation of minority shareholders on corporate boards of directors. Similarly, some local municipal and county governments have adopted cumulative voting to ensure representation of minority voters. Instead of awarding political power to geographic units called districts, cumulative voting allows voters to cast ballots based on what they think rather than where they live.

Cumulative voting is based on the principle of one person–one vote because each voter gets the same total number of votes. Everyone's preferences are counted equally. It is not a particularly radical idea; thirty states either require or permit corporations to use this election system. Cumulative voting is certainly not antidemocratic because it emphasizes the importance

35

of voter choice in selecting public or social policy. And it is neither liberal nor conservative. Both the Reagan and Bush administrations approved cumulative voting schemes pursuant to the Voting Rights Act to protect the rights of racial- and language-minority voters.

But, as in Chilton County, Alabama, which now uses cumulative voting to elect both the school board and the county commission, any politically cohesive group can vote strategically to win representation. Groups of voters win representation depending on the exclusion threshold, meaning the percentage of votes needed to win one seat or have the band play one song. That threshold can be set case by case, jurisdiction by jurisdiction, based on the size of minority groups that make compelling claims for representation.

Normally the exclusion threshold in a head-to-head contest is 50 percent, which means that only groups that can organize a majority can get elected. But if multiple seats (or multiple songs) are considered simultaneously, the exclusion threshold is considerably reduced. For example, in Chilton County, with seven seats elected simultaneously on each governing body, the threshold of exclusion is now one-eighth. Any group with the solid support of one-eighth the voting population cannot be denied representation. This is because any self-identified minority can plump or cumulate all its votes for one candidate. Again, minorities are not defined solely in racial terms.

As it turned out in Chilton County, both blacks and Republicans benefited from this new system. The school board and commission now each have three white Democrats, three white Republicans, and one black Democrat. Previously, when each seat was decided in a head-to-head contest, the majority not only ruled but monopolized. Only white Democrats were elected at every prior election during this century.

40   Similarly, if the black and white students at Brother Rice have very different musical taste, cumulative voting permits a positive-sum solution to enable both groups to enjoy one prom. The majority's preferences would be respected in that their songs would be played most often, but the black students could express the intensity of their preferences too. If the black students chose to plump all their votes on a few songs, their minority preferences would be recognized and played. Essentially, cumulative voting structures the band's repertoire to enable the students to take turns.

As a solution that permits voters to self-select their identities, cumulative voting also encourages cross-racial coalition building.

No one is locked into a minority identity. Nor is anyone necessarily isolated by the identity they choose. Voters can strengthen their influence by forming coalitions to elect more than one representative or to select a range of music more compatible with the entire student body's preferences.

Women too can use cumulative voting to gain greater representation. Indeed, in other countries with similar, alternative voting systems, women are more likely to be represented in the national legislature. For example, in some Western European democracies, the national legislatures have as many as 37 percent female members compared to a little more than 5 percent in our Congress.

There is a final benefit from cumulative voting. It eliminates gerry-mandering. By denying protected incumbents safe seats in gerry-mandered districts, cumulative voting might encourage more voter participation. With greater interest-based electoral competition, cumulative voting could promote the political turnover sought by advocates of term limits. In this way, cumulative voting serves many of the same ends as periodic elections or rotation in office, a solution that Madison and others advocated as a means of protecting against permanent majority factions.

A different remedial voting tool, one that I have explored more cautiously, is supermajority voting. It modifies winner-take-all majority rule to require that something more than a bare majority of voters must approve or concur before action is taken. As a uniform decisional rule, a supermajority empowers any numerically small but cohesive group of voters. Like cumulative voting, it is race-neutral. Depending on the issue, different members of the voting body can "veto" impending action.

Supermajority remedies give bargaining power to all numerically inferior or less powerful groups, be they black, female, or Republican. Supermajority rules empower the minority Republicans in the Senate who used the Senate filibuster procedure in the spring of 1993 to "veto" the president's proposed economic stimulus package. The same concept of a minority veto yielded the Great Compromise in which small-population states are equally represented in the Senate.

I have never advocated (or imagined) giving an individual member of a legislative body a personal veto. Moreover, I have discussed these kinds of exceptional remedies as the subject of court-imposed solutions only when there has been a violation of the statute and only when they make sense in the context of a particular case. I discuss supermajority rules as a judicial remedy only in cases where the court finds proof of consistent and deeply engrained polarization. It was never my intent that supermajority requirements should be the norm for all legislative bodies, or that simple majority voting would ever in itself constitute a statutory or constitutional violation.

Both the Reagan and Bush administrations took a similar remedial approach to enforcement of the Voting Rights Act. In fact, it was the Reagan administration that *approved* the use of supermajority rules as a remedial measure in places like Mobile, Alabama, where the special five-out-of-seven supermajority threshold is still in place today and is credited with increasing racial harmony in that community.

But—and here I come directly to the claims of my critics—some apparently fear that remedies for extreme voting abuses, remedies like cumulative voting or the Mobile supermajority, constitute "quotas"—racial preferences to ensure minority rule. While cumulative voting, or a supermajority, is quite conventional in many cases and race neutral, to order it as a remedy apparently opens up possibilities of nonmajoritarianism that many seem to find quite threatening.

Indeed, while my nomination was pending, I was called "antidemocratic" for suggesting that majority voting rules may not fairly resolve conflict when the majority and minority are permanently divided. But alternatives to majority voting rules in a racially polarized environment are too easily dismissed by this label. As Chief Justice [Warren] Burger wrote for the Supreme Court, "There is nothing in the language of the Constitution, our history, or our cases that requires that a majority always prevail on every issue." In other words, there is *nothing inherent in democracy that requires majority rule*. It is simply a custom that works efficiently when the majority and minority are fluid, are not monolithic, and are not permanent.

50   Other democracies frequently employ alternatives to winner-take-all majority voting. Indeed, only five Western democracies, including Britain and the United States, still use single-member-district, winner-take-all systems of representation. Germany, Spain, the Netherlands, and Sweden, among other countries, elect their legislatures under some alternative to winner-take-all majority voting. As the *New Yorker*, in a comment on my nomination, observed, President Clinton was right in calling some of my ideas "difficult to defend," but only because "Americans, by and large, are ignorant of the existence, let alone the details, of electoral systems other than their own."

No one who had done their homework seriously questioned the fundamentally democratic nature of my ideas. Indeed, columnists who attacked my ideas during my nomination ordeal have praised ideas, in a different context, that are remarkably similar to my own. Lally Weymouth wrote, "There can't be democracy in South Africa without a measure of formal protection for minorities." George Will has opined, "The Framers also understood that stable, tyrannical majorities can best be prevented by the multiplication of minority interests, so the majority at any moment will be just a transitory coalition of minorities." In my law journal articles, I expressed exactly the same reservations about unfettered majority rule and about the need sometimes to disaggregate the majority to ensure fair and effective representation for all substantial interests.

The difference is that the minority I used to illustrate my academic point was not, as it was for Lally Weymouth, the white minority in South Africa. Nor, did I write, as George Will did, about the minority of well-to-do landlords in New York City. I wrote instead about the political exclusion of the black minority in many local county and municipal governing bodies in America.

Yet these same two journalists and many others condemned me as antidemocratic. Apparently, it is not controversial to provide special protections for affluent landlords or minorities in South Africa but it is "divisive," "radical," and "out of the mainstream" to provide similar remedies to black Americans who, after centuries of racial oppression, are still excluded.

Talking about racial bias at home has, for many, become synonymous with advocating revolution. Talking about racial divisions, in itself, has become a violation of the rules of polite society.

We seem to have forgotten that dialogue and intergroup communication are critical to forging consensus. In my case, genuine debate was shut down by techniques of stereotyping and silencing. As Professor Randall Kennedy observes, I was "punished" as the messenger reporting the bad news about our racial situation. I dared to speak when I should have been silent.

My nomination became an unfortunate metaphor for the state of race relations in America. My nomination suggested that as a country, we are in a state of denial about issues of race and racism. The censorship imposed against me points to a denial of serious public debate or discussion about racial fairness and justice in a true democracy. For many politicians and policymakers, the remedy for racism is simply to stop talking about race.

Sentences, words, even phrases separated by paragraphs in my law review articles were served up to demonstrate that I was violating the rules. Because I talked openly about existing racial divisions, I was branded "race obsessed." Because I explored innovative ways to remedy racism, I was branded "antidemocratic." It did not matter that I had suggested race-neutral election rules, such as cumulative voting, as an alternative to remedy racial discrimination. It did not matter that I never advocated quotas. I became the Quota Queen.

The vision behind my by-now-notorious law review articles and my less-well-known professional commitments has always been that of a fair and just society, a society in which even adversely affected parties believe in the system because they believe the process is fair and the process is inclusive. My vision of fairness and justice imagines a full and effective voice for all citizens. I may have failed to locate some of my ideas in the specific factual contexts from which they are derived. But always I have tried to show that democracy in a heterogeneous society is incompatible with rule by a racial monopoly of any color.

I hope that we can learn three positive lessons from my experience. The first lesson is that those who stand for principles may lose in the short run, but they cannot be suppressed in the long run. The second lesson is that public dialogue is critical to represent all perspectives; no one viewpoint should be permitted to monopolize, distort, caricature, or shape public debate. The tyranny of The Majority is just as much a problem of silencing minority viewpoints as it is of excluding minority representatives or preferences. We cannot all talk at once, but that does not mean only one group should get to speak. We can take turns. Third, we need consensus and positive-sum solutions. We need a broad public conversation about issues of racial justice in which we seek win-win solutions to real-life problems. If we include blacks and whites, and women and men, and Republicans and Democrats, and even people with new ideas, we will all be better off.

60   Most of all, I hope we begin to consider the principle of taking turns as a means to bring us closer to the ideal of democratic fair play. [Supreme Court] Justice Potter Stewart wrote in 1964 that our form of representative self-government reflects "the strongly felt American tradition that the public interest is composed of many diverse interests, [which] . . . in the long run . . . can better be expressed by a medley of component voices than by the majority's monolithic command." In that "strongly felt Ameri-

can tradition," I hope more of us aspire to govern like Madisonian Majorities through "a medley of component voices." In that "strongly felt American tradition," I hope more of us come to reject the "monolithic command" of The Fixed Majority.

After all, government is a public experiment. Let us not forget [Supreme Court] Justice Louis Brandeis's advice at the beginning of this century: "If we guide by the light of reason, we must let our minds be bold." At the close of the same century, I hope we rediscover the bold solution to the tyranny of The Majority, which has always been more democracy, not less.

Questions for Discussion

1. How do the personal examples that begin the essay, as well as her citing of James Madison, help Guinier to make the point that rules of competition can promote fairness and the avoid undue division among winners and "losers" that can ultimately result in majority "tyranny"?

2. Describe the "positive-sum, taking-turns solution" that Guinier poses to guarantee minority voting rights and representation. How would it work in practice? How practical does such a solution seem?

3. How does Guinier try to refute critics of her ideas on cumulative voting and the "supermajority"? Did you find her defense of her position clear and convincing? Does she seem merely to be asking for racial quotas?

4. How effective is Guinier's self-defense against the charge that her ideas are essentially "antidemocratic"? Does it help her cause to quote Supreme Court Justices and turn the words of her critics around so that they seem fundamentally to agree with her?

Ideas for Writing

1. Try to put Guinier's ideas about assuring minority representation through "cumulative voting" into practice by devising similar systems to deal with the "winner take all" approach to voting in your school or community organization. How would you convince people to accept your proposal and put it into action?

2. Write an essay in which you examine some of the reasons for the low voter turnout in recent elections, taking into account

especially Guinier's explanations and proposed solutions for this phenomenon. Do you think more people would vote if Guinier's ideas for voting were widely adopted? Why or why or not?

Extending the Theme

1. West, Derber, and Guinier present different approaches for encouraging citizens to become more actively involved in the responsibilities of living in a democratic society. Contrast the specific ideas that each writer presents. Write an essay that discusses whose ideas you found most viable and appealing. Explain why you think which of the solutions proposed are most likely to work. You can refer to your own experiences when relevant to support any of your claims and do further research on the effectiveness of the solution or solutions that you have chosen.

2. Discuss Streisand's and Jones's ideas on the role and importance of vision and artistic creativity in affecting positive social change through heightening citizenship awareness on vital issues of concern in our democratic society. Do research to find out how artistic events such as art shows, films, plays, novels, poetry, or songs that have inspired activist groups or individuals to effect change.

3. In her essay, Pharr confronts specific problems involved in organizing for social justice. Discuss several of the most important obstacles to organizing and overcoming resistance to social change that she raises. Which solutions seem the most viable?

4. Visit an organization dedicated to organizing citizens to work for a common objective such as passing or defeating a ballot proposition, electing a particular political candidate, changing an environmental issue or regulation, protesting, or supporting an armed conflict. Research the organization's history and philosophy, interview leaders and participants in the organization, and/or work for the organization in some practical way. Write an essay that discusses what you have learned about the organization and its impact on your community. Do you think that this organization is effective in bringing about social change?